T0343681

When Life Gives You Lemurs

When Life Gives You Lemurs

How saving animals saved me

TIM HUSBAND
with DEBORAH KANE

ALLEN&UNWIN
SYDNEY·MELBOURNE·AUCKLAND·LONDON

First published in 2024

Copyright © Tim Husband and Deborah Kane 2024

Some names and identifying details have been changed to protect the privacy of individuals.

All uncredited photographs are from the collection of Tim Husband

Allen & Unwin
Cammeraygal Country
83 Alexander Street
Crows Nest NSW 2065
Australia
Phone: (61 2) 8425 0100
Email: info@allenandunwin.com
Web: www.allenandunwin.com

Allen & Unwin acknowledges the Traditional Owners of the Country on which we live and work. We pay our respects to all Aboriginal and Torres Strait Islander Elders, past and present.

A catalogue record for this book is available from the National Library of Australia

ISBN 978 1 76147 152 0

Lemur illustrations on chapter openers: AlphaVectorStd, Shutterstock

Set in 12.5/17 pt Adobe Garamond Pro by Post Pre-press Group
Printed and bound in Australia by the Opus Group

10 9 8 7 6 5 4 3 2 1

The paper in this book is FSC® certified. FSC® promotes environmentally responsible, socially beneficial and economically viable management of the world's forests.

To the people who I have crossed paths with over the years, both good and bad, wise and ignorant—you have helped me become the person I am today.

—TH

I think I could turn and live with animals, they are so placid and self contain'd,

I stand and look at them long and long.

They do not sweat and whine about their condition,

They do not lie awake in the dark and weep for their sins.

They do not make me tired discussing their duty to God,

Not one is dissatisfied, not one is demented with the mania of owning things,

Not one kneels to another, nor to his kind that lived thousands of years ago,

Not one is respectable or unhappy over the whole earth.

—from Walt Whitman, 'Song of Myself'

Contents

Readers should be aware that an incident of sexual assault is included in this book.

1

In the beginning, there was God

Swallows, a pair of them, probably breeding, perched up on the phone line like full-bellied ticks. Plastered up against the window of the old Morris, I always looked out for birds. But not swallows, because I knew swallows perched on phone lines, and phone lines led to Hell.

It was steamy inside the car—mid-January, Whangārei, New Zealand, 1973. Mum and my sister Rachel were wrapped in cotton frocks on the bench seat in the front. Dad was driving, and brooding, as always. In the back, my two brothers, Daniel and Steven, and me. Every weekend. Always the same thing. It was what we did as a family. We would drive the back roads of Whangārei bush country searching for phone lines. When we found them, we would follow them, because phone lines led to houses, and houses led to forgotten congregations of the unenlightened, and we were there to spread the Word of God to these poor, ignorant folk hunkered in the bush—the poor, ignorant buggers whose lives were about to change because we were about to bring the light of Jesus into their kitchens. We were Jehovah's Witnesses. We believed we carried the Word of God with us and, as His messengers, we were there to save people's lives.

Steven was digging the end of his pen into my leg to see how long I could go before I hollered. I never hollered. I was digging the corner of my Bible into the spotty, spongy skin under his kneecap. He always hollered. Sniggering and whimpering and dread were all tied up in that little Morris Oxford, on its way to save people's lives.

'Why don't we celebrate birthdays as Jehovah's Witnesses?' When Dad bellowed, it was always an interrogation more than a question. He'd spotted the phone line, and so our test of Jehovah's Witness scripture had begun. We had to be ready for any questions that might be fired at us by the poor, ignorant bush folk.

'Because nowhere in the Bible does it say to celebrate birthdays!' Steven always shouted the answers first. He was always keen for approval. More from Dad than Jehovah.

'Correct. And why don't we believe in using another person's blood?'

'Because the scriptures say . . .'

Steven attempted a swift reply but Dad was quick to interrupt: 'Tim. Why don't we believe in using another person's blood?'

I was still looking at the birds. Perhaps they weren't swallows, perhaps they were starlings. Did starlings perch on phone lines? Starlings and swallows kind of looked the same. Starlings were

2

bigger, I knew that, but sometimes they had the same colours . . .

'Tim!'

'Because the scriptures in the Bible say that we should not drink blood.' My answer was more of a blurt, a well-drilled bullet of a blurt, but I believed the answer to be correct.

'Aaaannd . . . aand . . . what else, Tim?'

Trawling through replays of our nightly scripture readings in my head, I tried to find the answer, but it wasn't clear. 'Sooo . . . when a person is in a coma they would be fed through the veins?'

'Correct!'

And so it continued, as the old Morris and its family full of rookie Jehovahs turned down a gravelly winding road to Hell.

'Daniel, who are the only people in the Bible who celebrate birthdays?' Dad throwing in a real curly one just as a house came into view.

'Kings?'

'And what rights did they have when it was their birthday?'

'They had the right to put the apostles, or prophets, to death,' offered Mum. Her replies were always dull, like she was working on a switchboard or something. You'd think that a birthday present like that might have thrown up a few questions for Mum, I mean if she was a REAL Christian. But there were no questions in Mum anymore, only answers. And only ones that she could come to easily. Mum felt to me like she was just hanging on. Like a hamster on a wheel.

We pulled up in a cloud of dust. The lawn was all car parts and chooks. The house was old, corrugated iron peeling away from hardwood. Poor, ignorant bastards. Thank God we were there. But it wasn't all salvation and white light in my head, because it took only a second for shame to sweat hot through

3

my whole body. Happened every time we spilled out of the car, like oil. I pulled my fringe down over my face as far as I could and sank into my cheap black nylon suit. Too big. It had been Steven's before it was mine and Steven was seventeen. I saw a stain on the leg of my suit, with a bit of dried sausage in it. A sausage roll stain on my knee. A fleck of tomato sauce on my white collar. Another sauce smudge on my tie. Felt good. Stains kept me grounded.

As much as I could, I always pushed to the back of the evangelical flock. Dad didn't let me stay there, though. He always noticed. He lined Steven, Daniel and me up in front of the door like boys in detention. Each of us had a Bible. Mine was torn. Thank God. Mum and Rachel hovered at the back like afterthoughts.

Knock knock.

Blowflies buzzing. Why were there always blowflies buzzing around when we waited for the ignorant folk to come to the door? I reckoned they had an inbuilt shit detector. I laughed a little at that. I liked my own jokes. Dad pushed me in the back again. But what if the fly thing wasn't really a joke? Maybe flies did go where they thought dead meat was, or was going to be.

The door slowly opened. 'Good afternoon.' Dad was always breaking the awkward fat silence first.

The doors only ever half-opened, sometimes not even that, while reluctant, ignorant folk collected behind them in shifting shadows. I prayed for two things at these times, knowing full well that Jesus was on our side of the door and most likely listening. One: whoever opened the door had better things to do today. And two—and this was the big one: I prayed that it wasn't a kid from school behind that flyscreen, someone who would recognise me and tell someone else at school.

'Good afternoon, madam. We won't take much of your time. We have just come to share some Good News with you today! My boys and I bring blessings and light and the possibility of a life without fear.'

Another two thoughts came to mind. I wondered why Mum and Rachel bothered coming at all. And I realised Dad had just dropped the big one, the tried-and-tested door-opener: Life without Fear. Dad always delivered the offer of salvation while choirs of blowies buzzed requiems around the four of us. Actually six of us, if you included Rachel and Mum.

Even though I was only eleven—actually, eleven and a half—I had witnessed the power death had over people. It made religion so easy for us kids to sell. When I said that to Daniel, I'd have a smile on my face stretched like a frog's from one of my ears to the other, and I'd follow up with, 'Death is like a gift for a budding Jehovah's Witness, Dan!' I'd heard that from Grandad and I repeated it whenever I could. Whenever Grandad said it, all his mates laughed, and I always wanted to make people laugh like my Grandad could. But I'd also noticed it myself. About death I mean, the power it had over people, how it plastered fear all over their faces. And I knew that Dad knew that too.

When death got dropped into Dad's speeches, we knew we were at the business end of the sales pitch. He always dragged death out by its ear when none of his other arguments worked. Arguments like neighbourhood crime or potential disease. If the door was still only open a crack at that point, he'd pull out his trump card. And it always worked. Maybe people they knew had died, or they were about to die, and we, as Jehovah's Witnesses, very luckily for everyone, could offer the ultimate comfort for their fears. It was always the same line that Dad delivered, and he'd say it in a weirdly gentle voice that we never heard at home: 'You WILL see your loved ones again after your death, should you decide to follow God's Word.'

That did the trick most of the time. It was then that we were usually allowed in behind the flyscreen door.

This particular January day was a good and a bad day. The woman quickly identified herself and her boys, then said she wasn't interested in anything we had to offer. 'No thanks. I've got my own religion.' Her response was swift and timed perfectly with the closing of the door.

'That's too bad, I've gotta share mine.' I said it loud enough for Dad to hear. The cuff over the ear stung like hell. This outcome was a good thing as far as I was concerned. It meant this phone line was a dud as far as saving anyone. But the bad thing was that the school bully—whose real name I'm not going to use, so he doesn't come after me in another life; instead, I'll call him Nathan Barrett—had been standing beside his mum, staring at me through the flyscreen like a boobook owl. Staring at me at the exact moment his mum was telling us to bugger off. Nathan Barrett, Grade 7, my class, had to repeat, built like a brick shithouse, ugly. Nathan Barrett had stared at me as if I was dead meat. Maybe I was the dead meat the flies had been waiting for.

We got back in the car, Bibles soiled in sweaty hands. I chucked mine on the floor. Steven clutched his while he jammed the pen into my leg again. Mum and Rachel were already in the car, silent. Seemed God had chosen his messengers carefully again, leaving Rachel and Mum in their sweaty, crumpled pastels, voiceless in the front seat.

'What went wrong there, boys?' Dad was snorting and frothing as the recriminations began. It was like a half-time pep talk. 'None of you offered your scriptures when there was a pause. We've gone over that! If there is a break, when no one is saying anything, you come in with your scriptures!' He was sweating and irritated, like my footy coach from Wednesday afternoon Rugby.

The car began overheating during our exit from the driveway of another mob of the unenlightened, all exhaust burps and blue smoke. We pulled off the main road, making sure that we were well out of sight of the ignorant bush folk, who were clearly destined for Purgatory after rejecting our salvation. We had our own Purgatory, with Dad under the bonnet, steam spewing out each side of the car and both of his ears. We sat in a line on the verge like penguins waiting for the tide to turn. Tired. Hot. Waiting for the Morris Oxford to cool down. Waiting for Dad to cool down.

Dad didn't believe in buying new things. Especially cars. Our cars were old cars even when they were new. Old English cars. They always had rust and needed to be bogged up. Our Morris Oxford was a really heavy-looking car, thick with twenty coats of primer and a hundred coats of marine-blue steel paint. The only seatbelts were for the driver and front passenger. It had a column-change gearstick. The dark-blue upholstery was torn. Mum was always trying to fix the roof by painting sunflowers over the holes on the inside, although she did that less and less these days. The painted flowers never stopped the rain, so we never knew what the point was. It was always a sticking or tacking job to keep our cars going—exhaust pipe putty, containers, clamps, manifold tapes and water bottles, rolling around in the boot.

Dad was always in the middle of 'patching up'. Today was no different.

We all got back in the car and Dad tried to turn it on. No connection. The petrol pump in the boot of the car was playing up again.

'Get in the boot, Tim.'

Still a shit day for me. With the boot snapped firmly shut on top of me and seeing nothing but black and smelling only exhaust fumes, I listened for the car throttle to sputter to a start. It was my job to tap the petrol pump when the ignition was just about to take. It was my job every time. Every weekend, I would end up in the pitch black of the boot with my nylon black Jehovah's suit crushed up against fuel and tools, pumps and putty, clamps and manifolds, and oil cans. Just waiting in the dark for Dad's instructions. Like usual.

⟶

After a day of preaching to the sullied and unenlightened, we rolled into our driveway in the late afternoon and the dry, dead scriptures leached from our exhausted brains like beached seaweed pulled back on a sliding wave. It was then that I could finally take a long deep breath. This was my favourite time of the day. Not just because the work of spreading the Word was over, but also because I was looking after a brushtail possum I had saved from certain death when a cedar tree, ripped apart by a storm, crashed at the end of our driveway. I kept him hidden in a box in the toolshed, behind the lawnmower. Dad didn't let me keep animals, but I did anyway.

Ted was mostly pretty quiet. That was what I called him—

Ted. For a month I fed him old fruit and bits of egg. He would eat tucked up under my elbow. I would think about penguin parents I'd seen in the animal encyclopedia at school. They tucked their chicks under their wing when they were regurgitating their food for them. Felt a bit like that. Not the regurgitating bit, just the under the wing bit. For now, Ted was warm and safe under my wing. I would slip out just before tea, curl him round my arm and sneak down to the river. Swinging on a dipping branch of willow, with Ted the brushtail possum tucked under my arm and the reek of the rabid midday heat gone and the soft red of the Auckland sun setting off for sleep at the river mouth, I reckoned I could call myself lucky.

Dad had heard me coming back up the path beside the house and burst out the back door. 'Your mother put tea on the table twenty minutes ago! Where've you been, boy?'

Ted was up my jumper and I was hulking over like a question mark. Dad leant into me, his leaky bug-eyes wobbling like sea slugs.

'Nowhere.'

'Look at me!'

But I wasn't going to look at him because that would mean straightening up and that would mean Ted could fall out and that would mean losing my friend and also that would mean just having to look at Dad—and, having considered myself lucky only minutes ago, I didn't want that feeling to go away. So there was no way I was going to look at my dad. Then Ted's little grey fluffy tail-tip dropped out the bottom of my jumper.

'What the hell is that?'

'Nothing.'

And I turned around and ran inside to my bedroom,

slamming the door behind me. Steven was in there because he shared the room with me. He was lying on his bed reading his Jehovah's scriptures. I lay on my bed and curled myself around my little friend—we were both curled around one another, like overseas pastries. It wasn't long before Dad exploded through the door. He leant in and tried to grab Ted. The bite was swift and deep and bloody. The warning raspy snarl coming out of my little mate sounded too old for him. It sounded dangerous and prehistoric.

Dad hollered like a crazy man. 'Jesus Christ!'

And it was a welcome reminder to be thankful to Jesus for being with Ted and me at this crucial moment when Dad was going to snatch away the only thing I really cared about. And I was thankful to Ted, too, for being able to tell good from bad, right from wrong. It was the first time in my life—although not the last time—that I realised animals could sense the good and the bad in humans.

I charged out the back door and back down to the river, where I settled my little mate into a hollow in a branch of the willow tree. I reckoned he wasn't quite old enough to be on his own, but if Dad got to him he would have a hammer in the back of his head and be put in the bin. Plus, I knew there was no place in Jehovah's Kingdom for dead animals, so I wanted to give him as much of a life as possible. Besides, this way, I'd get to come down here every day and be in the place where he lived. Even if I didn't ever see him again, I'd still know he was there somewhere and not in a bin.

Dad came into my bedroom at three in the morning. I pulled the blanket over my head and scrunched up my eyes. I knew what was coming, I felt the fear filling me in just before he got to me. He was dragging his belt on the floor behind him. Same as usual. My old man, dragging his leather belt, buckle tinkling and slithering over exposed nails. He yanked me from my half-sleep, pushed me over my bed, and whipped my arse. He used the buckle end this time, so I knew there was real hot blood in his angry that night.

2

Jehovah's scriptures

Everyone in our Jehovah's Witness community started their day reading Jehovah's scriptures and ended their day reading Jehovah's scriptures. Other stuff, life stuff, only happened in-between. Scripture reading was strictly monitored in our family. Every day we had to finish reading a certain number of chapters in the Bible. Sundays we would meet other Jehovah's families at Kingdom Hall, the church of the Jehovah's Witnesses, for an hour of Bible study. Kingdom Hall was a red-brick box at the end of Evans Street. Could've been someone's house except for the Jehovah's billboard on the front lawn. Every week the billboard offered a different message for the ignorant ordinary folk passing by. One week's message was, 'Don't let worry kill you, let God help'. Grandad and I seemed to be the only ones in my family who found that funny.

Kingdom Hall was where the old blokes of the church, who

were called the Elders, met and talked about how to run their religion. All the news from Kingdom Hall was covered by the monthly magazines *The Watchtower* and *Awake!* Dad would make us study them from cover to cover and learn everything in them. I hated it. It was shit. While other boys from school were thumbing through Marvel comics or sneaking *Playboy* magazines from under their mattresses or doing nothing with words at all, I would be learning scriptures by heart. Getting lessons on what levels of Purgatory awaited us kids for the sins we committed. And we were always committing sins. Especially after reading King Solomon's words from the Song of Songs 7:1–3, when he was praising his new wife:

> Your navel is a rounded bowl,
> It never lacks mixed wine.
> Your waist is a mound of wheat surrounded by lilies.
> Your breasts are like two fawns, twins of a gazelle.

On Wednesday nights we all went to the Ministry School for two hours, where the Elders would teach us how to knock on doors and answer questions. One of our teachers, someone I'll call Elder Winston, was always punctual. He was also fat and white. His chins would roll around the top of his white collar like a toppling pancake stack. He always liked us to be 'orderly and alert', and he didn't like us asking questions. When Elder Winston leant into his lesson, his voice would climb to a whine and he would land his unblinking glare on each of us, holding us like we were in a spotlight.

'We all have a difficult time starting a conversation with someone we don't know. Isn't that right, children?' His dark-grey eyes were fixed on Rachel, a butterfly pinned to a board. 'But because of love for God and for our neighbour, Jehovah's Witnesses make an earnest effort to learn how to have a conversation with the other in order to share the truth of the Bible with others. Do you understand, Steven?'

Steven copped the glare this time. It was some time before Elder Winston resumed his talk. Horrible, slow, terrifying time.

'Philippians 2:4 is instructive. It encourages us to keep an eye not in personal interest upon our own matters but in personal interest upon those of the others.'

I thought he was talking about the ignorant bush folk. I sank further into my seat, praying that I could duck the awful dark light of Elder Winston's eyes.

'If you are observant, you too can discern what the man may be thinking about. Does the man look happy or sad? Is he elderly? Possibly infirm? Do home decorations or personal jewellery indicate a religious influence? If your greeting takes such things into account, the man may view you as someone who shares an interest in common with him.'

But, I thought, what if a woman came to the door? What would you say then? And if the man *did* seem to have a lot of personal jewellery and an unusual interest in decoration, what then? Besides which, looking around for personal jewellery and home decorations was just creepy.

Elder Winston finally drew a breath. And then, there was silence. He was scanning again. He zeroed in on one of the older girls, an eagle about to prey on a small bird. But this time he had chosen his victim poorly. She wasn't ordinary prey but rather a raptor herself. I'm going to call her Jenny Falcon, because a fully clawed falcon preparing to launch an attack is the image that came into my mind when I watched her stare, dead straight, into the Elder's eyes.

'Jenny. Do you remember what Jesus did when he met a woman at a well in Samaria? John 4:7–26?'

Jenny Falcon shuffled in her seat, but it was all adjustment. There was no fear in it. 'I don't remember that piece of scripture, Elder Winston.' I was seeing something that I had never before seen from my siblings. A quiet defiance.

'John 4:7–26 . . . let me continue FOR you. What Jesus did, when he met a woman at the well, was to observe that her mind was on drawing water. Jesus initiated his conversation with her on that basis, and he was soon able to turn it into a lively spiritual discussion. That is the piece of scripture you have forgotten, Jenny. It was only three weeks ago we studied this in the Kingdom Hall. Where was your mind then?'

'Probably asking why it was that women are always the ones having to fetch the water. They ARE always the ones fetching the water aren't they, Elder Winston?'

His glare was fierce and deep and unforgiving. 'That is an incorrect answer and an inappropriate question. Please see me after scripture class, Jenny.'

The drone from Elder Winston's voice continued. It was an idling truck. 'Be alert for an opportunity to introduce the Good News, but do not be in a hurry. Allow the conversation to develop naturally.' Blah blah blah.

I couldn't take my eyes off The Falcon for the rest of the lesson. Her strong chin, her hair black and thick, her nose straight and long like an apostle, her skin soft, almond, velvet, warm. She was older than all of us. And she didn't seem to give a shit what anyone thought of her. She was going to be my hero. She would be in my head most days for a long time.

———

Monday morning, and it always felt like there was a rock in my guts. Monday morning, and I got to see how many schoolkids had talked to other schoolkids about the visits to their homes from me and my family. Mostly I tucked myself tight into my too-large school shirt. Head and long fringe down, staying small, staying quiet. Nathan Barrett and his buddies came from nowhere that morning in the playground. It was so quick, I never really had time to get scared.

'Who do we have here, boys? Oooh, I believe it's Pastor Tim . . . or is it the POPE!'

His gang of mates were cracking up laughing. Nathan had his hand around my throat and had me pinned up against the wall, my feet were off the ground. His eyes were a toad's breath away from my own. Two thoughts came to mind: one, *Nathan Barrett really IS as ugly as all fuck*, and two, *It's weird how his mates hang around him in a pack.*

Nathan started slapping me. Not hard, but over and over again. Annoying. Really annoying.

'Good Christians turn the other cheek, don't they, Pope? My dad says you guys don't fight. He says you're all cowards.'

The slapping didn't stop. It was getting harder, like he was trying to kill a fish on cement. So I T-boned his nuts with my knee. When he loosened his grip, I hit him as hard as I could with a right hook, which surprised both of us. He sank down and all his ugly buddies backed off.

Jehovah's scriptures

One of the playground teachers grabbed our shirts and cut a straight line through all the gawking kids, marching us to the headmaster's office. The headmaster demanded an explanation, never once taking his eyes off the swelling, bleeding welt around Nathan Barrett's eye.

'He was teasing me, so I hit him.' I wanted to give my story first, anticipating the headmaster's early take on what had happened. When the headmaster turned to me, it was like he'd already made up his mind. 'He started it!' I continued nervously, sensing the wrong conclusion growing in the headmaster's sheepdog glare.

'Good Christian boys don't go around punching other boys, do they, Tim?'

This would not go well for me. I knew that much already.

'I'm no Christian.' Got that in at least. Felt good to say that. So good.

There was a silence that went on for a while. The headmaster eventually broke it: 'Nathan, you can go back to class.' He then assigned me afternoon detention for the rest of the week and proceeded to give me six of the best.

As the whip chewed away at old scars, I soothed myself by quoting the Bible back to the old fuck. It was a mumble to myself, puffing and broody, never quite loud enough: 'And Jesus said, "Thou hypocrite, first take out the log from thine own eye," you old fuck, "and then shalt thou see clearly to take the speck in thy brothers."'

When it was done, I stood up, pulled up my pants and walked out, mumbling, 'Matthew 7:5, jerk.'

3

Loves an underdog

John had found a couple of branches of tea tree. Ten-foot long, with pointy ends that he'd taped up. He sat on his saddled black brumby, holding his tea tree spears, waiting for me at the bend in the river. He'd led a spare horse there for me, a bottom-of-the-barrel brumby called Cyrus. Mongrel eyes. Almost three times my height. Always needed to be somewhere else. I threw myself up on Cyrus as though I was a potato sack being thrown on the back of a truck. John's horse was called Diesel. He was higher, stronger, blacker, faster.

John was my only friend in the world besides Ted. I thought he was a fucking legend, but that hill wasn't a steep one for me to climb. Anything or anyone with a smack of free spirit I stuck to like a cockroach on sticky paper. John was a Māori mate from Rugby. He didn't say much—we had that in common. He liked me though. He quickly recognised and laid claim to an underdog. Saw himself in an underdog. He was always going to back an underdog.

John held a spear high above him like it was the staff of Moses, demanding the sky open. And I swear the skies did bloody open right there and then, as a bowel-twist of thunder rumbled across the hills. We galloped through teeming sheets of rain and thick fog along the riverside track. Galloped as if the whole world order depended on our safe arrival somewhere. Anywhere. John rode his horse like he lived his life: hard, determined, fast. I rode Cyrus like someone hoping to one day ride and live like my mate John. I rode beside him, filling up with all his courage the closer I got to him. The wind blew us from behind and through us, and we rode fast with its weight like we were gods. I thought I must be the fastest, bravest kid in the whole of New Zealand, as flies and wisps of tussocks and dandelions flew into my mouth and slammed against my skin.

When we rode like this it was hard to pull Cyrus up, but he knew the circuit. He knew that when we got to the cedar tree at the river mouth, we needed to turn sharply, 180 degrees. John pulled up next to me, throwing peat mud bullets in a spray over my face. He chucked a spear to me. Somehow I caught it.

'Stay there and wait till I call you!'

John and his horse flew away. Same mess of mud spray when Diesel morphed into a gallop from a standstill. After twenty seconds, John and Diesel were facing me from about 200 metres away. John called for combat as he held his jousting spear in the air. I swear the thunder was still rumbling when Diesel reared on his hind legs, looking just like the Flying Horse in Revelations 19:11–18, only Diesel was black. 'Then I saw heaven opened, and behold, a white horse! The one sitting on it is called Faithful and True and in righteousness he judges and makes war.'

I could feel Cyrus beneath me, rippling, excited. He knew this game. And Cyrus always knew it was a game because John and I had rules so the horses would never get hurt. Cyrus was busting to get going. Trembling. Thousands of pounds of muscle and nerves just waiting for a suggestion.

'Go!'

I was barely aware of my intention before Cyrus took off. I looked up to see Diesel and John galloping towards me. Cyrus and I were also galloping flat out, faster than I'd ever gone. Maybe we were going 60 kilometres an hour. Faster even than the Morris Oxford at top speed. All the same shit was hitting my face—dandelions, mud, tussock, flies—but this time my jaw was clenched, and my body was pure steel. Cyrus and I were like a single body.

The rolling mud spray that was Diesel and John was nearly on me. John had his tea tree spear aimed squarely at my chest. I tried to do the same, but I couldn't seem to get a grip on mine. John was faster and passed me in a flash. Somewhere in that blur, I felt his spear ripping through my shirt and jabbing hard into my shoulder, knocking me off my horse. Knocked me to the ground. Dead meat. Again. It hurt bad, but I wasn't going to show my mate John that. John didn't understand pain. No such thing as pain. Whatever didn't kill you made you stronger. His dad played for the All Blacks. Besides, I was starting to get a taste for pain. It made me feel alive.

I felt ready to have another crack and didn't mind letting John know that as he swung back and headed towards me, leading Cyrus at a canter behind him.

'You alright mate?'
'Fuck yeah!'
And we go again.

———

I was spending more and more time at the river. I made a little shelter down there for Ted out of willow roots and old fence palings that I stole from one of the Elders' yards when I went over to deliver a bundle of *Awake!* I seemed to collect small animals the same way other boys collected stamps. Trent Kilby's mum was giving away guinea pig babies. I took them all. I made a different shelter for them out of more of the palings, using nails and a hammer from Dad's shed.

By Christmas, I had Ted, my guinea pigs, three ducks and two rabbits. Every evening after supper, I would go down to the animals and feed them the leftover fish fingers and coleslaw that I'd snuck off my plate. Ted was always around somewhere. It seemed he was always waiting for me. After I cleaned out the cages and filled them with fresh grass, I'd sit for a while with my animal family. Those evenings I spent with them were some of the first times I ever felt like I actually belonged in the world, and I liked that I was responsible for all these little fellas.

I would curl up with Ted on the riverbank and watch the night take hold and wonder how a possum's fur got to be so soft. Sometimes I'd think about the pact God made with people about animals. About how, according to Jehovah's Witness scriptures, they weren't allowed into Heaven, but I reckoned I was doing some good things for God through my rescued animals, even if none of them got into Heaven. As far as I was concerned, they were still His creations and they still mattered, even if God didn't think so. John 1–3: 'All things were made through him and without him was not anything made that was made.' If I had my way, all animals would have got into Heaven.

—

Sundays were merciless, appearing without fail at the end of every week. One Sunday, rattling along in our patched-up Morris, we turned down a road—windblown, full of potholes—to follow a phone line that seemed about to fall over. But it was still a phone line, and for sure there would be a mob of sullied, ignorant bush folk at the end of it.

When we arrived, same drill. But this time my shoulders were curled around my chest like ram horns, and my eyes were crusty with sleep slime. I'd been reading late into the night, under my bed covers, learning about animal feed from a Reader's Digest book I'd borrowed from the library. Dad hadn't got to that one with his scissors yet. Dad's brown-nosing little foot soldiers, Steven and Daniel, raced to reach the flyscreen door first while Dad pushed me along at the back. I swore the push from Dad between my shoulders was becoming more of a punch.

'Get a move on!' It was always said under his breath and had hate-stink in it.

When we got to the front door, the platoon of blowies was there. The shadowy folk behind the flyscreen were also there. All us boys were lined up at the door. An old woman opened the screen door and stared at us kids. She looked surprised, maybe confused. I thought to myself, *What the hell must we look like to these people? Maybe like clowns in a sideshow, mouths swaying from side to side and with reams of old scriptures pouring out of them.*

'Oh, how lovely, look at you boys! Would you like to come in for some lemonade?' The old woman made the invitation after Dad had persuaded her with his story about Jesus and the woman at the well. That was after he had spoken about sharing Good News and giving comfort for the End of Days.

The house was all yellow, ageing linoleum and heavy, dark-brown vinyl furniture. There were doilies like the ones Mum used to knit, small circles of yellowing white cotton saving cheap furniture from cheaper five-cent trinkets. The smell in there was of dying flowers. Sometimes when I sensed loneliness in a house, I felt relief that Dad's Good News stories had brought in the light. I think Steven and Daniel also thought so. But this old girl seemed to lose the gist of Dad's spiel, unless there were hooks—words like 'light', 'hope', 'peace', 'joy'. When she did bring her attention back to Dad's sermons, it was brief and always with a twinkle and a giggle. Most of the time, her eyes, all milky and rheumy, rested on us three boys.

'What are your names, boys, hmmm?'

Dad, irritated that her progress to enlightenment was so easily derailed, reluctantly nodded at us to answer.

'I'm Steven, that's Daniel, and that's Tim.'

'Ahhh, that's nice. All Bible names. You are all good boys, aren't you!'

Dad slowly brought her back to the scriptures. He was patient. I wished he was like that at home. Then, just as the verse on the seven steps into Heaven was coming to an end, a young fella came in through the back door. He was built like a backhoe and was startled that we were there. It was pretty clear that he and the old woman didn't get many visitors.

'Who are you blokes?'

There was muscle in the question. He walked towards us, chest out, hands clenched into fists at his side. That happened a lot for us. Dad had often been on the point of making enlightenment inroads with some old codger at death's door when some smart-arse relative came in to save them from us saving them from themselves!

'We were helping your grandmother. Is it your grandmother?' began Dad. 'We were helping her see that there is a way to live without fear. When she lets the light of God into her life, joy will . . .'

'Jesus! You've got a fucken nerve you blokes, haven't you! Preying on old folk. Get out! She may be losing her marbles a bit but she's still got her dignity. Now, get the fuck out!'

I loved it when the shit hit the fan like this. I loved seeing Dad's face twitch with terror and dashed hopes and seeing the fight in the young fella looking after his nan—gave me a kick. I especially loved seeing Steven's face pruned up and petrified.

———

Mum stopped coming with us when we followed the phone lines on Sundays. Dad had decided that it was up to my brothers and me to spread God's word, and Mum did whatever Dad told her to do. She always seemed sad now. She seemed to be living her life under an empty thought bubble. I couldn't remember the last time I'd seen Mum happy. Maybe when she used to make doilies and paint sunflowers on our car roof. She used to be happy to see me in the mornings, and she was always happy when Grandad—her dad—came over. But somewhere along the way, she just stopped smiling.

Mum took to drinking sherry earlier and earlier in the day. I would sometimes get back from school and find Mum still in her nightie and dressing gown, passed out in front of our black-and-white TV while *Days of Our Lives* droned on, a bottle on the table beside her. Sometimes, before she passed out on the sofa, while still keeping half an eye on the soap opera tales of overseas people, she managed to remember us kids. She'd set out our dinner on the kitchen bench. Fish fingers on a tray, ready to be stuffed into the oven, along with cut-up tomatoes and chips. I never saw her do it, but at some point in the rat run of the living dead, she had remembered that she had four kids and they needed to be fed.

Those nightly feeds were the only times we kids noticed Mum in the house. Because Dad had stopped talking to Mum, I noticed that all four of us talked to her less as well. She was just a shape of a woman. Maybe even Jesus wasn't talking to her anymore. Grandad still talked to her though. He dropped into our house from time to time, always when he knew Dad wouldn't be there. He'd water the flowers, maybe put out the garbage. I saw how hard it was for him to see Mum fade away. He blamed my dad for that. I think he was looking for Mum, but he only found the shape of Mum carrying the weight of an empty thought bubble and a laundry basket full of clothes, or laying fish fingers out on a tray. He missed Mum, I think, missed her a lot. I wished I could have missed Mum the way Grandad did.

———

I'd sometimes skip going to school on Monday, just to let the shit show settle down from the weekend. I'd figure that by Tuesday, the stories of 'Tim the Pope' had had a good mauling from the kids in the playground, and those kids had mostly moved on. On those Mondays I'd go and hang out with Mum's parents for a few hours. They never asked why I was there. They never said much to me at all but I think they knew their place felt like a home for me. Grandad would be in his workshop whittling away at something. Nan would get me some sort of biscuit and a mug of hot chocolate as soon as I came in the door, then she'd go back to work.

Work for Nan was something like screwing an eyeball into a metre-tall plastic Wendy doll she'd been paid to restore. Nan was well known around our part of Auckland as the Dolly Doctor. Any time a part came off a dolly, the dolly's fretting owner could take it to Nan and she would put it back together. Nan's living room was a morgue of dolly parts. Spare arms with chubby pink plastic hands at the ends forked out of open drawers—to me it looked like the dollies were drowning in there, maybe screaming for help. Headless or armless or legless bodies were lined up along shelves above Nan's fish tank. On the shelves opposite, there were heads with their eyeballs missing or their hair shaved off or lips coloured over with black marker pen, or their skulls caved in from being run over by a laundry trolley or a car. They all lay there patiently in the Dolly Doctor's waiting room, waiting for treatment. I thought it was pretty cool, even if it was a bit kooky.

When I'd finished my biscuits and milk, I'd go and see Grandad. He was always making something useful for someone somewhere. Always looking out for ways he could make Nan's life easier. One day he was hammering tiny nails into a little wooden box with hooks on it. The look on my face must have asked the question.

'It's a box for pegs that will fit on your nan's washing line. She won't have to carry them in and out anymore.'

'That's a good idea, Grandad!'

I looked behind Grandad at the wall where he'd hung all his war medals in a line. They were shiny and obviously very important and valuable. They looked to me like they were the most important things in the world, and I could've stared at them for hours. Nan told me he'd seen a lot of war in his lifetime. He'd fought in both world wars and got medals for being a hero in both of them.

'A war hero? But he's so gentle! Grandad couldn't even kill a mouse, Nan!'

'Gentle doesn't mean you don't do what has to be done when something's not right, Tim. And trust me, my boy, some things aren't right! Hitler was not right.'

I didn't know much about Hitler, but I knew my grandad was a good and fair man, so I knew that he would've had his say if someone was a bully.

Grandad discovered my animal shelter. One day he followed me home after school. I didn't know he was there, but fair dinkum, that old fella followed me all the way down to the river. He popped out from behind a tea-tree bush when I was feeding my rabbits.

'You know rabbits are happiest when they are with their family group, Timmy.'

'Bloody hell, Grandad! Where'd you come from?'

'I had a feeling you were up to something down here.'

His eyes fanned over my refugee animal enclosure, with its refashioned chook-wire panels and old fence palings. He smiled, a beaming smile that spread like a beach across his face.

Happiness tugged at my insides, seeing him so proud like that. It was almost like a hunger pang, but more comfortable. His watery eyes twinkled green and blue. Two thoughts came to me: *maybe I got my love of animals from Grandad,* and *I wish Grandad was my dad.*

My words spilled out in such a crazy hurry that I could hardly keep up with them: 'And this is Jewel, this guinea pig is this one's dad, and this is Grit, he's a bush rat, I found him trapped in the riverbank. That's a family of five rabbits, and this here is Muddy, he's a gecko. Cool how they stand still like statues on rocks, hey Grandad? That one over there, that's a hedgehog and its back-leg spines were crushed by a car. Can't believe he's still alive!' Desperate to show Grandad everything, desperate not to leave anything out.

'Slow down, Timmy, I can see it all. Bloody hell! What a great job you've done down here, Timmy, to get all these little broken fellas going. I'm proud of you son.'

And just then, I knew I was the happiest kid in New Zealand.

After that, whenever Grandad came over to see Mum, he also brought leftover veggie scraps for my animals. He noticed the things I did. In a good way.

I reckon Grandad got me through school. He hated religion and what he called 'dogma'. He could see that school just seemed to be getting harder and harder for me. The headmaster had turned my name into trash, and I was a regular on the detention lists for most of the teachers. Branded a rotten apple, I reckon. Their judgement bit deep, like a bull ant. I never seemed to meet their expectations. They always said to me, 'We expected better from you, Tim', but I never knew why. Was it because God was meant to be on my side?

My English teacher was probably the worst. He eyeballed me through every lesson. He hated that I was a left-handed writer. Whenever I went to write with my left hand, he would smack me over the knuckles with a ruler, or a fist. When I clumsily gripped the pen in my right hand, my writing was always messy. I reckoned it looked like something left by a drunken spider with inky feet. Loved to think of a drunk spider with inky feet writing my English assignments for me. It made me laugh. On the inside.

'You've got detention!'

Most days I would get that from one of my teachers. I got detention just for having messy writing, or even something as stupid as staring at a teacher without blinking when they were talking or shouting at me.

I pushed on with telling Grandad how I was feeling: 'As soon as I think I'm a little caught up in class, I'm back to the bottom again. I've only just got my head around pennies and pence and now it's all decimal currency. Inches and yards are now the bloody metric system. I can't keep up. I'm writing something about my animals but the teachers say they can't read it. But I reckon it's also because they don't give a shit about my animals. I just can't keep up, Grandad.'

'Hang in there, my boy. I'll bet none of them know that parrots are allergic to avocados!'

We laughed. Together. I decided I was going to keep telling Grandad about shit that didn't feel right. 'I'm so shy, Grandad, I don't say anything. Makes the bullies think I'm a girl and the nerds think I'm weird. I've got no friends.'

'You know what you do about shyness, Timmy? You do the opposite. Be an extrovert! Say what you're thinking on the inside and say it loudly, son! Be a loudmouth, a show-off, a smart-arse. Show the bastards you're not afraid!'

Grandad's advice settled deep in my belly. Sitting on that riverbank with him beside me, and Ted wrapped around my arm, I could forget all the crazy people in my life. Just for a short time, but it filled me with a good feeling, like food did when I was hungry.

4

Beastly urges

Everyone knew that one of the people in our street was a paedophile. All of us kids were forbidden to go anywhere near his place. But he didn't seem that scary to me when he tried talking to me and Grandad as we walked along the footpath. And I knew he was good friends with the local greengrocer, so he couldn't have been that bad. That must've been how he knew that I needed vegetable scraps for my animals—the greengrocer must've told him. I only took scraps from this guy twice, but I did it because he seemed friendly and, like my mate John, I liked an underdog. Maybe it was my fault for talking to him. My fault for taking veggie scraps from him. We were all warned, so it shouldn't have been a surprise to me when he raped me.

He did it when I came to pick up vegetable scraps from him. It was a hot Sunday morning, in the summer of 1975. Everyone else had left for church, but I got out of it by lying to Dad, saying I had to deliver copies of *Awake!* I climbed over our back fence, went over his fence and then climbed down his orange tree. When I walked into his shed I shouted from the doorway, asking him if he had some spare scraps. He said there were plenty, but I had to wait while he finished cutting a piece of wood. I walked over to where he was working, and as soon as I got close to him he pushed me over the workbench. I tried to punch him but they were only airswings. One of his hands pressed the side of my face into the cedar sawdust, while the other pulled at the belt at my pants. I could only watch as long curly shards of freshly cut sawdust rose and fell with each of my heavy breaths. The smell was sour, rotting oranges, and old man stink.

'Keep quiet. Keep quiet and say nothing.'

I turtled into my own black-sky space, head hot with tears, thoughts crazy, bloodied with anger and hate, burrowing deep. I knew it was over when I could hear him buckling his belt. But the pain was still there, and I knew it would always be there. I knew it would hang around inside my body forever. What I didn't know was that its shadow would bully every one of my living moments from then on.

I went to the last part of the church service. I could feel my father's anger when he spied me slipping in through a side door. Brutal and unforgiving. Luckily, Steven was also late that morning, and because it was always assumed that Steven would have a 'good reason' for breaking any rule, neither of us ended up getting in trouble. All that day and all that night, I said nothing to anyone. No one at all. But it felt like a part of me had gone missing.

———

John and I rode like the fucking wind the following afternoon after school. John saddled the horses and we rode up into the hills. When the way ahead was flat, I kicked Cyrus into a gallop. Kicked him harder than I'd ever kicked him before. John and Diesel were always ahead of us, but this time, Cyrus and I took the lead. Cyrus and me, we were flying. But there was a darkness that afternoon. Inside me. It was like I was shut in the boot of the Morris Oxford. Every thought had a sharp edge to it and there was a fearlessness inside me that was new. I was driving Cyrus so hard he had white foam everywhere the saddle rubbed. Cyrus heard my war cry and, balancing on his haunches, raised his hooves in the air like Pegasus. I was a god, a god bitten by a devil's poison, and I was ready for war.

I turned to see that John and Diesel were about 100 metres behind us. Cyrus and I lurched into a gallop and charged explosively towards them. With one swipe of my willow lance, I clotheslined John from his horse, and we both crash-landed like shot-down World War II bombers. Crashed into the dirt. Rolling in a dust cloud like bombers. We were knocked out for a while, both of us, and I came to first. Something felt broken, maybe a wrist. Hurt like fuck anyway. I crawled over to John on one hand, dragging my body behind me. He had a cut across his forehead, must've been about six or seven centimetres long. He'd caught the edge of a rock, and blood dripped down his face over crusting red dust sealed in sweat.

John finally came to. 'What the fuck mate!'

'Sorry John, you alright?'

'There ARE rules bro, even though it's only a fucking game!'

'Sorry John, you okay?'

'Yeah, I'm okay. Bit fucked up, but alright.'

He was slow to sit up. His face was getting redder and wetter with blood. But he was smiling, and as he wiped blood off his face with a finger, a slow whistle escaped through the gap between two front teeth. 'You got the blood of the Māori in you today, bro! You got something you wanna tell me?'

'Nah, nothing to say. I'll be right.'

We didn't say anything for ages. Just sat there, staring at the dust.

'Alright then, let's go!'

We both wobbled across to the horses, who seemed entirely uninterested in our games, calmly grazing on poa tussocks. We slowly pulled ourselves up into the saddles. Then John raised a fist in the air and began hollering, 'Whatever doesn't kill ya makes ya stronger, hey bro!' and we took off for home.

Whatever doesn't fucking kill you makes you fucking stronger. But maybe not always. I would carry the real story of that assault inside me for decades, just waiting for its pathology to break.

———

I was nearly fourteen now, and I was learning to survive. I'd learnt to deal with the bullies at school by being a smart-arse. I'd learnt to deal with the headmaster by quoting scripture back at him. I'd learnt to deal with the nightly beatings from my dad because I had no other fucking choice. I didn't go anywhere near the back fence anymore. And there was good stuff happening around me, so I tried to focus more on that than on the shit.

My animal refuge was growing, and I knew I had a special

connection with all my broken and busted bush creatures. I always surprised myself by how I could make a fairly decent life for a hedgehog squashed by a car, and how I could make my bunnies so fat, fluffy and happy. Surprised to see the baby swallows that had fallen out of their nest get bigger every day, and watch them making friends with animals they had no business being friends with, like Ted the brushtail possum or Grit the bush rat. If it hadn't been for my animal friends at the river . . . oh, and John, and Grandad oh, and also Aunty Kez, Mum's sister, who wrote romance books, I reckon I would sum life up as being pretty fucking ordinary.

The best thing about turning fourteen was that I got myself a job with *The Dominion* newspaper. I was their new delivery boy. This job made good sense to me. I got away from the living dead in my home for longer, and I got $18 a month, which meant I could properly feed my animals. Sometimes I even got out of our Sunday enlightenment drives because I had to work. Also, Grandad found me another bike through a mate of his from lawn bowls. It was better than the old bike he gave me when I was eight, which was too small. Best of all, I felt like I was on my way out of being a kid who only got to do what someone else decided he could do. I was getting to the point where I could make my own choices, and soon I wouldn't have to take all the crap from the crazies in the Kingdom of Kookyland.

When Dad found out I had a job, he asked me how much I was earning.

'Not much, maybe eighteen dollars a month.'

That same day, he showed me a bill he'd been chalking up. He had written down every dollar he had spent on me for the fourteen years of my life.

'This is how much you've cost me. I think you can start paying me back now.'

He said that on his way out the door heading to an old folks home. He was going there to enlighten some poor dying bastard about the Good News about God's compassion. His words stung, like usual, but somehow my hide had grown as thick as a rhino's and my anger buried my hurt deep.

I also started volunteering at the local zoo, called Stagland. The offer was there for most kids at school, but I was the only one who took it up. I wanted to learn what to feed my bush animals, and even though I was amazed at how quickly I could get an animal to want to live again, I still wanted to learn how to look after them properly. So once a week, I would ride my bike to the zoo and spend two hours cleaning shit out of the animals' cages. I loved it.

Then Aunty Kez got married and we were all invited to her wedding. Aunty Kez had natural fight in her and rebelled against my family's religion as easily as Mum took to it with compliance. I loved her for that. I remember her once telling my dad that he was a weak man who used religion to hide the fact that he was a spineless bastard. And he was cheap. I was going to grow up to be just like Aunty Kez. I loved listening to how crazy angry beautiful words fell out of her mouth.

I also loved how Aunty Kez noticed me. In a good way. The night of her wedding, she poured some beer into my half-finished glass of Coca Cola. Filled up my glass. 'Drink it slowly!' Winking as she snuggled me close to her on a couch. I got lost in the stiff mozzie netting of her wedding dress. She stunk to high hell of synthetic vanilla or apple blossom or some other shit. She had her arms around me and I was swooning in those beautiful smells.

Her husband, Lou, was smaller than her, but that wasn't hard because Aunty Kez was over six foot. Lou was a fisherman. He had a big red bushy beard and a briny smell he couldn't shake, even when he wasn't working. He had an earring. Dad hated that he had an earring, but I thought it was the coolest thing I'd ever seen and I made up my mind there and then that as soon as I was out of the Kingdom of Kookyland, I was going to get myself an earring like Lou's. Lou was also steady and kind like Grandad. He was funny too, and he knew a whole lot of shit about music. All different types of music.

Sitting there tipsy between Aunty Kez and Lou, I thought that life was pretty good, the best thing being I was nearly not a kid anymore. I had a couple more of those beers without telling Aunty Kez, this time with no Coca-Cola, and when I got home I spewed all over Steven's bed on the way to mine. Dad beat me with his belt again that night. It was okay, though, because I had all of Lou's jazz music swirling inside me like soft caramel. I was going to be okay.

———

It was a Wednesday night, the night I maybe got to see Jenny Falcon in scripture class. Although I noticed she had been coming less and less. I reckoned that sassy mouth of hers could've been causing grief at home. I started wondering if a brain like mine, full of thoughts of wanting to see a girl, made you look different. Smell different. Different vibration or something. It was weird. It was just that, this particular night, I was getting lots of attention from the girls in the class. Especially from a girl who used to hang out with one of the Elders' daughters.

This girl mostly didn't say much in the Wednesday Kingdom class, but I do remember her being quite tall, and I remember her white neck seemed impossibly long to me. So much so that I thought of a tui bird every time I saw her. These birds are very common in New Zealand, and easy to spot because they have a long white tuft of feathers on their throat. So I will call her Tui, even though it's not her real name. Anyway, because Tui hung out with the Elders' daughters, she was considered, like them, to be a 'model of propriety', which is how the Elders—my dad included—saw them. I was never quite sure what 'model of propriety' meant, but I did know that one of the girls was called an 'easy lay' by John's mates, and I loved how mostly they seemed as messed up as the rest of us.

Tui was standing in front of the Jehovah's youth group, ready for her turn at the scripture recital. She was wearing a pleated dress with ugly purple flowers all over it. Her hair was pinned tight against her head, so tight the bun looked like it might tear her scalp open. When she looked out at the class, she found me in the back row and stared at me like I was the only bloody person in the room!

'Corinthians 4, chapter 12,' she began earnestly, 'we bless those who curse us. We are patient with those who abuse us . . .'

During that whole reading of the Corinthians scripture, when she wasn't looking down at her Bible, she was looking at me.

After the lessons, we all had a glass of an orange drink called Tang and inhaled lamingtons beneath a lemon tree in the backyard. Tui pulled at my elbow and told me she needed to talk to me. We went behind a flapping bedsheet hanging on a Hills hoist and talked—well, she talked, talked the whole time. Talked and smiled at me. Even though she was a lot older than me, she spoke strangely. More like my sister Rachel, who was only ten. She was giggling and excited. I hadn't collected a scrap of knowledge about anything to do with flirting and sex in my fourteen years as a Jehovah's Witness kid, other than watching the guinea pigs go at it and proverbs offering a spicy piece on laying your head on porcelain breasts, but I knew in my bones all this meant something. This was all body, all twisted smiles and half-closed eyelids, unfinished sentences and unfunny jokes. It had to mean something more.

'Wanna skip school tomorrow and go to the beach?'

'Yes.' My body made up its mind before my brain had any chance to think it over.

She picked me up in her sister's car. She'd partially released her hair from its prison, though it was still trapped at the back of her neck, and she'd replaced the stiff floral cardboard that was her Kingdom recital dress with a sack of white cotton—still stiff—that I guessed was her beach dress. We drove to the beach at Parua Bay, then she took my hand and we walked out to the sand dunes. I couldn't believe how everything felt, like I was hooked up to an electrical socket.

She set up a blanket on a flattish bit of sand in the dunes. Then there was some fumbling and kissing, and she took her top off. I looked at her boobs as though they were kneecaps at first. But then she took my hands and put them on her. I touched her boobs with a mix of shock and longing. Fucking terrifying longing. What followed was awkward and mostly clumsy. I ached for all the bits of her. It was a five-minute blackout. When I pulled my still-hard prick out from inside her, it was covered in blood.

'What?' I was confused and scared.

'It's okay, I'm a virgin.'

I had no idea that being a virgin meant there would be bleeding! I just thought being a virgin was a good thing for sex stuff. John had learned that from his *Playboy*: 'Blissed out with ten virgins!' Also the fact that Islamic martyrs died for the chance to meet 72 virgins in Heaven. John told me that being with a virgin was always going to be a good thing.

She used the edge of the blanket to quickly clean up the pooling blood. No sooner had she thrown on her white beach dress that she noticed the blood spreading in wider patches wherever the fabric touched her skin. She threw the blanket around her shoulders. 'I think we should go home.'

'Are you okay, Tui? I hope I didn't hurt you.'

She didn't answer. She just seemed anxious to get to the car as soon as she could. We both walked quickly, the flamingo dance going to the sand dunes replaced by a chook march to the car. Before I got in the car, I looked back to see a brilliant-red line of blood trailing back to the dunes. What looked like a thousand shockingly red drops on the white sand of Parua Beach. She dropped me home and then she went home. I was confused but thrilled. I had just 'had sex'—awkward, strange, clunky, wonderful sex! I had done it! I had a lot to tell John about.

———

It was Tuesday of the following week and Tui still hadn't come back to school. That was also weird. Kind of unsettling. Grandad found me with my animals after school. He had a strange look on his face, like someone had died.

'Timmy, come here, mate, I need to talk to you.'

This felt wrong. I thought maybe Dad had found out that I'd been collecting 'mostly dead' roadkill.

'There was an incident, son. I think you were involved in an *incident* where a young girl nearly lost her life.'

'What!'

He said Tui's real name. 'She is in hospital, son. She nearly died. Critical, apparently. Massive loss of blood.'

My thoughts fell in on one another like tiny grains in a collapsing sandcastle. It was murky inside my head. Memories popped up only in colours and shapes, textures. It was a mess in there, that was for sure.

'Son, she's what's known as a haemophiliac. Do you know what that is, Tim?'

He was so tender. I'd never seen that before. His ancient droopy eyes filled with tears. They looked like giant pools of ocean.

'No.'

'It's when someone's blood doesn't clot properly. Most people, if they have a cut, their blood seals the wound up pretty quick. Hers didn't. She nearly died because those stupid Jehovah's bastards refused to give her a transfusion. More blood, I mean.'

Now I remembered the darkening red-velvet blotches on the blanket, on her white dress, just getting bigger and bigger. I remembered the blood trailing back to the dunes like a giant bluebottle tentacle, only red.

'Is she okay?'

'She'll be okay, Tim. They gave her blood thickener. She'll be okay.'

I shut down. My head sunk into my shirt collar like a turtle. Everything seemed still. I could see ants in the dirt. Every part of them. Too much ant detail.

'She's saying you led her astray Tim. By making her have sex.'

'I didn't make her have sex! She wanted to have sex. How was I to know she was haema . . . whatever.' Fat hot tears started to roll down my face. 'My first go at sex and I nearly kill somebody!'

Grandad put his arms around me and held onto me. Tightly.

'It's okay, my boy. Wrong girl, wrong decision, that's all.'

I thought, *What the hell does a* decision *have to do with this?* 'She bloody asked me to go. Showed me what to do!' Held my hand, brought the blanket, showed me what bits to touch. 'Bloody hell, Grandad!'

Grandad got it, let my anger take its rightful place in my already sorely tested sense of justice. Thank God for Grandad.

'Thing is, mate, it's not looking good for you with the thugs who run the Jehovah's joint. What are they called, the Elders? That includes your goose of a father. They're gathering their heavyweights into something that looks like it's going to be a kangaroo court and they are going to come down on you very heavily, son.'

Angry, unfair, broken hurt feelings in my belly. A fresh batch. My first go at sex and I nearly killed Tui, a 'model of propriety'! Fuck! And the Elders, the people I hate most in the community, get to make a judgement on ME!

Fuck them!

It was hard to see my Grandad holding the weight of this thing in his eyes. 'I don't fucking care, Grandad. They're a bunch of hypocrites and she's thrown me to the wolves. Jesus, I didn't even know what I was doing!' I was pretty sure Jesus was no longer seeing the world as I saw it. But I had Rugby on Thursday and John was going to be there. I needed to talk to John.

Slow silent minutes passed. Too slow, and still too much

detail in the dust. I knew I was at the beginning of something truly horrible.

'So son, they have *summoned* you. Can you believe they even use that bloody word? To the Kingdom Hall on Thursday at four o'clock. They're going to go through your version of the story.'

'I'll bet they bloody will. Fuck, can't believe she said I made her do it. That I have to sit in front of the people I hate most in the world and they get to tell ME what happened!'

Because I knew it would go that way.

———

Thursday rolled around too quickly. I had skipped school to spend the day with my animals. Thoughts and feelings grew and swirled inside me the whole time. The 'courtroom' had been set up at Kingdom Hall. My father, the headmaster and Elder Winston were planted at a table at the front of the room. There was a single chair a few metres in front of them. Everything else in the room had been removed. The three Elders' self-assigned importance filled the room with a thick acrid stench that I was sure I could smell. The overhead fan was loud and slow and walloped away above us. The headmaster began proceedings.

'Sit down, Timothy.'

I sat.

'A very serious incident occurred this week, as I am sure you are well aware. A child nearly lost her life. Is it true, Timothy, that you took the young lady down to Parua Beach, where you then let your beastly urges overtake you? Is it true that you led her astray, that you had sex with this innocent child? Is this true, Timothy?'

My anger was ripping up the inside of my throat. I attempted to answer. It was grimy though. They had already made up their mind. They didn't want to know my story. I knew that well enough after fourteen years of being with these people.

'Yes, part of that is true. We did have sex down at the dunes.'

Silence. Then muttering, murmuring, everything too important and heavy.

'And are you sorry for what you did, Timothy?'

I waited a couple of seconds, staring at the faces of the people who had whipped me, beaten me, preached at me, the lines of righteousness in their faces chiselled in judgement. I made them wait, said nothing, just stared straight back at this mob of carnival clowns without blinking. There was a red-hot quiet. And then the words came to me.

'I'm not sorry that we had sex. I AM sorry about the mess it made though. Honestly, it looked like a car crash!'

Elder Winston sprang out of his chair. He clawed across the table, reaching for my throat, while the other two held him back. Only just though. His rage was only a toad's breath from finding me. 'You are a disgrace! You are a disgrace to your family! You are a disgrace to your religion, you are a disgrace to your school. The life of a young girl was at risk because you couldn't control your beastly urges!'

My father then spoke. I looked at him as if I had never known him and at the same time knew him too well. He calmed the room by carefully channelling the collective judgement of the Elders: 'You, Timothy Husband, have been disfellowshipped. You are no longer a part of our community. To do anything else means the chance of you corrupting others in the family and in the church.'

44

And then he quoted Corinthians, Chapter 5:13: 'Banish the wicked man from among you!' He hollered this into the ceiling fan as though he was giving a sermon on a mountain, his ugly lip line sagging in judgement, saliva frothing at the edges like decomposing fish shit. 'Go home, collect your belongings, and don't come back into this community. None of us want to see you here again. EVER again.'

I walked out of Kingdom Hall shutting the door carefully behind me. I walked through the streets. All the places I understood myself, all the places I didn't understand myself, I was leaving them all. I walked in a daze to the river, to my bush refuge. Grandad was there and he held me tight. I didn't cry though. I was numb. 'Please look after my animals, Grandad.'

I think he was crying. Then he shouted out in a voice I'd never heard before, 'Fucking crazy bastards!' It was pure anger. Hurting and spitting and loud. So very, very loud.

I knew there were things that needed to be done for the animals before I left. I told Grandad, 'I've made a list of all the things they eat, when they need to be fed, when the cages need to be cleaned,' handing him a scribble of lead pencil on a page torn from a school exercise book. Then I said, 'Thank you, Grandad. For noticing me. In a good way, I mean!'

Grandad pushed a few twenty-dollar bills into my hand and then gave me a tin box. It was battered and a bit rusty, and it was long, like my pencil box. Inside were all of Grandad's war medals and ribbons. It was like he was handing me the most valuable thing I could think of in the whole world. My mouth gave a twitch of a smile as I put my hand on Grandad's arm and leant my head on his old woolly flannel shirt. My head felt very heavy.

'This is your chance now, Timmy. Get out of this insane asylum. Make a good life for yourself, my son.'

I walked home. No one was there. Actually, the shape of Mum was there. She was passed out on the sofa in front of another afternoon soap opera. I didn't say goodbye. I chucked some clothes in a bag, just whatever was on the floor, and walked out of my house. I never returned.

5

On my own

All alone now. I am a young man leaving home. Leaving all those crazy fucks behind. Good riddance! It was quite clear to me that Jesus took sides and he wasn't taking mine.

'So fuck Jesus!' I shouted it into the darkening sky. Actually, I was excited! No more beatings, no more school, no more crazy stories about Jesus. 'Jesus doesn't live here anymore! No more crazy Jesus rules! It's my world! MY fucking rules!' Shouted that out on Stacy Street. Shouted it on Egleton Street. Shouted it through the suburbs of Whangārei so everyone knew the real truth about Jesus. 'Jesus is a LIE. You're never gonna see your nanna in Heaven. It's all a lie, a BIG FUCKING lie!'

Jesus never helped anyone I'd ever been close to. Not Mum, who was sucked out of her body by my dad. Not Grandad, with his daughter lost to the suburbs of Whangārei. Not the Falcon, who dared to ask questions. Not me, who had been abused, framed, raped. Where was Jesus then? 'It's ME bringing TRUE salvation to all you ignorant bastards because I know the truth.'

Dad's face was everywhere, scrunched in on itself like rotting fruit. Dad's face. Cracked. Violent. Everywhere. 'Aren't you proud of me, Dad, you old fuck?!' I think I was laughing, but it was a kind of lunatic noise that tumbled out. I hardly recognised it.

I wasn't sure where I was heading, almost like someone else was driving, and then I realised that I was making for Stagland—the only place I *could* go. Dick Brake, the man who'd owned the place for 25 years, was always letting off some backhander about the Jehovah scourge in town, and I knew he disapproved of my father. When one of the keepers let fly about the bastard Jehovahs who had come and hassled their mum on the weekend, I would see Mr Brake's face wince like he'd drunk a milkshake too quickly. He was my best chance of having somewhere to stay.

I wasn't taking my normal route to Stagland, though. I was stumbling around the back roads in a fog—back roads that spread like spilled spaghetti from the Whangārei suburbs into the bush. And I kept shouting, screaming stuff to the sky, over and over, because it just wasn't listening. Nothing, no one was ever fucking listening. Anger tore through me, spreading hate through my body and firing bullet tears down my face, as I walked hard into the falling night, hard into the wind, screaming into the sky so it fucking well listened.

'Fuck them all, I hate them all. Hate Dad, hate Jesus and hate the weirdo neighbour and fuck Tui for shafting me. SO fucked up. I hate them all!'

It was all shouting and gurgling and wiping tears away and wiping my nose across my sleeve and trying to catch my breath.

I sank onto the kerb at the bus stop on Kenny Road, not too far from Stagland. My head was heavy in my hands and my knees were tucked into my shoulders. Moans escaped my rocking body as I sat curled over my painful belly, keeping away the sharper of the pains.

'I hate them all . . .'

And then I became aware of a feeling I'd only ever had dressed like a penguin selling Jesus at flyscreen doors. Fear. Back then, it was fear of being recognised by someone from school. But sitting on the kerb, it dug deeper, like it was making tunnels through my body. I was really alone. Completely alone in the world. And I was always going to be alone. And it was terrifying. Then anger got hold of me again, and I started shouting more threats at the night. All the people I knew, except Grandad, had let me down. Oh, and Nanna and Aunty Kez. But other than them, I couldn't trust anyone anymore.

'I'm never going back! Never ever going back. No one can ever, ever make me go back.'

I ran from the bus stop, looking for some sort of shelter in which to hide. The possibility that anyone I knew might see me horrified me. I never wanted to see anyone from my other life ever again. On the old Silver Mine Road, I finally slowed to a walk, kicking at puddles. My body was numb. My head was dull and quiet. Nothing left to say.

The rest of the walk took much longer than usual. The 'STAGLAND' sign that hung from an old steel post at the corner of the highway and Silver Mine Road was a comfort when I finally came across it. For the last two years I'd turned down this road to do my volunteer shifts, but now it felt so very different. I stared down the long gravel road, the same road that I'd cycled down more than a hundred times. Darkness was starting to settle into the curves of things, and there wasn't a breath of wind. A couple of swallows were flying above, and I watched them glide around the tops of the pines and settle on a phone line. It was a strange comfort to know that birds were still showing me the way.

Walking down that road, I remembered how I used to imagine I was Dr Tracy from *Daktari* when I came to do my volunteering. I used to watch *Daktari* on TV after school. Rachel and I would never miss an episode. *Daktari* ('Doctor' in Swahili) was a TV show about a vet in Africa who would go everywhere to save animals—into jungles, into forests, into rivers. Saving animals that were hurt or trapped. I was always telling myself *Daktari* stories. Before I was chucked out of home, when I was on my way to Stagland, I used to make up my own *Daktari* stories in my head.

Daktari (me) *goes out into the wild world of Whangārei. He is part of the natural world, part of the natural order of things. He is an animal just like all the other animals he cares for in the wild. Daktari knows how animals behave in the natural world because he knows his world, watching with the keen eyes of an owl. The time comes for Daktari to leave his home. He must leave his home alone, just like the young male lions. He knows that young males often leave their pride and go out on their own. Out here Daktari is walking on the Auckland back roads, looking for his pride.*

But that was then. This was now. This time it was for real, and *Daktari* was just a show on TV at 4.30 in the afternoon.

'No more Jesus rules, no more school . . . no more crazy people . . . no more Dad . . .' I whispered it into the night as if to remind myself. Over and over like a prayer. A mantra. Trying to take back a shred of who I knew myself to be. All the while, I felt an undertow of exhaustion so intense that whenever I thought back to what had happened, I imagined what Lot's wife might have gone through when she turned to salt because she looked back at her home (Genesis 19:26). Unable to move. Dreading the next step. It took all my courage to walk up the stairs to Mr Brake's door.

6

Stagland

I waited for Mr Brake to come to the door. It was supper time, on that Tuesday 6th November 1976. My heart was beating as fast as a skink's in a closed hand. Then the man I'd only ever really known at a distance, through the mesh of animal exhibits, opened the door. He stared at me, taking in all of me. I knew instantly that he understood the story of what stood in front of him. My freckled tear-streaked face, swollen red by grief, anger, terror and wind. He could see it all. He looked worried. I had two thoughts: *I'm glad it's not God on sale this time when I'm knocking on doors,* and *he looks so different up close.*

'Come in here, lad. Come on in.'

In minutes, I was holding a hot cup of Milo in my hands, while the old fella and his wife, lit by a single cone of warm yellow light, peered at me across a flowery plastic tablecloth in their kitchen as though I was some kind of injured animal. Their concern was heavy but it wasn't uncomfortable.

Just as I went to spill my guts, Mr Brake said, 'We heard what happened, lad. It's all okay, you're safe here.' His hand was on my arm. The connection felt familiar for a moment, then I pulled away. Alarm running through my body. *How does he already know about it?* Everyone across the whole of Whangārei had to know my crimes. They were going to find me and drag me home for more punishment. Or maybe they thought I was just another kid running away from home. Another homeless juvie crim.

'Settle lad, your secret is safe with us.' He leant into the light. 'I don't know if you knew, but I am a friend of your Nan and Grandad. Your Grandad rang me to tell me what happened, said he thought there was a chance you might come here. You are safe here with us, lad.'

If a feeling could be a temperature, then I had a tiny spark warming the inside of my chest. Seeing Mr Brake's face up close was a comfort. It was wrinkled and pocked and weathered. Like the corrugated potholed asphalt on Smith Street. Like my Grandad's face. He had light-blue eyes the colour of the oceans I'd seen on the travel posters at Tony's Travel World in the mall. Dick Brake seemed kind, an old armchair kind of kind.

'You know me, obviously,' he said, 'but I don't think you know my wife. This is Sandra.'

I lifted my face into the light and nodded to his wife. It was hard to look at another person, especially these adult people I'd never really known before. But the eyes that met me were warm. They were kind, too. Still seeing me. In a good way.

Suddenly, Mr Brake clapped excitedly. A single clap. 'I'm going to give you a full-time place here at Stagland, Mr Tim Husband!' His voice had changed now his mind was made up.

He was speaking a bit like a TV show host, almost too happy, excited by everything. 'You will work alongside our head keeper, until you learn all there is to learn about Stagland. You will answer to him, and if he isn't around you will come to me. How does that sit with you, Mr Tim Husband?'

I sat more upright, my shoulders pulled back, with every mention of this adult version of Tim Husband. Had to, because I had a job now, and maybe a place to stay. I was sitting tall because I was a young lion making my own way. Daktari poked holes in my pain and lines of light peeked through my body.

'I only have one requirement before I give you this job, Mr Tim Husband.'

I was confused. What else could I possibly offer? All I was, owned and hoped for, sat in a kitchen chair in front of Mr Brake at that moment.

'I want you to continue with your schooling. You are only thirteen . . .'

'I'm fourteen.'

'Yes, well, you may be, but ten years of education is not enough to get you started in any way once you leave Stagland, lad. I want you to finish your education at night school. Here in the TAFE at Whangārei. I am a good friend of the teacher at the TAFE and we will work out how to proceed. I will call him tomorrow.'

My first thought was to question whether Daktari should be required to finish his schooling before entering the jungle and saving animals, even though entering jungles to save animals didn't seem to be on the table as one of my options at this time. Also, I never ever ever wanted to go outside the fence of Stagland again. TAFE meant town, and town meant maybe coming face to face with my family, and family meant anger, and anger lived as hate in the termite tunnels of my tummy.

'Are we agreed, Mr Tim Husband? I will provide all your food, your accommodation, your textbooks. All in exchange for a full day's work, every day. You will have Sundays off. You can choose whatever you would like to do that day. We are happy for you to join Mrs Brake and I and our family for the day. It is up to you.'

There was a long silence that I wasn't sure if I was supposed to fill.

'Well, how do you feel about this idea, Tim?' Mr Brake's TV voice was gone.

'Thank you, Mr Brake. I am very happy to stay here with you, and yes I will go back to school, and I am even more happy to be helping you with your animals. Thank you. Thank you very much, sir.'

They both sat there. They looked satisfied. Quiet and satisfied. Very worried too.

'You're a good lad, Tim. You don't deserve what happened to you back there.'

That came from nowhere, but he said it like he meant it, like he knew what had happened. Like he actually cared. Of course, he couldn't really know what had happened, and why should he care? It's like I couldn't put that sentence anywhere in my brain or my body. But my head hurt, and I was as close to a feeling of being safe as I could get after I had just had every door of my life slammed shut.

'Come with me, lad. I'll show you your new home.'

We followed a line of torchlight through the downy darkness of that long night, down a path sodden with black soil and kauri pine needles. My new home soon appeared, an old caravan. Briars clambered up the back end, and the roof at the front splayed off into two crooked star posts and a tarp covering. Steel buckets were piled on top of one another around what looked like a watering trough. I could hear the low breathy roaring of lions. It felt like they were only metres away.

'This is one of our watering stations for the lions, and don't worry, they are at least fifty metres from here and all safely locked up. Later, you can clear the buckets away and make a smoko spot for yourself out here!'

He chuckled. I liked that Dick Brake enjoyed his own jokes. Like Grandad.

We stepped up into the caravan. The walls bubbled with peeling lime-green vinyl. Two gas rings held up an old kettle and an iron frying pan. There was a fixed table covered in tan linoleum, one cushioned vinyl bench behind it. At the back, tucked under a line of cupboards, was a bed with a cover on it—a sun-bleached, tie-dyed cover, once loud with rainbow mandalas, still held the shape of the last person who'd slept there. There was a long window behind the bed, glass etched with the dark soil and branches of kauri pine whipped up by north Auckland westerlies. The smell was familiar, similar to my animal refuge. Mould, sweet pine, rat shit, and hot plastic sweating after days of summer. All mingling with the fetid farmyard smell of animal dung. My Daktari cave.

'Home sweet home. What d'ya reckon, Mr Tim Husband?'

'It'll be fine for me, I reckon!'

And I did reckon it was great. It could have been a shed-sharing thing with the chooks and it'd still have been great. Great because there was no Dad there. Really, really great because Jesus wasn't there. No Elders, no headmaster, no Tui and no fucked-up neighbours. Besides that, it was as close to a home as I was going to get, and I was safe. AND I was brave. AND I was free.

I took a breath. It was shallow and sat in my throat as if undecided. I was still so fucking angry. And sad and frightened. My throat burned. Courage and fear seesawed in my head, busy with all their blustering, and gave me a terrible headache.

Mr Brake put his hand on my shoulder and I instantly flinched. That was new. There was some sort of shutting down happening inside me.

'Try and get some sleep, lad, though I know it will be hard. When you wake up tomorrow, go over to the big feeding shed. You know where it is. You'll find the head keeper there. Remind him also to give you a jug of milk every morning. Hope you like milk! Goodnight lad.'

Mr Brake left and I sat on the bed. I was tired. Bone tired, as Grandad used to say. I lay back in the soft flickering light of the overhead bulb. I pulled the rainbow cover around my body. My thoughts were still tangled, like clothes in a washing machine. Their wrangling efforts to get my attention were inner monologues that would become my only company for many years ahead. But not even being excised from my own life could stop the steady drum roll of sleep, and before I knew it, I was in deep dark damp jungle sleep.

I am a young Daktari, a young lion man just making my way in the world. I'm surrounded by sky-reaching jungle trees and horizon-stretching savannahs. There are animals as far as I can see. Some I don't even recognise. My school encyclopedia has broken into 3D. Grandad is here, stirring something over a campfire.

John is here, hunting for our dinner with a spear. Ted is swinging around Grandad's arm. I am stalking an antelope. I think it's an antelope. Could be one of the kooks from the Kingdom. I have a spear too. Occasionally I stand up to look over my new world. I am strong, tall. Bloody strong like Daktari. Dad is also here, in the dark shape of a hovering cedar tree, reaching into the sky. Behind him, the man who hurt me, a darker tree shape, taller than my dad. When I look up at the trees towering in the black sky above me, it is as if I am the size of an ant. The Dad-tree has begun to fall, and everything in my world is scampering in its growing shadow. The tree behind is also falling. Its shadow is longer deeper thicker. Even the black sky is falling. One of the branches on Dad-tree is a willow spear. It's jabbing at the dirt, looking for its target. Looking to crush everything beneath it, crushing all my world beneath it . . . I'm running, running. Sometimes Dad's spear turns into a belt and its buckle whips at the air behind me . . . I'm running, running . . .

I woke in terror. It was still dark and I had no idea where I was. My rage had abandoned me and all I could feel were the tendrils of my dream disappearing from my mind like snakes down holes. It left behind a shivering cold shape of me. The night had emptied me and I felt utterly alone. It felt like the black sky lived inside me now. Memories of yesterday began to surface, and they felt like broken glass inside my head, sharp-edged flashes of colour and shapes that hijacked my thoughts.

The emptiness was so overwhelming I could hardly move. How I hated them all for hurting me so much. The tears flowed again, stinging like hell as they leaked across skin raw red from yesterday's hammering. But the sun had snuck through the blinds into my caravan in lines of soft warm light across the lime-green vinyl. That was soothing. The day had found me, and I was relieved that at least I could take one step forward.

I met the head keeper that first morning at the feed shed, a man I'll call Mick.

'How ya doin' man? I heard a bit about what happened. Sounds shit.'

'I'll be alright.'

Fuck, how does he know what happened? Pissed off that he knew. There were a few other keepers milling around but they kept to themselves. I bet they fucking knew as well.

'It's alright, bro, everyone in town knows. Between you and me, it's fucking shit what happened to you. You're gonna be okay here though, bro.'

Mick put his hand on my shoulder but all I felt was cold and empty inside. Something was happening to my body that didn't feel good. Things were sealing up. Airtight.

Mick took me around all the animal exhibits I never got to see as a volunteer. We saw a couple of lions, some monkeys, deer and bison. He showed me what my job was. Which exhibits had to be cleaned, and how to clean them. How to prepare the midday meal for the animals. How to feed it to them. I was relieved that I already knew a little of what it took to keep animals well and alive, because of my little refuge for bush animals at home. The day was full of jobs to be done, jobs to remember how to do, so many routines for animal feeding and watering that had to be organised. Daktari appeared a little more, and the emptiness and the hate hurt a little less. For just a while I could hold myself still and not think about yesterday.

Getting used to my caravan home was hard in those early months. Just learning to live alone. No brothers, no sister, no mother. Not that I'd liked any of them much, but they'd been family. They'd been all I knew and all I had. I did know a little about looking after myself, because I'd had to. I knew how to boil water for hotdogs and how to cook an egg and make toast. But that was all. Mum had hardly been there for us because she'd walked a weird tightrope: trying to be some kind of mum to us as well as trying to be everything Dad hoped for in a Jehovah's wife. And being a good Jehovah's wife basically meant doing what Dad told her to do. Dad, along with all the other male Elders, were the only ones who truly understood God's Word, because they were his trusted messengers.

'Mums and kids use only their ears, not their mouths,' Mum used to say to us. 'It's not our place to question why,' she'd often add. And it was always the case that 'Dad'll know what to do'.

I used to ask Mum, 'Why don't you ever stand up to Dad? He's a bully, Mum.' But she'd ignore these questions, if she was ever sober enough to take them in.

Each day of my new life started with a piece of toast and Marmite. I taught myself how to drink the gravelly coffee that had been left in a jar. I reckon some of it could've been straight mouse shit. It was okay with three teaspoons of sugar, though. I also drank milk. One of Mr Brake's kids brought me over a fresh bottle every morning after the keepers had milked the dairy cow from Friendship Farm, and they'd leave it at my door. Knowing my creamy bottle of milk was waiting for me made me want to get out of bed every morning. I'd never tasted anything as delicious before, drinking most of it the same day it arrived. I was also slowly getting the hang of cleaning out the enclosures and preparing frozen chunks of horse carcass for the lions. I'd get the horse legs from the freezer. The bales of hay for the stags came from the shed. Soon, Mick didn't follow me around anymore because he could see that he didn't need to. I was getting better at doing my jobs, mostly because Mick was such a good teacher. He was always very clear with his instructions and I often tried to remember them by repeating them in my head.

When lunchtimes came around, I would always take my spam and tomato sauce sandwich to the lemur exhibit. There was a viewing bench in front of it. I'd sit on that and watch a single lemur who, most days, was draped over a dried-out old slab of kauri pine. There were a few other lemurs in the exhibit and they too were often asleep, on the hard cement. The single lemur on the kauri branch looked like a blob of wax melting over the wood slab in the summer sun. We would both sit quietly, staring at each other in the midday heat, separated only by a fence. I noticed something hollow in his eyes, something dull and resigned—the same hollowness I'd seen framed in Mum's eyes, the one in my own eyes. I wished that the hollowness in the melting lemur's eyes would fill up, as I didn't like to see the despair in there. As we watched one another, I'd think about how we were the same in so many ways, but also different. He was still trapped in his enclosure but I was free, and brave. But still so angry. I took a deep breath in. So very angry. I wondered how free I really was. The breath out was long and laboured as I thought about how trapped I was. I couldn't seem to do much about my anger but I could make his life inside his enclosure better so he would be happier, freer. Then I thought about how I could actually make that happen. I decided I was going to watch the lemurs really closely. I was going to learn how they behaved, what made them excited, what upset them, and what calmed them down when they were distressed.

Sometimes, if the lemurs were mostly asleep, I went to hang out with Len, the old European keeper who looked after the geese. His real name was long and hard to pronounce, so everyone called him Len. He was always patient and tried to teach me things. Len had a way of talking that was almost like the preachers in my last life, but somehow different. He didn't stare into me when he spoke and he never pointed fingers at me. He didn't really mind if I listened or didn't listen to him. He was just telling me how he saw and understood life. How different this was from the Elders, not only because it was stuff I was interested in, but Len wasn't demanding I listen—he was talking to me, not at me. He explained how every animal had so much to teach us and we could only really learn by watching them closely, which I found fascinating. He told me how important it was to learn about animals, especially now that the number of humans on the earth was increasing so much that animals had fewer and fewer places to live.

'That's why zoos are so important, lad,' he would say, because we could conserve animals in zoos until such time as they had safer places in the wild to thrive.

It was my first real introduction to how important the conservation of animals was, and why zoos played such a big part in protecting them. It was weird to think that what we did at Stagland every day actually made a difference to someone in the world rather than just me and the Jehovahs. That I was no longer missing out on having a useful life because I was too busy preparing the unenlightened bush folk for their next life.

Another reason I liked to hang out with Len was because

I knew that, unlike some of the other keepers, he didn't know many people in town, which also made him the better choice for a lunchtime companion. Some of the other keepers gave me weird looks, like they knew the worst of my crimes. I always preferred to be with the animals or with Len at smoko rather than listening to Mick and the other keepers chewing the fat about what had happened at the pub the night before, or make fucked-up jokes about how girls looked, how big their arses were, who had done what to them, and where to find them in which pub. I hated talking about them. Girls, I mean. Besides, whenever I spoke to other people, I felt the same old burn crawling up my throat. An anger so explosive, so close to the surface, that it never took much to get me stirred up.

As it turned out, I hardly spoke at all in those first few months, unless it was to ask about animal behaviour, so no one took much notice of me. I liked it that way. I was always much happier with the lemurs.

—

Afternoons, I'd use my rake and clear out the night shelters for the deer and antelope, which I'd let out into their day paddocks that morning. The stink in the night shelters was especially sour and pissy—like the changing room at school, only with animal shit in it.

All the animals at Stagland were locked away in shelters at night. Mick said it was so you could check them and make sure they were all in good health. This gave me a chance to clean out the day enclosures. The day paddocks were bigger enclosures and weren't covered by a roof. Mick told me to call them 'exhibits' as that was the official name for animal enclosures at zoos. Sometimes, stags or does walked closely around me or stood silently beside me, chewing hay as I raked. They seemed to only be interested in keeping me company. At those times, I would feel some of my loneliness fill in, a warming inside. I'd believe I might be happy again one day. I would daydream that I might even own a farm, with lots of different animals to look after. Some days I dreamed that I would run a zoo, as one of the best zookeepers in the world, with lots of exhibits full of contented animals. I would know how to do everything: collect amazing animals from all around the world, work out their diets, observe and understand their behaviours. Well enough that I could make better habitats for them, which would mean happier animals more of the time. My zoos would also be better because I'd learn which animals liked to live with each other, and I'd try to mimic complex habitats that were closer to the wild ones I'd seen on *Daktari*. I'd get lots of people to come to my zoo and learn about animals. I would explain why we had to look after animals, because so many of them were disappearing so fast. I would be so good at running the zoo that I would get the job of director of the zoo, and then I'd be the best director of zoos in the world. I might even build a zoo one day, better than any other zoo in the world . . .

'Tim. Tim. Tiiiiim!' hollered Mick from the bison exhibit. 'Come over here, bro, there's some cleaning to do!'

My daydream evaporated and I walked over to him with my wheelbarrow full of shovels.

'You with us, Tim? Where'd ya go? I've been watching you for half an hour and you've been somewhere in Zanzibar, given how little your rake moved!'

It was a good-humoured jab because he knew I was a very hard worker. He also watched over me like the protective silverback gorillas I knew from my encyclopedia. One day he said to me, 'You've taken to this like a duck to water, young Tim!'

Confused, I asked him what he meant.

'The whole zookeeper thing I mean. You've taken to it like a duck to water. You're a natural with animals, young fella.'

Well, that filled me to the brim. For a few days I had a spring in my step and probably asked quite a few more questions than I usually did.

My endless questions about animal behaviours used to annoy some of the other keepers, however. I knew that because they'd often laugh among themselves, then look at me and stop laughing. One of the lion keepers decided a good name for me was 'Jockstrap'. I reckon he decided on that as a way of embarrassing me to get me to shut up.

'Get any on the weekend, Jockstrap?' That sometimes got thrown around on Monday morning when I walked past the feeding shed with my wheelbarrow while the other keepers were having smoko.

'Got some sleep if that's what you mean.'

'Bit of a smart-arse, aren't ya Jockstrap!'

'Fuck off.'

Wasn't the best way of communicating with the outside world, but it was all I had for a while. It would be many years before I realised that I was purposefully keeping people as far from me as possible. My anger was both my armour and my friend, and it was all I needed for company. I even got used to 'Jockstrap'. It was better than 'Pope', and besides that I had no idea what it meant— I thought it was maybe something to do with horse harnesses.

My nights were often the same, with me not finishing work until it was dark. The day's work would have so consumed my attention that there was never enough time to write down all that I'd learnt from the animals before sleep fast-tracked me through to morning. But some nights, when I wasn't so tired, I'd go into my caravan, put a pot of water on the stove to boil, then dump in spaghetti. After that I'd throw an egg into a frying pan along with one of the half-dozen sausages that Mr Brake gave me at the start of each week. Then I'd get busy writing about and drawing all my observations from that day. On those good nights, I was often excited, as the animals seemed to be showing me new behaviours—or maybe it was just that the more closely I watched for new behaviours, the more I noticed. On those nights, as my dinner cooked—and it was only ever sausages, eggs and spaghetti—I couldn't write down everything I'd discovered fast enough. I didn't want to forget anything, including stuff I picked up by listening to the other keepers.

People's behaviour interested me too, but only in that I had to learn how to be with them. I hadn't had much experience with 'normal' people except for Aunty Kez, Grandad and John. The rest were all freaks. Religious freaks with their freakish rules and stories. Even outside the Jehovah's Witnesses, people seemed to carry on in a way that was far more baffling than how the animals acted inside the zoo, but I still needed to know how to be around people, and I was always impressed with how Mr Brake and Mick seemed to have the respect of all the other keepers, so I watched them carefully. I put a new heading in my notebook, 'People behaviour and respect', and I wrote down weird behaviour by any of the keepers that would trouble Mick, like laziness or their having big egos, and I watched how he dealt with those keepers and how he worked to resolve any fallout with the other keepers. I also wrote down any clever ideas that Mick or Mr Brake told me about management, and tucked it all away with my animal books.

On those good nights, when I'd finished all my writing and drawing, I would lie on my bed with the two animal books Len had given me: *The Pictorial Encyclopedia of the Animal Kingdom* and *Wild Horses of New Zealand*. As I drifted off to sleep, I'd memorise whole paragraphs of *Wild Horses of New Zealand*. It was the second book I'd ever read from cover to cover. The first was the Bible. I also found myself wondering if escaped lions were strong enough to tear down caravan doors. Their blood-curdling roars often ripped through my home like thunderclaps just as I was falling asleep. Thankfully as the months passed, I got a lot more used to it.

The bad nights outnumbered the good in the early years at Stagland, and they followed the same script. I walked into my caravan like there were a thousand lead weights in my pocket. The single light in the caravan would flicker yellow and blotchy in the evening when I came in from work. As I laboured to work up an appetite, a dread would crawl over me as predictably as it had during Sunday sermons in my other life, and I came to fear it nearly as much. The pain came in streaks. Like the storms John and I used to ride the brumbies through. The loneliness came in streaks too. It was a dark loneliness, no floor to it, no ceiling, like black sky. But not the night sky, twinkling with stars or lit by the moon. My lonely feelings stretched further than my courage could hold. I was not Daktari at night, I was a tiny piece of space junk floating to nowhere. I was flailing in that black sky. My hot fat tears exhausted me into sleep on those nights.

But just when I felt completely overwhelmed, my Daktari mantra would return, as though something was holding me together. I am brave and free . . . and I'm tired . . . and . . . it would be so good if Aunty Kez and Grandad were . . . And then I'd fall asleep with the scented memory of Aunty Kez's artificial apple blossoms and a soundtrack of rumbling lions.

Some days were a surprise, the days when my emptiness was interrupted. Like the day Mr and Mrs Brake had me over to the main house for a cup of Milo. After quick questions and answers about my job and which animals I most liked working with, this came: 'I never liked your dad.' Mr Brake just went right for it! 'Hated seeing him in town. But the Jehovah's breed like bloody rabbits and the place started filling up with him and his kooky disciples. Can't stand all their dogma. The community just isn't the same anymore. They're like bloody weeds.'

Suddenly, the faces of the three Elders bellowing at my 'banish the wicked man' hearing, especially my Dad's, filled my head like they'd never left. The passing of time had no power over these gut ghouls that came up when called. They were broken images, chopped up in space, but when called on, they were just as clear as the day I'd left. Faces too close and bloodied and monstered. I dropped my head. My chest felt tight. Locked in and sore and tight.

'Oh boy,' continued Mr Brake, 'it is a good, good thing that you left that lunatic asylum of a home. He is a hypocritical bastard, your father, that's for sure. And cheap! All his talk about charity and his own family gets around in a broken clapped-out old car. He doesn't even have the balls to buy your mum a house but takes her and his four youngsters from council house to council house. Sucking off the very welfare his religion is supposed to provide for. I'm right behind your grandad when he rages about your dad, mark my words!'

A pause let us all take a breath. And then he took off again. 'And no playtime for any of you! Weekend after weekend, vacation after vacation. All devoted to Spreading the Word. Four little kids preaching to strangers! It's no life for anyone let alone a youngster! You poor kids. You're better off without those Jehovah's jokers, charlatans all of them.'

Mr Brake turned to me. He was sweaty from all his ranting. It was like he'd changed channel on his brain's personal TV again and he'd got his normal, gentle voice back now. It was deep and Grandad-like, almost pleading: 'Don't end up a dumb fuck like your brothers, Tim. Don't just finish school and start preaching. You've gotta finish your time at TAFE, get a decent education and take up a trade, son. Do you hear me?'

I hear you, Mr Brake. I hear you. That filled me up like a glass of milk from Friendship Farm, and it kept the emptiness away for weeks. After that, I spent more and more time staring at my lemur friends and imagining climbing structures, and that kept my emptiness away for more and more weeks. Slowly, as my days were filled more with thoughts of how to improve life for the lemurs and how to get bored lions back into play, the day's jobs stuffed the black lonely night sky back into the empty termite tunnels deep inside me.

———

Wednesday nights I'd turn up at Whangārei TAFE. I would cycle there and back with the old bike Mr Brake had given me. The thought that I might come across someone from school, or worse, my own family, made me so shit-scared that I would always wait until nightfall to get to TAFE, often turning up half an hour late. It was a real mix of people in my Wednesday night classes. Single teenage mums trying to get ahead for their kid's sake, kids who'd lost their interest in Shakespeare to coke and dope, the abused kids who had become the abusers, the kids who had 'let their beastly urges get the better of them', all the juvie crims. They were all there, laying puzzle piece next to chewed-up puzzle piece, trying to get a better picture of what their broken lives might look like if they just managed to pay a little attention. I always felt safe at TAFE, even though I never talked to anyone. We were in the same boat because we were all survivors. I think we knew that about each other and it gave me a sense of connection. We seemed to offer one another the best version of social interaction, and it was as much as any one of us could manage.

For me, TAFE was also good in that I got to go to the library and borrow every animal book they had on the shelf. In my last life, I was never allowed to bring books home from the library. Dad would throw any animal books I brought home in the bin or just rip them up in front of my brothers, Rachel and my mum. Sometimes he used scissors. But the TAFE library books always had a safe journey to and from my caravan, and every one of the books I borrowed taught me a little bit more about how and why animals did what they did. From *The Pictorial Encyclopedia of the Animal Kingdom* to *Watership Down*, I scoured every shelf for every tiny morsel I could find. I would tuck *The World of the Honeybee* inside a heavier textbook on English grammar. Inside my algorithm folder, a Reader's Digest book on camel nutrition would find its way to the caravan.

My mate John seemed to often be in my thoughts. I wondered

if he'd finally made the first-grade Rugby team. I wondered if he'd found another jousting companion. Whether he'd got together with the girl who'd just started at the front desk of Tony's Travel World. I wrote to John over the first couple of years of my free life—it was hard to visit him because of all my jobs at Stagland and because it was hard for me to feel safe anytime I left the zoo compound. He wrote back to me at first, and I loved getting his letters, even though most of them were about stuff I didn't know much about, like different plays for a left wing on a Rugby field, or treating saddle sores on Diesel's back. He was always blabbing to me about which of his brothers was the latest to hook up with one of the girls on his street.

Very occasionally, I got the courage to go out of the gates of Stagland to actually see John in person. Getting around the back streets of Whangārei on my bicycle without being recognised required stealth, but I was starting to think people might not even recognise me anymore. A couple of times I met John at the river with the brumbies. But we would just ride hard and joust harder. John would never talk about what had happened to me other than to say that it all sucked, and somehow my anger had built walls blocking where our conversations used to flow. Besides that, John had actually got together with the girl at Tony's Travel World and he told me it was serious. Even though John and I would always stay mates, I reckon whatever I was going through was too much for either of us to handle. Our talks became stilted, pocked with pauses and smothered secrets, eventually forcing more and more months between our meetings, and then we only communicated if there was news John felt I needed to know—like when my nan had breast cancer and they were going to do an operation.

I was sad for Nan, sad for Grandad. I knew Mum'd be on her knees praying for Nan. 'Jesus isn't listening, Mum! Don't know why you bother!' I'd shout that at my caravan roof while I cooked dinner. I wished I could help Nan like she had helped so many people and their dolls as the Dolly Doctor of Whangārei. But I never did go and see Nan and Grandad again while I was at Stagland. Somehow that was just too painful. A year after the operation, John told me Nan had died, and the news blew softly and sadly down the empty tunnels inside me and slipped quietly into the painful pool of my past, as if it had always belonged there.

Loneliness continued to live in me like cold in a freezer— 'symbiotic' was the word my encyclopedia used. I had learnt to rely on myself for everything. I was my own best friend, my own worst enemy, my own teacher and my own family. With my stories sealed safely inside me, oyster-shell tight, I was able to keep everyone I knew at arms-length. Anger had locked in hate, trampled on trust, and governed them both in a self-styled dictatorship that kept me from getting close to anyone in the outside world.

It would be many, many more years before any of my gut secrets would see the light, and in the meantime, anger morphed into both my companion and my jailer, and he lived in my brain. He was me, but somehow not me. I called him Tom because it sounded like Tim. I replaced the 'i' with an 'o' because the 'o' had a hole in the middle. And that was more like Tom. No centre. Tom always told me he was there to protect me. He always turned up when he wanted and left when he wanted. He was his own boss and I was never allowed to ask anything of him.

7

Learning from lemurs

Every six months, all the keepers were assigned different animals. Except for Len. He was only ever 'Keeper of the Geese'. Apparently, having looked after all the animals at the zoo throughout his life, Len had decided he had the most to learn from geese. The keepers would gather at the feeding station to hear Mick read out who would be assigned which animals, and in my second year at Stagland, I was officially invited to the gathering. It was the first time I had been 'assigned' anything other than Bible stories. The air was sharp that morning, acrid and heavy with the bloodied stink of freshly butchered cow and horse carcasses. We'd all got used to that though, it was all part of living tough as keepers. Daktari tough.

Mick reeled off the list of changes for the senior keepers before he finally got to me. 'Tim, you will be responsible for all the ungulates. All the deer, the antelopes, the three bison and all the yaks. They'll all be relying on your good husbandry skills. What you say goes, okay lad?'

He shouted his instructions a little too effusively. I think it was because he knew the other keepers would feel challenged by how steep my very first promotion was. He wanted to be very clear about how things stood with management.

'Also Tim, Mr Brake and I would like you to start working with the primates. You will be assigned the lemurs.'

It was as much as I could do to stop myself jumping up and down, like I had when I was eight and Grandad appeared at our front door with an almost-new bike for me. My *officially* assigned animals! I was totally in charge of ALL the ungulates and my very favourite of all the animals, the lemurs, my lunchtime mates! While eating a spam sandwich, I had watched them play—or not play as I came to notice—for nearly two years, and now I would get to go in and feed them. Get to go in and look after them. Get to just be with them. I got even more excited when Mick told me quietly that now that I'd been assigned animals, Dick Brake wanted to start paying me a wage.

I'd have loved Grandad to see me. Tim Husband, almost sixteen years old and *Keeper of Ungulates and Lemurs, STAGLAND*. I repeated it over and over in my head all afternoon. I could hardly believe it.

My daily routine was now fixed. For me that was good. Fixed long hours, hard work. No time to get lost in my thoughts. It was always a good thing for me to have a routine. I'd let the ungulates out of their overnight shelters in the morning and go in and clean up their night-time shit pile. A rake and a wheelbarrow were all I used. I'd rake up around their feed trough, then I would put out some pallets of fresh straw and put hay in their basket.

Afternoons, I'd spend with the lemurs—cleaning, observing, 'being responsible for them'. Months flew by, and I felt stronger and stronger.

There were all sorts of rules around animals 'coming into season' or 'coming into rut'. Mick explained to me, in my early days at Stagland, that 'coming into season' meant they were ready to either get pregnant, if they were female, or get a female pregnant, if they were male. I knew the stags were 'coming into season' because their normal sleepy cud chewing turned into crazed eyeball rolling, snorting, ground-pawing and stinky piss. They spent the whole day eyeing up other stags who had been their cud-chewing mates only the week before! Mick taught me that in rutting season you had to lock the stags away, otherwise 'they'll be fucking the females like drug-crazed rabbits!'

One day I asked him, 'Do y'reckon that's the same thing as being driven by their beastly urges?' I knew I'd fucked up before that even came out of my mouth, but my brain was still trying to make sense of what was Jehovah's dogma and what was normal.

Mick stood still for a second, just staring at me. He was often still like that when Jehovah's scriptures rolled out of my mouth without my consent. It was like they were stuck somewhere inside my brain just waiting to get out for a piss.

'That's one way of putting it, mate!'

I sometimes got edgy when my childhood crazy came up. At those times, my brain would get stuck on catastrophes, and rolling thoughts always gave way to panic. This time, a violent ghoul of a memory crashed across my vision so fast I had no way of stopping it. 'You took that poor innocent child down to the beach and then you let your beastly animal urges take over and you nearly killed her!' Elder Winston from Kingdom Hall was there, bug-eyed and wobbling with rage, pointing his finger at me from across the table. This damning ghoul was as loud and clear as it had ever been, still living inside me, still leaking its poisonous judgement into my veins.

Mick noticed that I was sweating and panicky, and put his hand on my shoulder. 'Hey! Tim, mate! You okay bro?'

I was pretty sure Mick knew my whole story. I was pretty sure most of the guys at the zoo knew my whole story. They also knew that Mick kept a close eye on whatever was going on for me, so for the most part they didn't bully me when I said stuff that seemed weird for a sixteen-year-old kid. Sometimes the Bible even got a run and I'd quote whole scriptures, which stopped conversations.

When one of the older stags died—one of the gentler stags who would always come up to be fed and who I'd shared quite a few of my morning thoughts with—I became concerned that he might not get a chance at the Next Life. When I'd asked one of the Elders in my last life why it was that animals didn't get into Heaven, he'd said it was because they hadn't been enlightened, and there was no place in Heaven for the unenlightened. He added that they had no soul—they were just worm food. I thought maybe Len might have a different take on this, so one day when we were sitting together, chucking the bread crusts from my sandwiches for his geese to snap up, I asked him if maybe there was another Kingdom of Heaven for animals where the stag might go now that he'd died.

Same reaction as Mick. Len's jaw dropped open. He eventually replied but it took too long. Long enough for shame to fill me up. I tried to distract him by kicking gravel into the pond.

Len said, 'The Kingdom of Heaven and unenlightened animals! That's a hell of a complicated afterlife you've got to figure out there, son!' Even though Len was about 65, I reckoned he looked like he was 105. 'You sure have a weird way of putting stuff, young fella. Don't get me wrong, I love it! It's just that you say stuff that sounds like it's from another world!'

I wanted to tell Len that I *was* from another world. He hadn't answered my question but he was still chewing on it, I could tell.

'It's hard when an animal that we've looked after dies, Tim. That's for sure. And who knows where they go when they die. Maybe somewhere even better than Stagland! Maybe they do just turn into worm food, but even if they're just worm food, why is that any less important in life's cycles than our human existence? I think humans are a little arrogant about how much they think they know, Tim. You may find that out on your travels. But you know, we, as keepers, are only the custodians of these animals. It's our job to look after them and give them the best quality of life we can while they are with us. It is our privilege to look after them. We don't own these animals. To my way of thinking, if we can give them the Kingdom of Heaven while they're still living, then I reckon we've more than done our job, and it's as close to a Kingdom of Heaven as any of us will ever get!'

When I wasn't cleaning and feeding, I continued to learn as much as I could about animals. I watched them when I could between jobs, filling up my little behaviour book, which I kept in my back pocket, with all its written observations and

77

drawings. I'd even written down Len's Kingdom of Heaven on Earth advice on my 'People behaviour and respect' page, even though it didn't really fit there. I just never wanted to forget it. For me, it was very comforting, and I was trying to fill up my black sky as fast as I could.

Every morning, after the park had opened to the public, another of my jobs was to stand with the tourists and watch the animals for at least ten minutes. The idea being, according to Mick, that when we looked at the exhibit from a tourist's point of view, we got a better idea of what they were actually seeing, which could inform our decisions. But the main reason was to look for injuries or to see if any had become unwell. I liked getting another chance to observe the animals' behaviours, also to see if any looked injured, but I much preferred being with the animals themselves inside the exhibit. It felt safer that way round. Sometimes I'd look out at what the animals observed when watching humans and think about how actually the humans looked pretty injured. Way too much work to be done on that side of the fence.

Once a day, as manager of the lemurs, I got to go in the enclosure with them. This was my favourite time of day, so I would stretch the time out as though I was pulling gum. The lemurs were usually gentle and curious, but they would come alive when I joined them. Excited, jumping around, playful. One day I took some currants in with me, tucking them into the top pocket of my uniform. My lunchtime mate was the first to come towards me, then the others followed. All the lemurs seemed to overcome the shyness that was characteristic of their species. I was surprised how close they came to me, close enough to actually scratch around at my jacket and sniff my chest. But my sleepy mate was the one whose long fingers stretched into the pocket of my coat and pulled out the currants. One by one.

'Hey! Pretty sharp for a slob!'

We were sharing the space between us, right up close. No bars, no cages, no history, only two broken animals meeting for the first time.

From then on, I would often sit down among the lemurs and share currants. And I started noticing new behaviours. When I was working one day, a couple of excited lemurs started climbing up the cage mesh, and whenever I bent over to clean their benches they jumped from the mesh onto my back, onto a driftwood bench, then onto the ground. That night, when I sketched these behaviours, I particularly noted the mesh-climbing and the lemurs' love of leaping. The following day, I noticed that the description of the lemurs on the information boards at the front of their exhibit was wrong. This text described them only as 'terrestrial', meaning they didn't climb, that they lived on the ground. But my observations proved they were also clearly 'arboreal', which according to my encyclopedia meant they were tree-climbing animals. I made a note to talk to Mick about the error in the Stagland description.

I also observed that, whenever there were big groups of tourists watching them, the lemurs would gather behind the kauri slab in an effort to hide. This seemed a completely understandable instinct to me given that in the wild, they never would have been in a situation where they couldn't get away. Besides which, it was an obvious behaviour given how naturally shy they were. Sometimes I was struck by how much I had in common with the lemurs, as I had lived a similar life as a shy Jehovah's Witness kid. And so creating a screened area where the lemurs could retreat from human view became a priority in my notebook. I put this observation at the top of the list of things to talk to Mick about.

Every day, I was excited to observe behaviours that I hadn't seen before. I was even more excited to try out new ways of helping the lemurs with difficult behaviours that had evolved from them being enclosed. One thing I did was to start hiding their food. I would cut up their lunch and hang it off a bit of string, making a fruit necklace. They then had to pick at it rather than just scooping it from a bowl. I got Len to help me set up another kauri bench, higher than the old one, on which I set up a platform where I hid little stashes of food. This meant that the lemurs had a few more challenges every day, and it also meant they had more climbing possibilities.

In the week after I made these changes, I watched closely to see if the lemurs' behaviour was different. What happened was astonishing. Whenever I passed their exhibit, they appeared to be doing far less lying around looking exhausted on the cement. More often than not, they were leaping about or looking around curiously. This simple change had injected life into their confined existence. I wondered if the lethargy that I had observed for two years in the lemurs was actually a hopelessness or a resignation that had developed from not having enough structures to climb or objects to interest or excite them in their enclosure. The structures in their enclosure were definitely not designed for lemur behaviour. It occurred to me that the hollowness in their eyes was actually depression. I knew it because, without my connection to animals, I could have been there too. We were all in the same boat because we were all cast-offs.

If I could improve the lemurs' behaviours with a few simple modifications, surely there were more possibilities to do so throughout the park with the other animals. I began watching for other animal exhibits where I could make changes. One of the first things that came to my attention was how the lions walked a balding path to and from each end of their almost one-hectare exhibit, barely registering tourists along the way. Watching these carnivores sluggishly pad up and down their fence lines, with little attention given to any form of surprise, unsettled me. I felt a deep sadness when I passed by them on my way to the feeding station each morning. I wondered if the tourists felt it too. Surely there would be an instant recognition of a life force lost.

Earlier that year, I'd noticed that when one of the lion keepers had thrown a big yellow plastic fishing buoy into the exhibit, the lions had tossed the object among themselves for hours at a time. It had taken a few weeks for the fun of the game to wear off, and the plastic buoy ended up sitting abandoned in the corner of the exhibit like a sun-bleached swing set in suburbia. Now I asked the head carnivore keeper to pull the buoy out of the lion exhibit for me—I had an idea of what might inject more 'life' into the object. I put it in with the stags, who, in the language of the Jehovah's Witnesses, were letting loose their 'beastly urges', so they were releasing all their pheromones. The stags loved the distraction, having something to fight over. They kicked the toy around for weeks, poked it with their antlers. They loved the possibilities for fight and tussle that the buoy presented. When we eventually put the buoy back in the lion enclosure, because the smell of the stags was all over it, those carnivores got months more play out of it, sucking every last scent of pheromone from its scored plastic surfaces. I kept this cycle going for the lions at Stagland, throwing the buoy in with different animals that had come into season and then returning it to the lions for play.

The head carnivore keeper wasn't threatened by new ideas and invited me to keep coming up with them for the lions. 'You've got an eye for this stuff, young Jockstrap! Very cool. Very, very cool.'

Because he was open to my suggestions, I tried out another one on him. My reading on lions' 'love of the hunt' in the encyclopedia had inspired the idea. 'Why don't we try dragging the horse leg around their paddock before we let them out of their night den?' I said. 'That way they get to follow it, and they get a sense of a chase for their prey.'

The head carnivore keeper had a go at it and over a few months noticed not only a decrease in the lions' fence pacing but also a lift in their play levels. He said to me, 'Love your weird little brain, Jockstrap. You've got quite the way of thinking, that's for sure.'

———

In my third year at Stagland, when I was almost seventeen, I took my collection of drawings and written observations to Mick and Mr Brake. There were sketches of lemurs hiding themselves behind logs with their backs turned to the tourists, sketches of the lemurs climbing the fencing of the exhibit, sketches of the lemurs jumping from the fencing onto my back and then onto the ground, sketches of lemurs searching for food in holes in the timber, and descriptions of them spending more time looking for hidden morsels. Beside each picture I had scratched out a rough explanation or two of what I thought it was that the lemurs were responding to and how their behaviours had changed. Even though my sketches looked more like stick figures with tails, they told the stories I needed to tell.

I strode into the office, where the two men were chatting to each other about something at the filing cabinet, and declared, 'I want to show you both some ideas I have had about the lemur exhibits.' My excited pronouncement silenced them both. They turned and stared at me like I was an escaped animal, giving me the time I needed to jam more of my discoveries into the silence left open by their surprise.

'I've been watching the lemurs for years now and I think I can make their exhibits a lot better. Better for them. More interactive. They'll be happier, I think. I want to build a climbing structure for them. A complex one, more like a tree. A 3D kind of structure. I've discovered that they climb, that they leap! Have a look at this.'

I pulled out five pieces of foolscap. They were crumpled and scrappy with bits of egg on them, but the drawings were easy to make out. Mick and Mr Brake continued to stare at me.

'This is what I have in mind. Take a look!' I pointed to my drawings, stabbing the illustrations with a finger more than once to get their attention. 'It's not just good for the lemurs but it means the public will get to see them from lots of different angles. It's a three-dimensional exhibit. Cool, hey!'

'I think you better sit down, lad,' said Mr Brake. 'And I think you and I both better sit down, Mick.' He gave Mick a wink. I'd never before seen Mr Brake give Mick a wink.

Mr Brake ironed out the papers with the back of his hand. He was surprised by my suggestions, I think. But mostly he was just a little bit proud. I could tell. I knew when those turquoise eyes twinkled that there was joy in there, joy at how this broken kid was growing strong. I liked seeing the jostling sparkles of pride and surprise in the old fella's eyes because I was still hell bent on getting not only his approval but his affection. It somehow took the place of not having my grandad around.

'You can have all you need, Mr Tim Husband. What's more, you will have it within the next two weeks!' said Mr Brake, using his TV show host voice again.

'Thank you. You are going to be amazed at how much happier the animals will be. I promise you that.'

I swept up my papers and left with a determination and optimism that had seemed out of reach for so very long.

Steel poles and lengths of kauri pine were dropped next to the lemur exhibit only a few days later. It dead set looked like I was about to build a house inside there. Some of the other keepers sneered and talked behind their hands as they passed me and Len and Mick as we were banging and screwing and lifting and glueing.

'What have we here? Is it Dr Dolittle or is it Noah himself? Jockstrap seems to have outdone himself, fellas!'

I knew the tone well. Sarcastic. Bullying. Bullshit tone. Didn't touch the sides though. I had a long history with industrial-level bullying and theirs was child's play.

The climbing lemur tree took us three weeks to build. It was about twenty metres square and three metres wide. It looked like a huge timber teepee, but between all the angled logs I'd put branches and wires. This meant the primates could live and play in a place that was multidimensional. They could fly backwards and forwards and sideways. At the base of the teepee I'd pushed two logs off to the side of the exhibit. The logs faced flat to the public, giving the lemurs a screening area to hide from the interminable gaze of the humans on the other side of the mesh.

Learning from lemurs

It was only a couple of weeks after we put up the 'treepee', as I called it, that I noticed that the lemurs were no longer lying around at lunchtime staring into the abyss. In fact, I'd noticed there was no staring at all. The lemurs had adopted a routine of play, rest and sleep that had brought life into their apathetic bodies. Their curiosity drove them now in a way that only hunger could have a month earlier.

8

Broke open

For me, the years rolled by unmarked. Unless you measured time as increased horn length in bison or the continued expansion of the ungulate families. Other than that, there were few external markers for time. There were changes to my face and body that I'd figured out had already happened to most of the other keepers at Stagland. My face was all outcrops of downy blond hair, and I seemed to have shot up to be taller than any other keeper. Len reckoned I must've been almost six-foot-three by the time I was seventeen and felt excited enough to tell me so. There were other changes too. Not good ones. I was becoming broody and irritable. I was calling on Tom, my mate in my head, for company more these days as he remained true to his habit of warning me off people, which suited me.

Mick told me it was a hormone thing and it wasn't unusual. 'You're in musth, mate!'

'What?'

'Yep, like the bull elephants. Hormones have got a hold of you and you'll have a go at just about anything. Nothing to worry about, mate. We'll just keep clear of you!'

'Suits me. Now fuck off!'

I knew there was more going on though. I knew the ghouls of my past were still haunting my insides and creating havoc. Whenever I thought of the people who had condemned my life to a living hell, hate and anger blew up inside me as though all that shit had happened only yesterday. Even Len was less inclined to spend time with me as, according to Mick, I had developed a tendency to answer in less than the monosyllabic three-word offerings I was already known for. A single grunt was more usual, and that was often an effort. If anyone tried to intrude into my silent world, they got an earful. Not even the animals seemed to quieten the stone-kicking aggression that was growing and trapped in my body.

Dick Brake asked me to come into the office for a chat one day. He had been made aware that whenever anyone tried approaching me for a conversation, even if it was just to say hello, I would blow them off, sometimes with a look or by turning my back on them. Both Mr Brake and his wife were in the office that particular day, which made the 'chat' particularly uncomfortable for me.

'Being told to fuck off all the time isn't pleasant for anyone, Tim. I know it's hard for you, son. I know the years have been hard on you when you've been all alone, but I can't abide you treating other staff or visitors this way.'

Dick Brake was being as firm as I'd ever known him to be, and I was suffering a degree of what was possibly shame. But I wasn't sure. I only knew that I did not enjoy upsetting him.

Mrs Brake jumped in to fill the difficult silence that followed:

'You need friends. You need to be social, Tim. What about a youth group of some sort? Not a Christian group, obviously, after all you've been through, but maybe something else. Maybe darts? Or tennis. Maybe even line dancing at Whangārei hall?'

Darts I knew about because there was a board in the keepers' common room. Tennis was foreign but only a little less so than dancing, the ethics of which had always been tricky as a Jehovah's Witness person. We were always required to do 'all things to the glory of God' (1 Corinthians, 10:31). So dancing could only be undertaken in celebration of God's glory and should we ever be tempted to take to the dance floor, we were required to ask ourselves two questions. One: was the type of dancing we were considering participating in viewed as sexually suggestive or sensual? And two, was the type of dancing we were considering viewed to be a distraction from our worship of the one true God? I imagine the Whangārei line-dancing group would not have had the same head scratching before toe tapping with their mates. I did eventually come up with my own idea for a hobby, or should I say, it came up to me.

I tried riding my first bronc not long after my conversation with the Brakes, after a travelling rodeo pitched up in Whangārei. The idea of spending another Sunday either on my own or with Mr Brake and his family was not appealing. All I ever did was sit and listen to the Brake family anyway. Mostly never said anything. Just saw what a happy family should look like when it was working. It used to comfort me, just to sit and watch, but it was always from a distance. Like seeing *The Waltons* on TV. Still someone else's story. Mrs Brake was right, I did need something else to do on Sundays, but line dancing or tennis sure as hell weren't it. Besides, I knew that rodeo riding would piss my dad off should he ever find out, and that still rumbled inside me as motivation for just about anything I did.

My jousting history with John on the brumbies was recorded as 'past experience' when they registered me in the novice class at that rodeo in Whangārei in 1979. It was a comfort to remember the brotherly mantra we bonded over as we tried to clothesline each other off our horses. 'Anything that doesn't kill you makes you stronger, bro!'

I repeated this to myself as I climbed over the railing and got on top of my first bronc. All I could see was a black mane and a muscle-strapped backbone rippling power through a speckled silky grey hide. The bronc's head was down, pushing at the spaces between the railings, which I heard as the crash of bone on metal. The noises coming from the bronc beneath me were primitive and blood curdling. If crazy power had a smell, then it was there that day. The horse's anger, my fear. Yesterday's stink was there as well. The stink of frightened sweat from red-blooded young cowboys and bulls and horses, hanging in the air. My hand, wrapped around the halter, gripped it even tighter and I squeezed my legs as hard as I could around the bronc's ribs. Adrenalin threw me between its poles of terror and exhilaration, and already I knew that whatever this was, I was never going to be able to get enough of it. Christ, did it feel good!

'You ready, son?'

It came from one of the chute bosses. Cowboys were everywhere, and as busy as blowflies on old meat as they got the chute ready for opening. Lunatic anger and pent-up power in the trapped bronc beneath me, all ready to meet my mad.

'I am!'

The gate exploded open like a bullet from a gun barrel, but

it was over almost before it began. The bronc reared out of the chute like a breaching whale and, in mid-air, it twisted on its back feet, making my trajectory end in the dust. Because the bronc hadn't even planted his front hooves after coming out of the chute, I didn't make the first mark. No score. One of the chute bosses gave me a hand.

'Bit steep to put you on Gun-Drill first up, I reckon.' Knowing I'd had no chance. 'Good for you, kid!' Respect as he pulled me up out of the dust.

When he followed me over to the railing, I asked him, 'Hey, that horse is gonna be okay, right? He had a bit of trouble in the crush.'

'Brother, these animals are athletes. We look after them like gold. Don't worry about him, mate.' Then he looked at me with a bit of surprise, slapped my back and went back to the action.

I was okay. A bit dusty and bruised, but not bad for a first go, and it was wild! Adrenalin coursed through me in waves all the rest of the day. I was still riding its sets even as I crashed out in my caravan that night. My brain replayed each moment of the failed ride. Over and over in a loop. I was finally feeling something—I loved that I was feeling anything at all.

As I stripped off my jeans and threw on a T-shirt, I laughed out loud. Mrs Brake's advice for staving off my depression had been to take up a hobby, and she'd suggested gems like line dancing or tennis. The image of me dressed in tennis whites, sipping tea with my fellow staffers and pitching in for another set of doubles had me rolling around my bed laughing. What might Sandra Brake have thought of my hobby of choice? Then again, knowing the Brakes, I reckoned anything that moved me along my journey they would be happy about.

Broke open

I eventually slipped softly into the first gentle sleep I'd had in years, but not before sending a gratitude prayer to a non-existent God. I thanked my non-existent God that animals were still showing me the way. The broncs, and later the bulls, in some fucked-up way, were going to help me calm all the angry and crazy in my body. Their crazy angry would meet mine in a wild ride that pivoted around mutual self-destruction and self-preservation. Week after week, it would be the bronc, the bull and me, trapped and kicking like fuck, just to stay sane.

I found a way of getting to wherever the travelling rodeo was going. I was now receiving a fairly decent income from Stagland, so I could afford the third-hand Yamaha motorbike that was for sale on a street corner in the bush suburbs of Whangārei. That first year of my rodeo career, I must have registered to ride in over thirty rodeos. I only placed twice, but I was getting the hang of it all, and I was up for everything. Bareback bronc riding, saddle bronc, calf roping, bulldogging. Totally driven. And even after all the wild riding, after all the wrecking and wrangling, the best part of it was that every Monday morning, on my return to Stagland, I still got to be with the animals that were my family. They were all there doing the things they always did: swinging around on my treepee, chewing hay, playing with tree trunks, tearing around after each other, scratching each other, digging for smells. I even started talking with the other keepers a little again. The certainty of my Monday routine and the simple joy of seeing the animals anchored me in a way that I wasn't entirely aware of at the time.

My bronc riding started to improve. Bronc riding had technique written into it. I knew that to have a decent ride on a bronc, I had to follow the horse's head as soon as it was out of the crush. That much I got from talking to other cowboys. But I also taught myself a lot through observation, as I was very keen to avoid another pulled shoulder ligament or swollen wrist, from the countless times I'd been bucked off. If my first mark was good, meaning that the horse had planted both front feet on the ground, I would set my heels above the horse's shoulders, then the rest of the journey would be about following the bronc's head. Wherever the head went, the horse's body would follow, so I would know which way to lean. The better I was at anticipating where the head went, the more chance I had of staying on the bronc and surviving the eight seconds required to begin registering a score.

Bulls were different. Bull riding was considered the most dangerous of all the events on the rodeo circuit. Still, wherever the adrenalin frontier was, I was going to be there. So one day I climbed the rails and straddled the broad brown hide of Wrecked, a thumping muscle-bound beast from Wellington. The ride blew my mind. While Wrecked was spinning on the spot, his hide was rolling around him like it was detached from his body. Riding Wrecked, I felt like I may as well have been in a washing machine. There was no following the head like in bronc riding. There was no technique I could identify and then repeat on the next ride. I was completely out of control as I could never figure out which way the bull's rump was going to roll as it twisted and turned around a single point of rage.

With no pick-up riders, no MC and only the rodeo clown to watch out for me, the sense of vulnerability I felt was extreme.

My heart may as well have been pumping pure adrenalin around my body instead of blood. It was as close to bliss as I had ever experienced. I knew that when I successfully got myself off the beast's back, I needed to get the fuck out of there and quickly. Not easy, because I was tied in. And on. I had a thick rope tied around my wrist and another extended eight feet around the bull's rump. When the lassoed rope pulled tight in a vice grip, like a belt around a fat man's belly, the bull began his maniacal bucking.

I would never fully remember that first bull ride. When the gate burst open, sheer terror and its chemical circuitry must have blocked out any of my normal brain function. I only registered reality again when I heard the blast of the eight-second horn and I heard the clown yelling at me to 'Get the fuck off!' It was then that I realised the thick wrist rope seemed to have tightened noose-like around my arm and wouldn't release. All the while, the bull's head was flailing around my peripheral vision, throwing putrid bovine snot in the air in wads like chunky sea foam. And sometimes, fleetingly, I'd catch the whites of his lunatic eyes and their black-holed pupils searching around for my body, to horn the crap out of it. They couldn't find me though because, trapped in my hand rope, I was hanging off the side of his rump and bouncing around his belly like a Christmas bauble. Eventually the rodeo clown distracted the bull enough to release the too-tight knot and give me time to escape to the closest fence railing. I was wasted and rattled, but buzzing. I was so high that all I wanted was to get right back out there and have another crack.

Fear, excitement, power and pain were all explosively at play in my life every weekend, and I loved it. Straddling any one of the beasts in the crush and feeling the power below me was like being hooked up to the mains of some sort of primitive circuitry, and all the pent-up aggression and hate in my body were explosively released through its wiring. The eruption from the crush, the broncs, the bulls, me, together, flying, sometimes as high as three metres in the air before taking our chances with the landing. Locking horns with death meant adrenalin was on tap for me and I could get my fill of it weekend after weekend. Unbridled terror. Unbounded excitement. And as real as it was to go through that fear, even better was knowing I had conquered that fear. I needed to feel fear in its most elemental form to know what it really meant to conquer it. Raw fear and vanquished fear defined me—I needed them both.

Every rodeo, I would take my saddle blanket and camp under a tree to wait out the hours until my ride. Or my rides. Often, when it was crowded and the attention of the audience was on the action, I'd just go down to the pens themselves and hang out with the brumbies. I noticed that other cowboys would often go down and check on the animals. One of the chute bosses had once told me that a lot of the cowboys had a real connection with the brumbies and bulls they rode. He told me that they would often check on them after a ride to make sure they were okay.

Another amazing thing about the brumbies and bulls was how the animals seemed to be used to the theatre of the thing. I was always curious as to why they settled down so quickly after their ride. Sometimes I'd even see them rolling around enjoying a dust bath after they came in. Could it be that the animals themselves perhaps understood the spectacle as a performance?

—

I was slowly becoming known as a someone. A lanky, downy, quiet upcomer. Never said much. Steadily worked my way up the cowboy rankings. I was 'Most Improved Cowboy' after my second year, and more and more people on the circuit were starting to sniff around me like I was 'in season', as Mick put it. Managers, other cowboys, sponsors, women. I bought myself a cowboy shirt and a cowboy hat, because sponsors had started introducing themselves to me after rides. I'd sometimes have a beer with a couple of other cowboys and then get on my Yamaha and ride home, drinking in the black night at speed like it was straight liquor. At first I avoided the night-time events after the rodeos because I couldn't cope with the fact that I'd have to talk to other people, especially women. As the years rolled on, however, my rodeo riding gave me confidence. When I started regularly placing first or second, I would hang around for just a bit longer after each event. Slowly, I let myself stay a little longer at the yards, then longer again. Maybe hanging around for a third beer. Then maybe for a bourbon or two.

I even started talking to women. Actually, they started talking to me and I would mumble something back. Usually only a couple of words at a time. At least we weren't exploring Corinthians anymore, and thankfully Genesis didn't quite have the sticking power it once did, and that was always a relief. But even as the alcohol helped soothe the terror of actually speaking to women, I would notice the first bellicose rumblings of a rant starting in my head: Tom, grumbling about me needing to be more careful around women and not give up too much of my story. He would whisper warnings to me about the woman I'd just been introduced to before I'd even got a chance to talk to her. She would either be too dumb, too dull, too fat, too much of a princess, too slutty, too short. There was always something. They were never good enough. Not even for a conversation, apparently. Women seemed to be stuck in two dimensions for me. It was as though all the distress and anger I felt for Tui, and the disappointment I still felt for what was left of my mother, had found a way into my adult world. They had found new life in the stories Tom told me about what was happening to me when I was with women. He'd often remind me that women were the 'ones who couldn't be trusted'. His rants were strings of insulting jibes about women, all while he insisted he was only keeping me safe.

I reckoned a part of me was putting up a fight though. What right had I to judge? Jesus Christ, this group of girls was nothing like the so-called 'models of propriety' I'd known in my last life. There was not an ounce of what I understood to be Jehovahly virtue in this mob, and as far as I was concerned, that should've made me trust them more. These women were as much on the wrong side of right as I'd ever been, so I had every reason to keep Tom's opinions about them out of it. And they were feisty! Of that, there was no doubt. They were all buckles and bourbon and dust and gum chewing. They were known among the local cowboys as the 'buckle bunnies', although some of them were better known among the bronc riders for their 'happy endings', which meant a blow job or hand job for the cowboys after their daily stoush with death.

I was getting better at staying put when these women talked to me. With enough bourbons inside me and the monstrous memories of my early sexual encounters tucked deep enough, I could take a connection with a woman a little further. It was still a struggle though. The reality of this new world played out in my life as if it was happening to someone else. It was almost like thumbing through a *Playboy* as though it was a *National Geographic*. There was a part of me that was never really there. Still, the women kept checking in, kept having a crack. We would talk about my ride. They usually told me how they'd watched the full eight seconds. Then they asked how I managed to stay on that 'fucken crazy animal'. Then they talked about how much they 'loved rodeos'. They talked about how it was cool to watch the cowboys, and how much they loved to hook up with them after their ride. One of them said, 'If you can stay on that fucking bronc for eight seconds, then surely you're gonna know how to ride my bony arse for eight seconds.' Another offered, 'Are you comin' cowboy? Throw yer spurs in too, I'll show you a real ride.'

Sometimes they told me that I turned them on. I'd have a few more bourbons and then often I was turned on. But without the bourbon, these interactions with women were more terrifying than any bronc or bull ride I'd ever had. I hated them and loved being with them all at once, but I'd have to remind myself of what Aunty Kez used to say to me sometimes when I didn't want to go home after hanging out with her. She'd snuggle me into her favourite T-shirt, the one with the laughing hedgehog on it, and she'd say, 'There's no way around Hell but through it, Timmy, so be brave.'

Mostly it was just hand jobs or head jobs behind the corrals. It was always a relief when I started to feel anything in my body when I was with a woman, because there was another narrative in the mix whenever I appeared to be coming close to having sex with anyone. Being raped when I was thirteen had seeded an idea in me that I could've been gay, that I must've been gay for a man to abuse me. How was I to know any other way? Nothing in my religion or my childhood was remotely like the actual stuff that happened to me. I had no idea. It was like everyone around me was speaking a language that had no words in it for the actual stuff that had happened to me in my life. And without a shared language, I could only make the obvious, and often the wrong, conclusions about myself. So with every hand job and blow job, I got to prove to myself I wasn't gay, but I never had enough courage to do more than that. I never had enough interest to go any further than that and I didn't trust enough to change anything in this routine for a few years.

Besides, I never remembered anyone's name—not the cowboys I competed against, and not the buckle bunnies who got me off behind the corrals. I reckon word had got around the rodeo circuit that I was a loner. Everyone knew the routine with me. Women knew what to expect. And I liked it that way. Some of the bunnies told me they thought I was cruel, but Tom usually set me straight. Kept me safe. If the buckle bunnies ever gave me any grief, he'd shout bimbo jokes through my head as I rode home, probably having just won another 'Best Cowboy' award at a rodeo. On those nights I would clock speeds of over 100 kilometres an hour on my Yamaha. Never any room for more than two of us in there.

It wasn't until I was twenty that I actually had sex with a woman. I mean real sex. A shared intent. The woman I had sex with was different from the others. For a start, she was ten years older than me and she seemed less interested in my eight-second bronc rides than anyone else I'd met in the past three years. I am going to call her Kea because John had told me that in Māori culture, the kea was known as a wise bird, and although my experience with any sort of wisdom was pretty limited, my gut feeling was that this woman had to come pretty close to it. Kea asked questions in a way that required more and reached further than any bourbon-swilling swamp of a conversation could cover. Her questions were all around what else I did when I wasn't kicking the shit out of myself. We talked about Stagland. I told her about the lemurs. She asked about my family. I stopped talking. I asked about her family. She told me they were around, she saw them regularly, they were all close. She asked if she could see me more. I said no. She asked if she could see more of me. We both laughed. She asked if we could just grab a coffee some day, she was only in town for a couple of weeks. I said sure.

We grabbed that coffee, and we talked more about Stagland, and also her dog. When she went to say goodbye, she leaned in to kiss me. Weirdly, I let her. It felt strange. There was a bit of movement inside me, and it wasn't just my dick. I felt like something was kind of flickering. A broken pilot light trying to start. We went to a motel and she showed me how to have sex. I felt self-conscious and vulnerable. Fear shivered inside me as deep cold. An atmospheric fear, more intense than anything I had known before. Something about her felt different. She did everything for me, just like Tui before her—took off my clothes, pulled me to the bed. But she also seemed to be showing me a way that was safe. Just by locking onto my eyes with hers, she was showing me a safe way.

When I entered her, my thoughts filled with blood trails and pain. With every movement, with every body shift, came a fear of hurting her. But I stayed there with her. And she looked at me in a way that held me, as if she had known every detail of my story and that I was going to be okay. That it was okay to keep watching her, to have the courage to go on.

After I came inside her, she still held me with her eyes, as if to say, *Pay attention now.* As if to say, *It's not over.* As if to say, *Feel how connection also happens all around us, not just in the body.*

'Can you feel it?' she asked.

What I felt was completely held and seen by Kea, but within that astonishing reprieve, I got a glimpse of something else. My story of abuse was losing its power. The anger that had held me hostage for so long was releasing some of its grip. Ice melting to water. For the first time since I was a very young boy, I *felt* my body, every part of it, awake and tingling. The blood trails and rotting oranges, the smell of cedar sawdust, the crazy Jehovah ghouls roaming at will inside me, they were all pulling away on a receding tide choked with rotten memories. I felt like I was inhabiting a bewildering new space in my own body, and it even stretched beyond my body to the space 'all around', as Kea put it.

'I think I can feel what you are talking about,' I said to Kea in a whisper, for fear I might scare away this new sense of belonging.

Was this trust? It definitely was a comfort to know that sex really was all that it was made out to be. It was a release, and it involved trust and desire gently shared. And that day, to my relief, I didn't almost kill her.

And then, it all stopped. I moved quickly to the end of the bed and sat there, naked, trembling. Then the shaking stopped. Then it started again. My head was in my hands. Trust flickered gossamer-thin in me, but I was breaking. I needed to get away. This was way too tender. Vulnerable. Exposed. This wasn't how the real world worked. Tom returned with his familiar alarm, warning this wasn't reality. I needed to move on. Snap. Bang. Closed. Move on.

Kea came over and held me like I was some sort of survivor. Her hug had moved from the sensual lingering touch of a lover to something weighted with the affectionate pragmatism that comes with hospital care. Longing had turned into concern in the time it took me to find the empty end of the bed.

——

Kea came to my next rodeo and found me after my ride.

'Can I see you more?'

'No,' I told her.

'Can I see more of you?' she said, laughing.

'No.'

She was okay with that. She already knew. I didn't need to say any more. It was too hard, it was too close, it was asking too much of myself to give up the bits of me that my anger had protected for so long. Give up bits of me to a thirty-year-old woman who could see all of me.

'I understand, Tim. I really do. Good luck and go gently, my friend.'

And she left my life with her thirty years of wisdom and integrity intact. For a short time she had held me with great tenderness and compassion, and she knew that was her gift to me. That's how she was able to leave me without looking over her shoulder. She had opened me to trust. Just a sliver. She had given me a tiny glimmer of hope. That was enough for her. And that was so much more than enough for me. It would be years before I understood how to allow that living connection into my body again.

Besides, I was feeling enough as it was. I'd just gotten my first sponsor and had made Broke Open, which was the semi-professional level of the rodeo circuit. The ride that opened the door to my becoming a professional rodeo rider was poetry. I knew that because that was how it was written up when I won the Wellington Rodeo.

Poetry in motion. Tim Husband. New Zealand's new rodeo rockstar.

Best ride of the year. Tim Husband. Eight awesome seconds sees in new international celebrity.

Everything fell into place during that particular ride. The bronc exploded out of the chute front legs first, so the way ahead was clearly marked out. From then on, it was all rhythm. Understanding a horse's movement after three years of bronc riding kept me completely calm. It was as though it all happened in slow motion. I was watching the head because I knew that's where the body followed. As I was watching the head, I laid back along the bronc's rump as though this had been rehearsed. Every one of the bronc's movements sent subtle messages about how to respond with my own body. It was a silent conversation between us. If the bronc's head went to the right, I knew I had to position myself to the left to keep us both in balance. I was in my own zone. There was nothing but complete silence. It was like the power of the bronc's eruption from the crush slowed into eight seconds of a sweet sleepy afternoon. It all seemed to flow so gracefully, something as true to its nature as it could possibly be. The horse and I were one, in rhythm, movement and intention. I heard the eight-second buzzer and then there was a pick-up guy beside me breaking my daydream. The sense of slow motion turned swiftly back into speed, danger and razor edges. The pick-up guy reached up and pulled me off.

That ride got me into the New Zealand Rodeo Team, and our first trip would be to the United States for a month. I had one more bull ride before heading for home, during which I managed to clip an eye socket on a railing when the bull crashed against the gate as I was trying to get onto his back. The socket blew up like a veiny purple plum, eventually swelling so much that it was impossible to open that eye. I rode my Yamaha home with single-eyed vision, replaying the 'poetry in motion' ride that got me into the national team over and over again in my head like a favourite song. Nothing was going to take the edge off my selection.

The following Monday, as happened every Monday, I was hobbling around forking hay out for the animals that I was responsible for and who were my mates. My work colleagues at Stagland had gotten used to watching my post-rodeo Mondays as though they were watching a car crash: 'What the hell's going on for you, Tim? . . . Thought you'd grow out of this rodeo gig . . . Bit of a sucker for punishment, hey? . . .' Mick, though, was tired of me turning up at work injured. For three years, I'd been riding broncs and bulls on my weekends off, then turning up to work with screws in joints, hips pinned, legs broken, elbows strapped, wrists and fingers sausage-swollen, eyes bleeding and bruises in puffy meat mounds.

Mr Brake called me into his office and talked to me in his

concerned fatherly way: 'I don't like to see you so broken up, son. What is it with this rodeo thing?'

'I dunno. I love it. It makes me feel stuff.'

'Stuff like broken bones and twisted limbs, you mean? Stuff like that swollen sausage of an eye you've got there?'

'No, stuff like alive. It makes me feel alive!'

'Stagland animals not enough for you, Tim?'

'No. Yes. I mean, I don't know. I know it sounds kind of weird, but I like the pain. Besides, I've just been chosen to represent New Zealand in America at the end of the year!'

Mr Brake took a deep breath and raised an eyebrow, though he also did that when a new truckload of lion feed came in. He didn't understand the power of pain. Didn't understand how much I loved pain. At least it was a feeling, and without feelings I was just a living stack of meat. Also, surely Mr Brake must see representing New Zealand as an achievement. But there was little acknowledgement of any success on this old familiar face, only concern as he watched me struggle to get out of the chair. That cut me up. Cut me up severely.

That night, as I nursed the painfully swollen stretch of weeping skin across my eyeball at the same time as readjusting my sleep position because of a two-month-old hip injury, I lay awake. Thoughts tumbled around my brain. Tom and I were fighting like pig dogs. What was it that I really liked in the rodeos anyway? Why was I hurting myself so much? Seemed like all I wanted to do was damage myself. Tom made some good points though. He reminded me that I was representing my country riding the rump of a Brahman bull, and that in itself was awesome. Tom also knew how much that would have pissed my dad off. He would have fucking hated that I was making a living riding bulls. So too bad if Dick Brake hated it. I was good at this and it made me feel stuff. Fucking FEEL stuff, and that felt so fucking good! Bourbon always helped with competing pains, both in my body and in my brain.

———

Somewhere in the lead-up to representing New Zealand, when I was preparing for the nationals, I suffered an injury that put a whole new spin on what it was to feel stuff. It happened at a rodeo that wasn't even on the circuit. It was a smallish rodeo outside Auckland, at Taupō, and I thought I'd include it in a trip to the big smoke of Wellington just as a little extra practice. I entered the bareback bronc ride, probably the wildest, fastest of rides. I reckon I was on the lookout for a bit more adrenalin to get me ready for the American tour. In bareback bronc riding, there's a harness that almost looks like a suitcase handle, which is strapped around the flanks of the horse like a saddle. That's all you have to hold onto. The beast was a scrappy scrawny red brumby that groaned like a carnivore in the corral. He was mad, but I knew mad. The horse's mad met my mad as soon as I straddled him, and the second the gate blew open, the bronc soared into the air. We sparred like eagles tussling in the sky. But this time it was edgy, really edgy. As we tore around the arena, lurching from buck to gallop, the bronc took off into the air again like a firecracker, white froth spraying from its mouth. On landing, a hoof found the bottom railing on the stadium fence, forcing the other leg to buckle underneath its hips. It reared back as far as it could, which meant I was going with it wherever it went. I made ground first, falling behind the bronc. He then fell in front of me. As I was flailing in the dirt, I turned my head and saw a dust cloud, horse limbs protruding, rolling towards me in what seemed like slow motion. The bronc's whole body rolled over me, nearly 500 kilos of equine weight, in one devastating movement. I lay there semiconscious, looking up at the blue sky, unable to move. Blue sky turned to black. I woke up in hospital, where a doctor told me I would walk again but I had snapped my hips open like a wishbone and they were going to have to pin me back together again. My whole lower back and pelvis were broken, along with any chance I had to go and see America while representing my country.

I spent long slow months recovering in my caravan. The physical pain was more intense than anything I'd ever known, but I was managing it okay—pain had long ago become a fellow traveller. A much more sinister pain was spreading through my brain. Tom was angry about everything during those days, even trying to find stuff about my animals to complain about. I was becoming more and more withdrawn from them. More withdrawn from Mick, Len and the other keepers. I passed the days and nights in my caravan reading *Playboy* and *National Geographic*. For hours and hours during the day and the sleepless nights, I lay on my bed curled around my broken insides. My split pelvis made lying in any position unbearable. The loneliness, anger and excruciating pain made pulling blankets over my head for days at a time my only retreat. Mick or one of Dick Brake's kids would occasionally come to the caravan door with a few days worth of food Mrs Brake had prepared for me. Sometimes they had cards and suggested playing a game as a distraction. Tom saw them off pretty swiftly.

Depression was taking a brutal hold of me again. I felt

like every time I moved I was wading through mud. I would often find myself drinking bourbon just to get to sleep. Whole bottles of the damned stuff. I was trying to drown out all the background brain noise, all the judgements and loopy reasoning Tom was constantly hurling at me. But the bourbon only made him more cantankerous, which only made everything worse. The more I drank, the louder he got, and the louder he got, the more I drank. I was on a spinning wheel. Trapped.

Somewhere in this time loop of the living dead, I remembered my mother. She was often drunk, and when she wasn't, it always felt to me like she was only just hanging on. Hamster on a wheel. Same as me. Did she have a brain bully running her life too? I knew she had a real bully running her life, so God knows she didn't need another one! I was hurting for the mother I'd never really known.

Tom kept right on telling me where I'd gone wrong: *Is all this worth it? You didn't even make it as a cowboy. Back to shovelling shit then? Is it worth all the effort if you're not even worth the effort?*

We had conversations about whether or not life was worth living. Daily, Tom would prod me about how life was meaningless, that I was a fuck-up, that nothing was ever going to work out for me. The black sky I'd stuffed away for so long blew up inside me like the massive ballooned body of a jellyfish. Its long lonely tendrils wrapped around my sleep in a chokehold and its venom leaked through my days as though death itself was biding its time. If I did get to sleep, it was always threadbare and broken. My tortured dreams were night hours spent in wastelands roamed and ruled by ghouls. Fragmented contortions of my father were the violent gatekeeping demons of this purgatory. The drawling baritones of the Jehovah's Elders were there too, judgements pouring from their soggy mouths in long ribbons of blood. Forever in flood. The gory trails they left behind were hungrily lapped up by abandoned broken-boned animals who devoured the message because there was nothing else to eat. Nightly, these foul ghosts danced their demonic lot in my head. Unchecked. It took all I had to hold on until daylight.

Then, one morning, a sliver of silver sun woke me through the blinds, and I caught sight of a swallow sitting on the power line outside the caravan. Then there were two, then three. It was an unusual time for them to be there, which is why I noticed them. And somewhere inside me, in the blur of hopelessness and self-annihilation, these swallows triggered a light, and then I remembered the lemurs, and all the other animals who had shown me which step to take next on my journey, and given me enough of a sense of security to bother to take it. I remembered that together we had worked out a pathway through this crazy mess of a world. I took it as a sign to get out of bed.

9

When the light gets in

I began venturing outside the caravan in an effort to walk a certain number of steps every day. Eventually, I was able to walk the 100 metres to the lemur exhibit, where I would sit for hours at a time watching the primates. From the human side of the fence. The lemurs would stare at me as though they knew that I was on the wrong side of the fence, that something strange had happened. I wanted to join them, but I couldn't risk another injury. And as they leapt with increasing abandon, swinging between the branches of my treepee, my lemur friends helped me chuckle for the first time in months. With their help, and by walking a little further than I'd managed the day before, and setting myself small physical tasks, I became stronger, both in body and in spirit. Over time, I was even able to teach myself tricks to deal with Tom's bellicose offerings. When his rants began, I'd take time out. Catch my breath. Then take deeper breaths. And as much as I could, I would just let him rail.

Same trick I used to use to block out Dad's yelling when I was a kid—although back then I'd put my fingers in my ears when he'd scream scripture at us from the front seat of the Morris Oxford. I knew Tom would eventually run out of steam.

A task I enjoyed was collecting the post for Mr Brake, because the walk to the letterbox was manageable, the ground being mostly flat. One day, a letter arrived for him from ARAZPA, his regular monthly subscription to an Australasian zoo magazine. This particular magazine caught my eye because there was a chimpanzee on the front, and across the top it announced that an inaugural international zoo conference was to be held in Auckland. Inside, there was a page calling for applications to present papers or perform administrative work at the conference. The challenge sat up like a primary school kid at the end of detention and I went straight at it. I tore the page out and dropped the magazine with the rest of the post at Mr Brake's office. Back at the caravan, I took out a pen and circled the details referring to applications for presentations, underlining all the requirements for proposing a paper.

I knew that was exactly where I wanted to go. Back into my animal world. The relief I felt that a path was opening up for me was overwhelming. In a good way. After months spent in the swamp of my own ruminations, this felt like a complete release.

I took all my drawings, all my notes, and spread them out in my caravan, then pulled out a clean wad of foolscap paper. Over the next couple of weeks I organised everything into an order that I thought would make sense. I figured my drawings of lemurs would have to be larger, so I expanded them, then ran over them with black Textas. Len lent me his Kodak camera and I took photos of all the lemur structures that I had built at Stagland.

Once I had everything together, I bundled it all up into a large package and sent it off to the address in the advertisement.

Three weeks after sending in my application, I received a letter addressed to 'Tim Husband, Zoologist, Stagland'. Mr Brake had opened it in his office, then given it to Mick to bring to me in the caravan along with a message.

'Mr Brake said this came for you. He wanted me to tell you congratulations.' Mick had given up even pretending to be interested in my life, as I hadn't been the best of company recently, so he delivered his message in a monotone. He walked off after throwing the envelope in through the door.

'Thanks,' I said sheepishly, remembering what a prick I had been over the past few months.

I took a deep breath. My heart was pumping hard up against my ribs. I can't quite remember how the letter read, but it went something like this:

Dear Mr Husband

Thank you for your submission to the ARAZPA board for a place presenting a paper at the upcoming zoo conference in Auckland on 15 November.

The board has reviewed your submission and were very impressed with the material proposed for presentation.

We are formally inviting you to present this paper on the morning of 15 November at Auckland Zoo auditorium for the inaugural New Zealand and Australia zoo conference.

Yours sincerely,

Executive Assistant

Office of ARAZPA

I sat down. There was pain, but I had little space to pay it any attention. My heart was still thumping against my rib cage like it was trying to get out, but another part of me was dead calm. Like it knew all along that this was the path I was going to take, and there was only the quiet relief that this moment had finally come.

Later that day I saw Mick's head passing by the kitchen window as he walked to the feeding shed. 'Mick, Mick! Come here. Come in, bro, feel like a cuppa?'

Although Mick was a little unsettled by the change in my mood, his curiosity got the better of him and he came over. Plus, he was still watching out for me, I reckon, and willing to take any opening he could get. 'Hey, whatever was in that letter, you need more of that!'

'Yeah, sorry, Mick, haven't been great company, that's for sure. I've been asked to give a talk at the Auckland zoo conference! A talk on primates!'

'Are you fucking kidding me, man!? Wow, that's great. Good for you! When is it? Are you going to present those scrappy bits of paper you showed Dick and me in the office? Bro, you've gotta do better than that. Have you got anything decent to wear? I swear you've lived in those shorts and that T-shirt for six years now. Take one of my shirts.'

Mick was genuinely excited about this new development, but I'd been so alone for so long it took me a little time to actually digest his reaction. I just always assumed nobody really cared about anything I was doing.

—

I arrived at the Education Centre at Auckland Zoo on my Yamaha on the morning of 15 November 1984. I was wearing one of Mick's freshly pressed Stagland manager shirts and a pair of my favourite Levis. I'd only done one rodeo in them since their last wash, so I figured they'd be okay. My Blundstone boots were polished, but that was only because they were new. Mr Brake had dropped them off at the back door of my caravan.

There were so many people there. Hundreds. Although whenever I saw more than ten people in a group at any one time, it always felt like there were hundreds. I later learnt there were only around 50. There was a table with conference programs on it. Complimentary tea and coffee and biscuits as well. You could get yourself a real drink from a barman at another table. As I walked in, an old codger asked who I was. When I replied, someone promptly pinned me with a name tag:

Presenter, Lemur Behaviour, Tim Husband

The old codger, decked out in a suit and tie, looking down his nose at a list of names while barely making eye contact with me, said, 'You're a very young fellow.'

'You're not,' I said without looking at him.

Two speakers went before me, laying out the dietary needs of reptiles and effective transfer methods for elephants. They were both probably around the Elders' age, both Aussies, with a few letters following their names on the program. Thankfully I didn't know what any of that meant. I was just excited to talk about all the observations that had consumed me for so long, to finally share years of sketching and scrawling notes on behaviours. My ideas on how to improve the lives of the animals at Stagland—in particular the lemurs. I also knew how to deliver a speech. Turning up to houses in the bush blocks of Whangārei from when I was six to deliver monologues on salvation had laid down a template in my brain, which, when revisited, numbed any nerves that I might have had when I got up to the lectern. And the best part was that this time, I was talking about shit I was actually interested in. In Grandad's words, 'If you can sell religion Tim, then for sure you can just about sell anything.'

'Hello everyone. Thank you for giving me this opportunity to share my observations. My name is Tim Husband . . .'

For the next ten minutes, I talked easily about the innovations we had made in the lemur complex at Stagland. It rolled on something like, 'If you, like me, have watched for hours while animals lose all interest in life, and in particular play, animals that spend days on end looking like a kid who's just copped their fifth detention in a row, then you are going to be amazed at just how much change in behaviour you will see when a few fairly simple changes are made.'

While I talked, I fumbled unashamedly with my piles of crumpled A4 papers, pulling out the transparencies for the overhead projector that I had created, after a little instruction, that morning. When I put them on the projector, I was able to see my stick figure monkeys expand into what looked like life-sized lemurs, their tails stretching across the screen.

After the day's program had been completed, all the speakers met up in the foyer for drinks. I ordered a double bourbon and coke and swallowed half of it in my first go.

'Interesting approach. I really enjoyed hearing what you're doing here in New Zealand.' A woman was talking to me.

'Thank you.'

'My name is Uli Ware. I'm Head of Primates at Melbourne Zoo in Australia. We've been implementing some of the strategies you talked about in your presentation for some time now. There's new research on how aggression can be contained between species when you use visual barriers. We have red-fronted lemurs and ringtail lemurs in the same exhibit.'

I mostly got the gist of what she was saying and offered more of my own observations: 'Well, I think I noticed that within single-species exhibits. They were angry yes, but also quite depressed. They were both, I think. I also discovered that when they were getting really upset by each other, having something to hide behind for a while really calmed them down. I noticed that when we were building the climber. They often hid from one another behind the piles of kauri we were using to build the treepee.'

'Yes, it's the new frontier in animal behaviour. Innovations in animal enrichment,' Uli added.

'Yeah, it felt like a no-brainer. They just looked so bored and depressed. For me, it was like, I would have loved to have a place to hide if I had people staring at me the whole time.'

She laughed. 'You're very refreshing, Mr Husband. Here is my card. Please stay in touch and let me know how you're going. Primates, particularly gorillas and lemurs, are my favourite areas of research.'

'Mine too, but only in that I like to hang out with them.'

'Right. We've still got so much to learn, hey!'

'We do indeed, Ms Ware.'

'You are quite young, aren't you?'

'In some ways. Not the ways that matter though.'

'I like you, Mr Tim Husband. Please stay in touch.'

I wouldn't see Uli Ware again for many years but that first

connection with her, a zoo professional who worked inside an international zoo, was a real buzz. We really seemed to understand each other.

I was enjoying myself very much. I was feeling seen. Many of the people at that conference appeared to be interested in my talk and, weirdly to me, wanted to introduce themselves to find out more about me. That was a first. I was starting to feel something that was quite new to me. Was it respect? Respect, not because I didn't mind beating the shit out of myself, but because I was contributing something to make the lives of animals—the lives I cared most about in the world—a little better?

'Did well out there, mate. Loved what you had to say. My name's Bazza. I'm an Aussie, but you've probably already guessed that from the accent! I'm from a place called Coolangatta in Queensland. We've got a zoo up there. I've got a lot of contacts in the zoo industry in Australia, mate. I'll keep an eye out for any openings that come up. I reckon we could do with a fella like you across the ditch!'

'Good to meet you, Bazza. Thanks for thinking of me, mate!' I excitedly replied despite the pinch of anxiety that came with it. It was really going to happen! I was going to work in an international zoo if Bazza had his way! There was so much to process.

I liked Bazza. Even though it wasn't his real name, I like the way 'Bazza' rolls off the tongue. I think it was a nickname. There was something about him that I understood, that resonated. Naturally curious, down to earth, loved animals, didn't take shit, looked like he didn't mind getting his hands dirty, probably liked beer. He bothered to write me letters after he returned to Australia. I wrote back. It was good to have a mate again.

Late that night, the back pocket of my jeans bulging with my presentation notes, I rode my motorbike back to Whangārei. So many thoughts were racing through my head. Despite the fact that my life still felt like it was tracking more like a blowfly's death spin, I felt a quietening. It felt like one door was closing and another opening at the same time. All my old dreams were still rumbling away, and now there was a tiny bit of hope that one day they might even get a foothold. Maybe one day I would be a zoo director and I would have all the authority I needed to make the changes I wanted to make for the animals. To improve the quality of their lives, and in turn give me a sense of success in my own life. Besides that, there was the satisfaction I'd get from showing my dad what happened to the wicked who were banished from the Kingdom of Chosen Ones. That was always pushing me towards being first whenever a finish line came into view. I got back to my caravan after a two-hour ride and went straight to bed, where I slept the sleep of a safe baby.

Dick Brake came over a couple of days after the conference. 'I heard you made quite the splash at the conference Tim! I've gotta say, I'm glad you're using your talents more usefully now, son. Breaking your body is a mug's game. You'd be no better off than those deadbeat preacher brothers of yours.'

'Thanks so much for the boots.' I stared at him and felt full of something. I wasn't sure what, but it was profound and powerful. It went deeper than the layers Tom took up in my head.

'Don't think about it, son.'

'No, thank you, Mr Brake. For more than the boots.'

'Tim, call me Dick. You're not a kid anymore.'

'Okay. Dick. Gotta thank you, Dick.' It was awkward. Didn't know what I was about to say, but it came anyway. 'Don't really know how to thank you, but here it is. Without you, I'd have had nowhere to go when I was thrown out of home. I wouldn't have known how to write that paper. I wouldn't have learnt anything about animals. Without you, I might not even be standing here.'

I love that Dick always showed his emotions in his face. His eyes were a bit watery. 'You're a good kid, Tim, even though you're not even a kid anymore.' He laughed, enjoying his own joke, as always. 'You are going to go places, son. I know that. I'm really proud of you. More so now that you are not trying to actively kill yourself. You know, I knew that I was only going to ever stay in Whangārei when I brought my first truckload of deer. Didn't have anything more driving me than Sandra and the kids, yeah, and the keepers and a few animals. And that was more than enough. But you, ahh, I don't know, with you, there's something else. Something I didn't have, and I want you to follow it as far as it takes you, son.'

We stood there together. I'm sure we were both remembering that grim drizzly dark night when I came and knocked on the office door looking for a home. I remembered watching his face up close, weathered like a tree trunk, watching his eyes tearing up with worry. But now his face was glowing, almost luminous. I put that down as love even though my experience of it was limited. It was either love or pride, but whatever it was it ran through every line on his face. Maybe love *and* pride were there in his face that night.

———

I pulled a duffel bag from under the bed and filled it with a couple of keeper shirts, a few pairs of jeans, Dick Brake's Blundstone boots and my animal behaviour books. I also pushed the tin with Grandad's medals down the side of my bag. My favourite Western saddle was coming too, and I slung it over my shoulder. Then I closed the door on my Daktari cave, leaving very little room for sentiment as I walked down the sodden kauri path towards the office. Dick was somewhere in town, Mick was in the shed. I walked past the lemurs, who were so busy playing they hardly noticed me walking past on the people side of the fence. I found Len at the goose pond.

'Aren't you sick of looking after geese, Len? You've been doing it for so many years.'

We sat together on a bench in silence for a minute or so. When Len finally answered, he did so without turning away from the geese. 'When I've learnt all there is to learn about geese, then I will move on to something else.'

I got up, briefly put my hand on his shoulder, then walked out of Stagland forever.

10

Keeper of primates

Stepping off the plane in Sydney in the autumn of 1985, I felt older, stronger, further away from my father. This was my first job with an international zoo—Taronga Zoo. It was likely I'd been offered the job as senior primate keeper because Bazza had put a word or two in for me, but I reckon my lemur talk in Auckland had a fair bit to do with it as well. The dry heat of Sydney was new. Eucalypts and faint wafts of sea-salt spray had replaced the damp suffocating weight of the kauri and manuka woodlands of home. Whangārei was hemmed in by mountains and forests, and the sky there seemed more like a lid than an escape, but this city was hectic, with spaghetti roads trailing chaotically over hills and ocean inlets, and everything seeming to open towards the sky or the ocean.

When I walked into Taronga the next day, it felt like one of my true Daktari moments. All those years before on that first bike ride to Stagland, the scripts of my future that swirled around my head had all kicked off with a scene where I walked into my first role at an international zoo as a keeper. And now here I was, doing it for real. Taronga Zoo scaffolded a cliff face backboned by slabs of chalky pink and white sandstone, and it overlooked Sydney Harbour, which on most days of the year when the sun shone, sparkled all over. Inside the zoo, everywhere I looked I saw exotic animals that I'd only ever seen as grainy faded photos inside my coffee-stained encyclopedias. Hippo, elephant, rhino, zebra, giraffe, wolves, kangaroos—they were all here. It was as if all my books were breaking out into the living world, and escaping with endless possibilities.

Brilliantly coloured Australian birds rose to heights in aviaries that hardly seemed possible for captivity. Primates loped along ledges, then disappeared behind sandstone slabs. Carnivores shaded themselves under rock platforms choked in climbing ivy. The rock outcrops themselves offered protection, not just from the sun, but also from the unrelenting gaze of tourists. Sometimes I couldn't even see any fencing around the exhibits because it was so neatly tucked away—that blew me away. Reptiles enjoyed waterways edged by sloping beaches of dark-sediment sand. Numerous saurians—alligators, snakes and lizards—shared their territory and were splayed motionless on the enclosure beaches as they basked in the Sydney sun, which on this March morning had already reached 33 degrees Celsius. The indoor exhibits were just as impressive. Aquariums offered expansive glass walls for underwater viewing. I watched while fur seals did their daily pirouetting performances for the public.

Possibility and excitement ripped through me like wind over flat water, and my body was flushed all over with goosebumps. I was only 23 years old, and yet the fourteen-year-old banished boy from Whangārei was here too. The boy who had spent the last ten years of his life talking to Len, Keeper of the Geese, and watching lemurs in his lunch breaks. That young boy, only slightly unsettled by all the changes, was experiencing a sense of arrival. No word from Tom that day. I was satisfied with who I was, where I was, right then at that very moment. And that was a first.

I made my way to the office, where I was to meet the operations manager. He greeted me with a strong handshake and a down-to-earth grin, then handed me my name badge. 'Welcome to Taronga Zoo, Tim Husband!

'Hi, good to meet you Mr . . .'

'Mate, call me Burnsy, everyone else does. Let's go and meet everyone.'

This guy had the same TV voice that Dick Brake had used all those years ago when he offered me a place to live and work at Stagland, and any memory of Mr Brake always had the effect of grounding me in every way possible. Especially since I was still wearing his boots.

'Everyone. Can I have your attention please?' That was all it took for people to stop speaking in the staffroom. To stop pouring coffee, laughing, eating. He had everyone's respect in that room. I noticed that. 'This is Tim Husband, Taronga's new primate keeper.'

There was a round of head nodding interrupted only by the odd hello, and then I saw a sea of curious faces staring at me. Panic grabbed me by the guts until one of the other primate keepers, Glenn Sullivan, bounced over to me and dropped into the awkward silence with an outstretched hand. 'How the fuck are ya!'

Wow! Was NOT expecting that! was what I thought but didn't say. I grabbed Glenn's hand in what I hoped was a convincing man-shake.

Glenn introduced me to everyone else in the room, people who, for the most part, had already returned to whatever they'd been doing. Then another of the managers, a tall lanky guy, offered to show me around the zoo's exhibits. I reckoned he must have been nearly six-foot-five, taller than any keeper or cowboy I'd come across before. While doing the rounds with me, he talked with barely a pause. His updates on new research were choked with micro-data. I was a little confounded by the many statistics that stood like sentinels around his animal knowledge. He also delivered his talk in a monotone, like one of the Elders used to do when covering the apostles' epistles in our Kingdom class. By the time this guy had left me, I hadn't opened my mouth once. I made a mental note to later write down in my 'People behaviour' list that if I ever became a manager, I would always allow a new employee space to feel seen and let them ask questions.

After the manager finished his rounds with me, I swung back to find Debbie Cox, who we had earlier passed in the primate section. She warmly welcomed me, talked to me about the Taronga primate collection, talked a bit about her own work, then went on to ask about my background. 'I heard you did an interesting job with the lemurs and their exhibits in New Zealand!'

My giant stick-figure lemurs with their fruit-looped tails swinging across the enormous theatre screens at the Auckland Zoo conference—that was the memory that came to mind. I chuckled and answered Debbie with a reference to her Jane Goodall work that Burnsy had told me about earlier.

'Nothing compared to the work you're doing. Jane Goodall! Bloody hell!'

'Hasn't happened yet, but I am in touch with her at the moment and I'll be spending a year with her, next year I hope.'

She talked about her research and her data on chimp behaviour. How time she'd already spent observing Goodall, in particular how the scientist quietly 'inserted' herself into the chimps' territory, had had a huge impact on her own understanding of how observation of animals should be conducted. Debbie, like Goodall herself, believed that observation was an art form of its own.

Debbie's knowledge of primates was astonishing. I was also struck by her steadiness, how she seemed to carry within her a stillness and unflinching sense of her own strength. It was something I hadn't come across since Jenny Falcon in Kingdom class.

At lunch that first day, I saw some of the keepers sitting around a table in the canteen: Glenn Sullivan and a couple of keepers I hadn't yet met.

'Tim, bring your Kiwi arse over here and sit down!' said Glenn. As I sat down next to him, he continued: 'This is Lisa. She's a senior keeper also working here with the primates.'

Lisa seemed to have the same steady focus that Debbie had. 'G'day, Tim. What's your history with monkeys, other than following directions from this idiot here?'

'Steady on, woman. We've gotta work together!'

Glenn and Lisa laughed with each other. They were obviously good mates.

'Nothing too impressive. I worked with lemurs for years. I learnt a lot about them. I don't know chimp behaviour well but hope to learn a lot here.'

'Lisa here is an orangutan tragic,' said Glenn. 'Can't say anything bad about orangs or she'll have you on a spit.'

Lisa rolled her eyes but nodded her head in acknowledgement.

'Sounds unpleasant,' I said.

Lisa got up to leave. 'Got quite a bit of stuff to catch up on. Catch you guys later.'

The third keeper, who I'll call Rick, was carefully finishing a small yoghurt. I leant towards him and asked, 'What do you do here?'

'Same as you guys.'

'Okay, so working with the chimpanzees?'

'That's right Tim. I'm a primate man.'

'More like a fully committed Jesus man.' Bits of pastry fell from the meat pie in Glenn's mouth as his mumbling interruption sized up Rick's faith.

Rick continued: 'I've been working with the staff here at Taronga for over three months now.'

'All the time with primates or with some of the other animals?' I asked.

'Yeah, mostly with primates, Tim.'

'Actually, it's human animals that he's really been working on,' said Glenn. 'He's been working to convert them to Jesus Christ. This mob of macaques here is a little more challenging than the kiddies at Manly's Sunday School though, aren't they, Rick?'

'You don't have to listen to him too much, Tim, he's got a mouth on him the size of a hippo and as dirty as elephant dung.' Rick's voice had begun to tremble a little as he tried to shut Glenn down. He was a kid on the ropes. I'd known that kid well.

'That's a good one. Why don't you tell him you're a Christian, mate. Be proud!'

Rick took Glenn's bait, turned to me and said, 'It IS true, Tim, I am a Christian. Did you know, Tim, that we are all made in the image of God? "Every person, from the womb to the tomb as human beings, bears the image of God." Book of Psalms, Psalm 139.'

It was all getting a bit heavy for a lunchtime chat over a mini-yoghurt, but Glenn seemed to find another gear, quoting from a different book: 'I, on the other hand, like to "think of my fellow man not as a fallen angel, but as a risen ape". Book of Desmond Morris, *The Naked Ape*, chapter two.'

Although slightly unnerved by being thrown back into a bit of textbook playground bullying on my first day, I wasn't going to get in the way when it came to the flattening of a Jesus zealot, particularly when I did think of humans more as risen apes than fallen angels.

Later that afternoon, I went on my own to the chimp exhibit. A few of the chimps noticed me sit down on a bench on the other side of the moat that ran around the perimeter of the exhibit. The water protected the keepers and the public, as mob violence among chimps is common.

'Hope you guys aren't going to go too ape shit on me, hey!' I called out. The chimps hooted as if they got the pun.

I had wanted to work with chimps ever since I'd heard the talks on them in Auckland, and I was excited to finally be sitting with them. The only access the keepers had to the chimps was through the animals' night den, although entry was restricted to the senior keepers. These particular chimps were obviously very used to people and, like all animals, they could sense empathy and the desire for connection in a keeper. A few more of them had now gathered at the moat's edge and were watching me intently across the water that separated us. I observed the troupe for a couple of hours that afternoon. Home again, just sitting on a bench watching primates in silence. Eventually I made my way to their night den to start work on their overnight exhibit.

———

My first rented flat was in the suburb of Manly and overlooked Sydney Harbour. Its narrow verandah had a red plastic chair and a wrought-iron table. Every morning at 5 am, I'd sit on my verandah drinking my sweet coffee and watch the sun's slow break across the ocean horizon. That was always a comfort, just like when I was a kid in my caravan and the first warm white shafts of sun found me after another night I'd spent in the wastelands. I was still feeling full with a satisfying sense of arrival, not only to a new country but there was a growing confidence that my path was opening up and I was just letting it live in my body as an unusual sense of quiet. At those times, Tom didn't have much to offer, and that was always a relief.

———

My early months at the zoo were mostly spent learning the ropes of primate keeping, so I worked very closely with the chimpanzee troupe. I would observe them for longer than the hours it took me to clean their exhibit and get their food. I learnt that they had intricate relationships within their family groupings, and I learnt how their troupe dynamics were based on cooperation as much as competition.

I witnessed the many ways in which the chimps watched out for each other's welfare. Members of a family within the troupe would help Mary, a blind chimp, whenever she needed to go anywhere. When Susie the diabetic chimp had an attack, her two adult daughters would drag her limp body to the night den, as they knew this was where she would get the treatment she needed. We were able to quickly treat her and return her to the troupe in the morning.

The competition for dominance among the males involved harder lessons to learn. It was interesting to observe that the male behaviours included cooperation to the extent that other males in the troupe could be politicised to create power blocs. This was especially evident when we acquired a pedigree chimp from New Zealand called Snowie. We watched while Snowie was targeted and consistently challenged by many of the resident beta males. Snowie was so heavily invested in maintaining his role as alpha chimp, spending the majority of his time fighting off rivals, that he only ever managed to father two per cent of the troupe's offspring. This meant we lost out on the gene line we were specifically seeking. We eventually lost Snowie. During his short life at Taronga, he was constantly stressed and then weakened by what was happening. His untimely demise came about when the mob of beta males pushed him into the moat, where he drowned.

This outcome was difficult for Debbie, Lisa and me. We had come to know all the characters in the troupe very well, and we naturally hated to lose any of them. But I was particularly hard on myself because I felt that there was something I had missed by not paying close enough attention. I couldn't accept Snowie's death as inevitable, and when I wasn't at work I kept revisiting the months leading up to the killing. What could I have done differently?

This became deep-seated doubt when Tom's low-pitched babble started up in the background of my day, droning on like the TV Mum used to leave on all day. He'd occasionally have a crack at me, saying stuff like, *Too busy being one of the boys to pay attention! Maybe you're just not up to it, it's an international zoo after all. Told you you should've stayed at Stagland.*

His accusation that I couldn't pay attention to detail really stung, because I knew that had always been one of my strengths. It was something I had come to value in myself after years of sharing my lunch with Len, whose lessons had been drilled into me since I was fourteen, such as, 'When you think you've learnt everything you can about geese, pay even greater attention, they'll show you something else.'

Tom and I sparred like feral cats in my head, and brooding and rumination took hold of my moods during the day. This internal head lock usually showed up for others as irritability and moodiness but I discovered it was much harder to hide my truculence at Taronga than when I was at Stagland. Such behaviour was deemed unprofessional at Taronga, and unprofessionalism was the last thing I wanted to be known for.

Debbie Cox noticed my tension when we went to review Snowie's body at the vet clinic. Being as empathic as she was observant, she suspected a tendency for self-blame and so reminded me that we were all feeling the loss. 'Go easy on yourself, Tim, everybody is hurting. It's natural. There's so much for ALL of us to learn, my friend, and there always will be.'

With the two people I trusted most with animal care, Len and Debbie, giving me the same advice, I knew I had to be careful about being too hard on myself. Besides, I felt I HAD learnt a lot, not only about alpha male chimp behaviour but also about how I handled situations. By 'going easy on myself', in Debbie's words, it helped me get through difficult emotional stuff more easily and I was getting better at not only noticing, but also accepting all the stuff that really *was* outside my control. There was something else, too, something new. I'd noticed at Taronga that when something majorly distressing happened with the animals, the staff looked out for each other. They seemed to care for animals as acutely as I did, so we all knew how profoundly each of us would feel the loss when something unforeseen happened. I was surrounded by like-minded people, particularly my primate colleagues, and so I was beginning to care about upsetting others at work. That motivated me more than whatever kind of crazy was going on in my head. I was sensing a connection to place developing. A sense of belonging.

———

The years rolled on at Taronga and I found myself drinking less bourbon. Much less. I'd also developed a friendship with Glenn that silenced most of Tom's destructive rants and allowed me to feel slightly human. Normal. Average. A good bloke with a good friend. I suspected I was becoming THAT zoo guy, the one I'd observed when I was growing up. The regular zoo guy who knew how to work hard but also knew how to play hard. Nowhere was that more apparent than in my interactions with the reclusive Christian keeper who, even after four years at Taronga, was still throwing casual Bible verse at me as though I gave a shit. Whenever he talked to me, he would lean in close, as though we shared a secret. I didn't seem to be able to shake him despite doing my very best to do so. If he found me before anyone else had arrived at work in the morning, he'd offer something ecclesiastical, like: 'This is the day the Lord has made, let us rejoice and be glad in it, Tim.'

Occasionally I responded, with something I knew Glenn would get a kick out of, like: 'Did you know that it's even harder for the average ape to believe he is descended from humans? The Book of H.L. Mencken.'

But mostly I kept quiet, mostly never even looked up, because Rick's velvet-toned offerings made my stomach churn. It was the same creepy voice Dad had used at flyscreen doors, and it made my blood boil and set its circuitry imploding through my body in search of something to punch. I wasn't sure why I couldn't shake him. Could he sense a fault line in me? How could he possibly know my history?

I was trying to rewrite some of the damage from my own childhood, and I consoled myself with the idea that anyone who had Jesus as a first line of defence was fresh bait for me. But I always felt unsettled after a lunchtime interaction with this keeper, and I only seemed to calm down by returning to the primates. The simple act of quiet observation was always my escape. All the cigarette flicking and sarcastic one-liners, all the nods and winks from our lunch break, would fall away as I became absorbed by the many layers of connection, communication and conflict among Taronga's chimpanzee troupe.

Glenn's colours also changed when he was at work as a keeper. Just when I'd picked him for a typical ocker, he would reel off reams of raw practical animal knowledge. I also continued soaking up behavioural anomalies about chimp family life from Debbie Cox. She would sometimes let me sit with her while she observed the more subtle interactions of the troupe she worked among. Debbie acutely grasped the importance of protection and enrichment in the design of sanctuaries. She cared deeply for the animals she kept and, from my observations, this allowed her to see more than those who simply collated data. One night, I was privileged to observe that connection firsthand. We were in the night house and on this particular night, the chimps were unusually unsettled, screeching, throwing sticks at each other. In the middle of the hullabaloo Debbie started laughing, very loudly and cheerfully. What happened next was astonishing. The whole troupe stopped their noise and ruckus to stare at Debbie laugh and then they watched on while she walked calmly out of the night house. She returned ten minutes later and had all the chimps calmly cooperating, not only with her, but also with each other. There was a connection there. I asked her if it was possible that the animals she observed showed more of themselves because of how they felt when she was there.

'Couldn't tell you that, my friend. Way too existential for me.'

After years spent observing primate behaviour, I was becoming aware that there were similar codes and hierarchies playing out at Taronga among the staff members. Although I enjoyed being one of them, rather than the weird dude who sat silently on benches watching animals, I did realise that inside the human ape troupe, I was both the watcher and the watched.

Taronga seemed to operate like any primate community: it had its village idiots, its leaders, the workers, the villains. I saw how staff members were drawn to their 'type' and spent a lot of time and energy preserving this. It seemed hard for people to reach across their character divide to someone who had completely different interests to them. They appeared to be separated not only by status but also by their interests. The carnivore keepers tended to be the big-ego guys who seemed to be playing out some sort of power trip. Not all of them were in it for the power, but the large open-mouthed carnivore tattoos they carried had to be either an aggressive power display or an homage of some kind to the beasts. Both seemed weird to me. I often wondered why the keepers who looked after birds weren't inspired to do the same. The aviary keepers kept to themselves and tended to be more academic. The aquarium keepers had an unusually close bond with their animals and knew their nutritional needs in microscopic detail, which they became very earnest about sharing with anyone who cared to listen. Those in the primate mob were mostly mischievous, naturally rebellious and perhaps a little arrogant. That seemed to be as far as I could get with observing my own behaviours when inside the troupe, but maybe that was the nature of belonging.

One thing I was constantly bewildered by was how the antics and politics of the overlapping tribes within the human troupe sometimes rivalled even the more extreme of the chimp behaviours. It was an echo of my very early intuitive take on the human species when I'd join the lemurs at lunchtime and watch the human exhibit from inside their enclosure. It seemed to me that ours was a complex and dangerous species with a high potential for self-destruction.

My Taronga adventure eventually started succumbing to the zoo's own, or my own, fault lines—I was still too green to know which. There were some in power at Taronga who couldn't understand why I spent hours observing the animals and recording their behaviours. Their need to adhere to regulations and rules often overrode the simple explanation I gave them: 'I learn most from connection and hands-on experience with the animals. This, I believe, makes me a better keeper.'

I started to feel micromanaged, sometimes over things I felt were relatively minor. On one rainy Sunday morning, I was challenged by management for not giving the set talk at the chimp exhibits—scolded for spending my time with the few tourists brave enough to face the rain answering their questions and pointing out behaviours as we observed the chimps together. I was reprimanded for speaking back to my unit manager about the poor health of some of the animals at Taronga's Friendship Farm, as this was 'not your animal division'.

It didn't help that Tom stood over conversations in an effort to intimidate and I became increasingly moody at work. I battled hard to stop his sly efforts at sabotage—especially when my state of mind was vulnerable—by spending more time with the orangutans, more time with the macaques and the squirrel monkeys. More time on the bench. On my own. Just observing.

11

Life force

It was the beginning of 1990, and this particular morning in January had begun entirely unremarkably—a night shelter clean, a restocking of chimp food and a car crash of a conversation with the Christian keeper. With my cigarette hanging almost forgotten from my lips, and an instant coffee in hand, I did the thing I always did—sat on the sandstone steps and soaked up the winter Sydney sun while watching the comings and goings of keepers. Glenn joined me for a while, we didn't say much, just enjoyed soaking up the sunshine. A group of people approached us, new horticulturalists. The head of horticulture was with the group and introduced Glenn and me to the new employees. Among them was Wendy Anthony. She had a no-nonsense beauty that struck me hard. Her dark-brown wavy hair came down below her shoulders. Handfuls of it had escaped the hair clip that hung carelessly, unsure of its job. Her olive skin was speckled with sparse black freckles. Her sharp dark-brown eyes met me fully dilated, the pupils collecting layers of information microscopically, methodically. My information. She pinned me to where I sat. A still, steady connection. Sensory, mind, body. It was mind-blowing.

I soon found any reason, every reason, to make my way to the horticulture area, or to take a break when the gardeners came in for lunch. For the first time in my life, I was thinking about a woman beyond a hook-up in a motel. Endlessly thinking about one woman. I turned over witty throwaways in my head after re-enacting chance meetings. I practised picking up a phone and leaving a message—again, all in my head. This was a completely new and bewitching hell. Tom chipped in as well, mostly telling me that my chances of getting her to take a second look at me were non-existent.

A couple of weeks after meeting her, I got the opportunity to try out one of my scripted pieces. I saw her outside the canteen talking to a group of people. As I walked past with my coffee, I felt a boiling inside. Uncomfortable. My heart was banging against my chest. Not even Wrecked, that bucking bull in New Zealand, raised my heart rate the way this woman did and even though I'd never taken a feeling for a woman outside a motel room or away from the bronc shed, I knew my appetite for dangerous edges was pushing me towards her.

'Nice day! When are you going to go out with me?' Apparently my self-styled 'cool' didn't even require me to stop and face her as I delivered my throwaway remark. I kept walking, turning around only once.

'When you ask properly.' She, on the other hand, didn't seem to have any problem facing me.

Once I was out of sight, I shouted at the sky. 'Fuuuck!'

When life was simple.
Me at eleven months old.

My first close encounter with an exotic animal, at age 9. The elephant had escaped from an enclosure at Wellington Zoo and I thought it a good idea to share some fruit and nuts with him. He was calm and welcomed my offerings, and I was hooked.

Was so chuffed to be asked to represent my school to lead the haka. My mate John gave me some of his Maori gear to wear.

School photo in the early seventies. I was too young to realise that the world could be your oyster.

My grandfather, my hero. Here he is as a young soldier.

Grandad was always ready to listen to or share a story. Here he is, as an older man, with a twinkle in his eye and a Lion Red lager in hand.

Leaning on my rake, otherwise known as 'a keeper's best friend'. This is the only photo of me at Stagland. I was nearly 19.

My short stint as a rodeo clown (right), in my last year on the rodeo circuit. Crazy adrenalin rush because nothing and no one stands between you and the charging bull.

Poetry in Motion. The winning ride, on a horse called Kiss me Goodbye, that got me into the National New Zealand Rodeo Team.

While helping out at Friendship Farm at Taronga, I began a lifelong love of Scottish Highland cattle. And hair-brushing.

When the days were long and the shorts were short. Between shifts at Taronga Zoo, aged 24.

Enjoying the arrival of a new Sumatran tiger cub at Taronga.

In 1996 we celebrated 50 years of conservation at Taronga. Glenn and I were asked to dress in the zoo's original keepers' uniforms for the day.

Two red panda cubs, only 6 months old. They climbed all over me, one down my back and one down my front, both looking for fruit stashed in my pocket.

Mini, the oldest-known spider monkey in the world, celebrated her birthday at Taronga. I was given the task of cutting the cake, which was to be shared equally between Mini and all her monkey mates. Unlikely, to say the least!

Willow, the three-year-old orangutang at Taronga, who I'd developed a close bond with. She was always ready to jump on board if anyone was carrying a bucket of fruit and nuts for a treat.

My first experience of holding a snake. Actually, my first experience of seeing a snake! There are no snakes in New Zealand so this was a heck of an introduction!

Wendy and me on our wedding day at Taronga Zoo, with a couple of unusual gatecrashers. PHOTO: BRIAN CASSEY

Newborn gazelle at Dubai Safari Park. Fleet footed and fragile, gazelle are one of the most graceful of all wild animals.

My Aunty Kez came to see me in Dubai. She was always in my corner.

Our first lion cubs born at the Cairns animal park, aged 6 weeks.

PHOTO: BRIAN CASSEY

Same lion cubs, at 12 months, not so easy to hold, but just as playful.

PHOTO: BRIAN CASSEY

Eight-year-old Jordan, our son, and his mate Nelson the rhino.

Watering the rhino to cool and calm him down in preparation for the trip to Indonesia after the new owners of the Cairns animal park sold up and transferred the animals to Denpasar Animal World. PHOTO: BRIAN CASSEY

A baby Malaysian tapir born in Denpasar Animal World. They are born with white speckles lining their body but eventually they turn into two colours: black on the front part of their body and their tail, with a broad white stripe around their belly.

At Denpasar Animal World we were hand-raising this 1-year-old leopard cub that had been rejected by his mum.

Me and my colleague Woko in the elephant exhibit at Animal World showcasing Wendy's elephant poo paper and leaning on a less-than-convincing lounge suite! PHOTO: BRIAN CASSEY

Teaching keepers how to catch a crocodile. It takes many keepers to hold down a big crocodile.

Preparing a crocodile for transportation. The jaws always needed to be secured first.

My colleague Essa and me reviewing progress at the Dubai Safari Park.

Preparing the lion crates in Cairns for their flight to Indonesia.

Handling giraffe is a special art. It is tricky to get the giraffe into a crate so we put a hood on the animal to help calm it down. We then run a rope gently up the giraffe's neck and around its head, allowing us to carefully bend its neck in the right direction to enter the crate. Johann (far right) is an expert at it. Here we are in Africa getting giraffe ready for their trip to Dubai.

Top: The early construction stage of Dubai Safari Park, which grew out of a sand dune in the desert.

Middle: Me welcoming a group of visiting dignitaries to Dubai Safari Park in 2018.

Bottom: The eagle has landed. My last day at Dubai and the education staff— as a farewell to me—called in their golden eagle to land on my arm.

Tup and Lady Gagulah, my two friends, enjoy a morning break at my farm.
PHOTO: BRIAN CASSEY

Me with Deb and Rob Kane, my neighbours, and Beannie the dog on their farm. They say 'no man is an island' but with a couple of friends like these, you can be an archipelago. **PHOTO: STEVE BATTEN**

What sort of man could get on a one-tonne beast of muscle-bound bovine power and ride its rump around a ring, then talk to a woman with a line you'd expect from a third grader in a playground! The soundtrack in my head was merciless. My heart continued its rib thumping.

I retreated for a day or two into self-recriminations while Tom railed against a settling of my mood and trawled through any combination of my character flaws. He even threatened a return to the nightly bourbon ritual, until a chance meeting with Wendy allowed a reprieve. The surprise itself handed me back my best intentions, and my words were gentler this time, and unrehearsed. 'Hey. Sorry about the other day. I meant it actually. I would like to take you out.'

Her colleague, who was pushing elephant grass into holes, choreographed a cough and moved further away from us. Wendy faced me dead-on. Took me all in. Shark swallowing a tuna whole. Her well-worn Levis were peppered with black soil, and I noticed she'd tucked them into her work boots. And then, I noticed her boots. They were made from leather. Old, soft leather that had been worked hard and well looked after. They were clearly loved. I rarely took my own pair off. Wendy's black full-moon eyes were still pinning me to the spot like an insect specimen.

'I'll check my diary and get back to you.' Said with a warm smirk.

After a few days, Wendy finally let me know she was happy to go to the movies with me that weekend. I didn't sleep much the night before, running conversational possibilities around the rat runs of my brain, and I was more than a little disturbed to notice they were limited to two or three subjects. Maybe my intellectual and emotional maturity had stalled at fourteen, when I first went into the caravan, planting telltale red flags in my difficult attempts at conversation and rattled nerves. But how was I to know what was weird and what was normal?

I picked Wendy up in Glenn's Ford Fiesta and we went to the cinema in Randwick. She had picked *Empire of the Sun* and spent the whole film completely absorbed. I, on the other hand, cherrypicked scenes and memorised lines, covering myself for conversation at the end of the film. Afterwards, we dodged the bullets of our family history over a beer in the pub and cautiously edged through safe zones like horticultural advances in desert rejuvenation and troupe behaviour among squirrel monkeys. We did have a moan about Taronga staff, some people's unhealthy appetites for power. Curiously, it seemed there was personal stuff that she protected with the same ferocity that I recognised in myself.

For six weeks we went out together. To the movies, swimming, to dinner. Our conversations covered primates, palm trees, composting half-lives of rhino manure, taming wild tussocks, enrichment for ungulates, fungal activity in soils, and observable symbiotic relationships between species. There was people stuff too, stuff about friends. It all seemed to run along as naturally as a seed spreading roots through good soil.

At the end of an evening, I often tried to kiss her, but time and again, she turned my attempts into an awkward cheek-butt by turning away. 'Nah, none of that. Not ready for that.' It was all she offered.

This response was always confusing and crashed up hard against my observations of 'romance'. Since my rodeo days I had often found that women, after a few shared drinks and a few stories told, were open to a hook-up, a one-night stand. But this time, the behaviours Wendy presented were baffling. Never before had sex been the last point of connection for me. Of course, whenever any possibility of intimacy had presented itself, Tom had been careful to wrap up parts of me airtight, limiting sexual encounters to a single night, and there was never any returning to companionship with me for the women who took that road. Wendy Anthony seemed to sense the danger and took a different path. The more she delayed the language of sex that I had learned to navigate so effectively as a means of self-protection, the more I turned inwards, and the more I turned inwards, the more tender stories escaped. I was defenceless against this woman, and it was impossible for Tom to protect me. These torn and tender stories that fed my depression and nestled for years in the curves of my black-skied lens emerged bit by tiny bit.

'I feel like I've been running my whole life.' That one escaped.

'What do you mean?'

'We used to follow phone lines as a family in Auckland.' I found myself telling Wendy how I was forced into selling Jesus.

'Selling Jesus? Is Jesus at the end of a phone line in Auckland?'

I told her how I would watch the swallows build their nests outside my caravan windows and then spend their days on the phone lines connected to the Stagland office. I told her that not only swallows but all animals felt like family to me. That they made me feel safe, and I worked out life stuff through them and with them. A broken description of my childhood followed, with all my ghouls tumbling out in mangled, hairless lumps. For the first time in my life I talked about my father. As soon as I started to expose these gut ghouls, I felt my body brace defensively, felt Tom stirring, putting his fists up. But I pushed through, hugging my chest, as I delivered my history to this strong, safe woman. It was the first time I'd told my story out loud since I had left 10 Smith Street, Whangārei, my family home, almost twenty years before. For so long, fear and anger had run the shit show that was my life, endlessly fuelling the drunk in my head. But that night, I was there only with Wendy and we were travelling through the chapters of my childhood and it all felt safely held in her presence, cocooned in the black corridors of those eyes. I was feeling heard and seen as if for the first time, and an emotion, touched on only once before by Kea, was starting to run warm through my blood, to run warm through my body. It could have been trust. Strange that we had not kissed, not had sex. But after six weeks the need for sex to legitimise who I was, and what this connection was, began to recede with this new sharing of a tender private space I had only before shared with my animals.

———

One Saturday in October, I slipped my Western saddle into the boot of my car, picked up Wendy, and we drove two hours out to Wollemi National Park, where we'd booked a weekend of horseriding with some Taronga colleagues. While the others signed in and gave details of their riding history, I went to the manager's office, gave her a brief account of my riding experience, and asked if I could be given a green horse. A recently broken three-year-old buckskin filly was led out of one of the stalls for me. Muscle bound and twitching, throwing her head, with her bridle bit jangling, she was already sweating enough adrenalin that white foam was collecting at the corners of her mouth. She was the colour of Sydney sandstone, and black socks ran from her knees to her hooves. I slowly walked over to her and took the reins from the groom. Moving in close, I slid my hand down the horse's neck and softly talked to her like I used to talk to the brumbies in New Zealand.

When I could feel her settle a little, I walked her out to the yard. The groom reached for a saddle on a railing. 'I'm okay mate, I've brought my own.' I slipped the soft oily leather of my Western saddle over my forearm and carried it lightly to the filly, letting her sniff it, letting her take all the time she needed before moving it away from her nose. Because she was no longer throwing her head around, I knew she'd accepted it. I slipped the saddle over her sandy haunches and stepped up into the stirrup with no more than a shuffle from the horse. When I finally pulled myself onto the saddle, she mostly stood still, but then she reared, just a little, then jumped sideways and back, breaking into a half-moon canter. I brought her calmly back to the spot. As the filly and I shuffled around in search of the still point of trust, I marvelled at how shy truths showed themselves. This single moment of connection, a silent conversation of signals with this animal, felt like another home for me. With every movement of muscle in her body, every twitch, she sent a message to me, and I answered her with a simple shifting of my own weight. I began to work with the buckskin filly by moving her around the paddock. Cantering, bringing her to an abrupt stop, encouraging sidesteps, then getting her to step backward. She and I continued to connect for some time, deep in silent conversation, oblivious to anything and everything going on around us.

I became aware of people clapping. My Taronga mates were all lined up on the railings, like oil-skinned starlings on a phone line. They were watching me work the young horse with looks that included shock and bewilderment.

'The horse whisperer, Tim Husband! Who knew!' Glenn yelled it loud enough for me to hear.

Eventually we were all set and we rode through the breaking fog over the peaks of Wollemi, through eucalypt forests thick with stringybark and apple gums. It was some of the most spectacular country I'd ever seen. Some of it was escarpment where vast sandstone cliffs dove down to babbling creeks rich with brilliant green lichens and tiny yellow native duck orchids. Wherever there was open country, I took my filly for a gallop and then met up again with the rest of the group. But mostly we all trotted together, following the well-worn tracks made by kangaroos or goats. Most of the time, I was in a blissful bubble shared only by me and this precious animal.

We decided to stop for lunch and a swim where the Colo River formed a billabong at the bottom of the escarpment, then we continued for a few more hours. When dusk started to shadow the tops of the eucalypt forests, we stopped, unsaddled the horses and built a bonfire. The fire took some time to calm enough for us to throw some chops and sausages on a grill. Ginger teas, bourbons and red wine were passed around in the firelight. The night, velvet and luminous, was ink-black peppered with a million of the Milky Way's brightest stars, the moon a sliver of silver in this pack of extroverts.

I sat in a camp chair that night, holding a tin mug full of red wine and staring at the roaring bonfire, my belly packed to the rafters with good feelings. Later, I left the glow of the fire and went into the night to check on my buckskin filly. When I looked back, I saw my Taronga mates cutting golden lines in the black night as they drank their wine and sang loud strange songs about swagmen and billabongs with the bonfire roaring behind them.

Wendy seemed to appear from nowhere and walked next to me for a while. 'Can I ask you a favour?'

'Sure.'

She stopped and turned to me with an urgency that surprised me. 'Will you kiss me?'

It felt like I'd just walked into a tree. 'Umm, I mean yeah, sure.'

And we kissed. It was remarkable. It was like I'd never actually really kissed anyone before her. She had already opened me to trust, to respect, to a living connection, but this kiss swept blood off the tracks. Within a few months, we were married.

12

Three's a crowd

'It's never been done before for a wedding!' John Kelly, Taronga's director, was excited when he gave us the okay to have our wedding in Taronga's walk-through rainforest aviary in January 1991. Bower birds and fruit doves flashed blue, pink and green across the shafts of white light that streamed through the aviary's mesh roof that summer when Wendy and I got married. King parrots and Eastern whipbirds swooped across the sunlit veils of looping tropical natives. Wendy's gardening team had dotted hundreds of moth orchids throughout the aviary. It looked like thousands to me. Their thickly fleshed petals of white and purple lined the pathway from the entrance of the aviary to the birdbath where we'd chosen to have the service.

That morning, I stood between Glenn, my best man, and the celebrant from Cronulla, waiting for Wendy to join us for the ceremony. We were the only people in the aviary. When Wendy finally appeared, she was wearing a simple white-lace wedding dress and she had a crown of tiger lilies on her head. The generous handful of egret orchids she was carrying looked like a hundred whitewater birds preparing for flight. A long golden snake had wrapped itself around her arm like some sort of ancient Macedonian jewel—as she came closer, I recognised it as an American corn snake. I watched while she walked through the orchids, their purple tongues trumpeting celebration with every step she took. Her long winding walk to the birdbath where I waited for her was time slowed for me. No picture of Wendy could have been truer. She was of the earth. Elemental simplicity. Beautiful.

As she approached, she looked at me in my slightly too small, shiny synthetic grey suit, one of her eyebrows raised. *It was all Glenn had*, was my silent excuse. I could tell that the vivid-green Fijian iguana that perched motionless on my right shoulder met with her approval though.

The ceremony began. Birdsong, both native and exotic, underscored the celebrant's words and the extravagant show of colour in the plant and animal life that enveloped us. I could have been in a dream. This setting was the perfect altar for my unlikely pairing with this extraordinary woman, and almost everything and everyone I held close was there to witness it that summer day. The only thing that could have possibly made it better would have been if my childhood mate John or Grandad or Aunty Kez had been there. But I knew they would have loved Wendy and would have loved that we were getting married, so in a way, they were there.

Wendy and I lived a blissed-out life after the wedding: surfing, making love and eating like kings. Wendy cooked with the same passion she poured into her plants. I was treated to culinary adventures that I had only ever imagined for normal families. Or *The Waltons*. Marinated chicken stews, apple and rhubarb pies with homemade pastry, fresh berry muffins and slices, soups made using the vegetables from Wendy's long wooden verandah boxes. Whenever she cooked, Wendy tried to use whatever she had managed to grow, and she managed to grow a lot.

I was always astonished at how much she could produce from just one little seed. She would return from Taronga with precious piles of what she called 'black gold' in the form of elephant and rhino shit, and work them into the lengths of the verandah boxes. In just a few months, zucchini, pumpkin and eggplant leaves had exploded from the narrow boxes, and only a few weeks later we were able to eat the vegetables that had been protected by the vast umbrella leaves. Our flat began to take on the silent sweet pulse of a greenhouse. Endless herb varieties spilled over baskets hanging from window frames. And there was always a row of embryonic seeds softening in wet tissue folds in egg cartons above the sink, each one ready to sprout once the first early sunlight hit the kitchen window. The same devotion she'd given to a growing seed she'd mothered from its first fledgling spread of roots, she'd then pour into her cooking, and the result seemed to bring the best out of every ingredient she used. It often occurred to me that Wendy quite literally brought life with her wherever she went.

We both knew early on in our marriage that life in the city wasn't ever going to be enough for us, so a small farm of some kind became a goal. It was particularly important to Wendy because her green thumb was always in need of more space but it was also important to me because holding Wendy's love of the living plant world was like trying to hold flowing water in cupped hands. A small farm also opened the possibility of me having a collection of my own animals. As well as my own space. And lots of it. Room for my unravelling. I intuitively knew that I needed both those things in my life if I was to ever pass as an unremarkable human being. Animals and space. Both were my refuge from people. We started saving for the deposit.

———

A couple of years slipped by. I returned to work with Debbie and Lisa with the orangutans, and I spent my lunchtimes observing the new exhibit of squirrel monkeys. We had introduced a South American rodent called an agouti into the squirrel monkey exhibit some months before, along with daily servings of macadamia nuts so the agoutis had something to gnaw on. I was interested to see if any mutualistic relationships had developed and was amazed to discover that the squirrel monkeys had figured out that once the agoutis had done all the hard work of gnawing and cracking the macadamia shell, the monkeys could land on them from above, frightening them off the macadamia and steal the nut. For the squirrel monkeys this was useful as they couldn't have opened the nuts themselves. It didn't seem to be a true mutualistic relationship for the agoutis as they never got the nut they'd worked so hard to crack. They did, however, get to gnaw on the shell of the nut so in some ways it did work both ways.

Homelife was a new frontier and it seemed that Wendy and I were fitting into the world in a conventional way I could never have imagined possible for myself. Work, swim, food, play, sleep, sex, work, food, work, sex, work. In any order. Whenever I was at work, I noticed that I was watching the ape troupe through a different lens. I looked more for cooperation and how the animals nurtured one another. It was around this time I decided to have a crack at applying for some promotions that had come up at Taronga, but it seemed that certain roadblocks I'd been facing were still in play with management. My applications kept getting knocked back. I was already aware that I continued to run hard up against the prejudice of some middle managers who knew I lacked the educational background of some of the other senior keepers, but I felt this new hurdle was taking it to another level.

At first, I was able to balance the frustration I had at work with the excitement I had for life at home with Wendy. All of my exasperation at Taronga, my frustrated ambition and its stalled clambering to find its place in the zoo hierarchy, turned strangely sideways when I was home. Wendy revealed to me an understanding of success that meant looking for meaning where no one else seemed to look—underground. Her efforts to further her understanding of the invisible connections and communications in the plant world gave Wendy all she needed for ideas of success to gain traction. Her composting compositions and combinations sat in lined hessian bags on the verandah, and she tended to them with a maternalism that I always found fascinating. She'd explain to me that, just as a zucchini vine explodes into vast leaf life after months of unseen connective work in the soil, work done below, we needed to follow meaning to all its invisible interconnective roots.

'It's not just a zucchini, Timmy,' she'd say. 'This is the end product of millions of microbial conversations among bacteria, fungi and root cells. All the stuff we don't see! They're all in there chatting away and weaving themselves into new life forms through their connections in the soil.' She'd chuckle as her freshly picked vegetables rolled from her basket in a cloud of black gold dust onto the table. She'd pick up a zucchini—or any vegetable that came to hand—and wave it at me, saying, 'Not just a zucchini, love!'

What really blew me away was that the connections needed to create the physical world were mostly unknown to us. All we ever saw was a zucchini, or a tree, and humans would give the zucchini and the tree so much meaning, even though they only ever played a bit part in a much bigger story. What happened underground seemed to me an undiscovered secret world, a complex web of connections that the human species still seemed to know very little about, yet without them, there was no world at all.

Over the following year, I pushed on with applying for promotions within Taronga to become the head of a department, but management continued to block me. I had to watch while many of my colleagues continued their inevitable progression up the zoo hierarchy as head keepers or divisional managers. It infuriated the hell out of me. It was Kingdom Hall again, it was my English teacher slapping my pen from my hand because I was left-handed, it was my father with his fist in my back pushing me towards a front door with my Bible, it was my headmaster trusting the word of a known bully over my own accounts of self-defence while his whip chewed away at old scars on my arse. A deadlock appeared in my body as my guts turned uncomfortably over their empty tunnels in constant protest. Unprepared, unarmed and no control. These were old ghosts with different masks.

All were in play, but when they blew up inside me, it was like I was encountering them for the first time. Forces outside my control were once again dictating my future. I felt suffocated and trapped around these management people with their inflexible grip on power and their ability to hold me in check. The fact that I was trying to pick up extra shifts to save for our farm only made everything worse. The same sense of helplessness that I'd felt when I was a boy returned. It felt like these people, just like my father before them, had me by the throat.

It was also becoming harder to keep Tom in check. Harder to stop him from plotting retribution against whoever he felt deserved it. The frustration built month after month, until the rejection of a sideways move to senior keeper of the macaques prompted Tom to release his full arsenal. I found myself in the zoo's public bathrooms one morning, throwing chairs against walls and punching toilet doors. Finally, when all the shouting was done and the punches thrown and the place was turned completely upside down, I slid slowly down the tiled wall to the floor. My head was throbbing, heavy as a bowling ball in my hands. My body was rocking like it had when I was at the bus stop at Kenny Road as a young boy.

In the weeks that followed that outburst, Tom's relentless ranting left me exhausted. I seemed incapable of silencing him. Worse still, he was on the move. Slowly and slyly, he found a way to sabotage life at home as well. He started with the odd whisper here and there, telling me that I was flirting with the edges of 'normal' with my life with Wendy, and that I was never

ever going to fit that mould. That I didn't even deserve to have Wendy in my life. His constant cautioning was unnerving. I had so much to lose. The last thing I wanted was him interfering with my relationship with Wendy, yet he persisted, and I was beginning to feel too worn down to put up a fight.

The first of his efforts at sabotage to appear in our marriage as a full-blown argument seemed to have resulted from something relatively benign. Tom was irritated that Wendy had insisted we share at least one meal together at the flat each day. Mostly it was dinner. But I had started missing a few because of the orangutan research I was helping conduct, and Tom had a go at me about Wendy, as he thought it unreasonable to tie ourselves down to an obligation like that given our various schedules. When I brought this up with Wendy, she was understanding, but Tom didn't seem interested in any sort of consensus. He insisted on having total control of the situation. *I'm only trying to protect you!* he reminded me.

Wendy and I began to argue about how much time we *thought* we should be spending together, a problem that had never bothered us in our first two years together, despite having exactly the same set-up for our work and home lives. We argued over my not coming home exactly when I said I would. Then disagreed over how late was too late. We argued over when it was too late to call. The understanding and flexibility with which we'd previously managed the same problems seemed to have evaporated.

As the months passed by, Tom continued to create scenarios for the growing disquiet within our marriage. His favourite game was to point the finger at Wendy and load her up with blame for just about anything she or I did or said. He picked out little things—stuff she'd left in the car, empty cigarette packs she'd left on the couch, gardening equipment she hadn't put away. Tom pushed further with his conspiratorial whisperings, often suggesting more serious incompatibilities, all the time reminding me, on a loop, about how much I had at stake. *Too much to lose mate, better insure yourself against it, hey. What was it she saw in you anyway? You're better off on your own.*

I began to second-guess stuff about Wendy. I constantly overthought everything. Tom methodically infected most of my thoughts, and although very occasionally the better part of me tried to put up a fight, I could feel myself giving in. Besides, what he was saying was probably true. I didn't deserve Wendy. That bum-fucked little kid who nearly killed someone didn't deserve anything, didn't trust anyone. My father had known the score when he screamed my failings at my face: 'Banish the wicked man from among you!'

Without knowing why and too scared to question anything, I continued the slow process of sabotage, both of my marriage and my own state of mind. My brooding moods made our dinners dull in their sharing. We would sit silently opposite each other with a glass of wine and escape to our hidden histories. The trips together to work were choked with endless 'nothing' chat. Appointments and calendars. Nothing. Gone were the easy flow and warmth of the space between. With my retreat in full flight, parts of me found old familiar hiding places in stifled silences and spasming guts. After all, roots that ran too deep had to come undone at some point for all the pieces of me that were still on the run.

I could feel Wendy's confusion growing. The better part of me knew just how hard this was for her. But even knowing that she was hurting, I didn't seem able to stop the slide. The only comfort I allowed myself was knowing that, thanks to a different God, Wendy had a father who loved her ferociously. He was as strong and steady as an ox and always encouraged her to grab life by the horns. So whatever this was that sat in front of her, whatever crazy I was dishing up, she only knew one way to handle it, and that was head-on with courage and authenticity.

'Talk to me Tim. What the hell is going on with you?'

But I couldn't find the words. I could only hope she had the strength to hang on until at least one of us knew what the hell was happening.

I told myself it was because of the deposit for our small farm that I needed the night job moving furniture. I wanted to spend less time at home, and I was able to justify that because of my second job. I worked some weeknights and one day on the weekend moving furniture around Sydney's suburbs, often averaging only three or four hours' sleep a night. Everything became about saving money, or so I told myself. I continued with Taronga shifts but I was withdrawing. I found all sorts of ways to get my work done and avoid having to talk to anyone or even see anyone, sometimes arriving early and leaving after everyone else. I'd only ever go home when I knew Wendy wouldn't be there. I even stopped spending time with the chimps, except to do what was required for work. I was on the run. From Wendy. From friends. From work. Everything and everyone. My black sky shadowed me like a vulture circling over a fresh carcass.

This was a path I'd travelled before, so I recognised it when it started. The rest was just another failed love story, or so Tom told me. A human story about the troubles inside relationships. Ours was just another ordinary story about a mismatched married couple in suburbia thinking their love was something unique. The stuff of romantic fiction. All the stuff Aunty Kez wrote books about.

———

The Golden Apple was a brothel in Kings Cross. When it advertised for bouncers I knew it was a job I could do. Sure enough, I got the job without too much hassle. It meant doing eight-hour shifts from ten at night until six in the morning. It paid good money so I'd quickly be able to come up with the farm deposit, and it was a perfect match for me as it gave me an excuse not to return to our flat at night. 'Saving for our farm,' I'd tell Wendy when I did overlap with her in the flat. She didn't say anything. I noticed she was pulling away more and more from any attempts at conversation.

The Golden Apple became a place for me to land. There, I was surrounded by people who hid from the world. Hid with their histories tucked behind habits, be it for silence, alcohol or heroin. My job there was to protect the working girls. If any of them were in trouble or felt they were in any danger with a punter, they would press a buzzer. It was then my responsibility to go up to the room, open the door and intimidate the guy who was harassing or bullying the girl. Tom and I were, for the first time, legitimately on the same professional page. With him in my head, I always felt strong, like I could do anything—it felt just like when I was riding bulls. I'd march up to a room and usually find a guy in the ruby smoke of the night-light with his pants down and his hands around the working girl's throat. It was never too hard, I discovered, to intimidate a guy with his pants around his ankles—usually suit pants, so there was always the stink of a secret around it. Most of the perpetrators turned out to be what I'd only ever imagined was a stereotype: well-heeled businessmen looking for an escape from marital monotony. My favourite thing to do was to barge in, blasting the door against the wall like it had been hit with a grenade, and stand over the trouserless bastard like a thug. I certainly looked legitimate enough, with my biceps buffed and overcooked from primate and bull handling. I'd hover over the guy with my arms crossed while he bent down to pull up the exhausted elastic waistband of his ageing underpants.

'Don't I know you from somewhere?' That always scared the shit out of them. It was with remarkable speed that the senior manager at some corporate finance firm would whip up his suit pants and scurry out the door. He'd be muttering something watery and threatening and litigious under his breath as he barged past.

Some of them even went so far as to make a final plea to me before going out the door. 'Just don't tell my wife, okay? She doesn't deserve this.'

'Just fuck off, mate.'

Mostly I chilled in the office, watching movies or reading books. Some of the working girls would come and hang out with me in the smaller hours of the morning, after their work. They'd have a cuppa, share a fag, and it would feel like we were all part of the same mob.

The sex workers from The Golden Apple were mostly single mums trying to support themselves or young students trying to pay for their education. As they walked towards my desk, I'd be reminded of a prepubescent kid going to the bathroom to take a piss before bed. The garb of sex—the silk gowns, the lingerie, the fishnets, the latex—all of it hung off them like they'd borrowed something from their mum's wardrobe. Plonking down on the office swivel chair and throwing their bare legs heavily up on my desk, they'd reach across and swipe a cigarette from my pack of Marleys. If they felt like a yarn, it was usually about mundane things, like kids at school, bullying husbands who drank the kids' lunch money, gambling partners whose jealousy sent them to work with bruises and broken wrists. These were hard stories. All these young women were just trying to make their way. Just like me. We were grown from the same seeds. All trying to pull the world back into a form that made sense to us. Working at The Golden Apple filled me in the same way food would, the ache of lonely soothed by the sharing of broken stories.

One of the best things about working at The Golden Apple, other than piling the bucks into the bank for the farm, was that I found I could also better manage Tom's company. There, Tom could comfortably take full control of the confusion in the crazy theatre of my brain. He would be in there, sinking another bourbon and screaming at the screen that was the live feed of my life, yelling, 'Deck him, mate, just deck him.' Tom was always ready to have a crack at any of the sadistic punters on the second floor if I needed him to. We seemed to be much easier with each other's company when we were at The Golden Apple. His interminable babble was less intrusive, less grating. Whenever I went back to the flat, however, I always noticed it was much harder to manage him. When I'd come home, Tom would go straight into sabotage talk. He'd rumble about a pot not being cleaned in the sink or uncovered compost piles spilling into mud on the verandah, and he'd always be telling me, *Three's a crowd.*

As we neared another wedding anniversary, I hadn't crossed paths with Wendy in weeks, and was in full withdrawal from our marriage. I completely missed the actual day and came home the following day to a cold casserole with a gravy skin dried so tight over it it looked like the hairless hide of a sunbaked carcass. There was an overflowing ashtray, a mostly empty wine bottle and two glasses on the table. One of them had been drunk from. My gut locked up when the full implications of the scene landed for me. I hurt for Wendy. Deeply. And flooded myself with recrimination and shame. Shame for the fucked-up mess that I knew I was. I thought she was home so I called her name. No one home, only dying zucchini flowers and the smell of unturned compost. I sat down and drained the wine dregs.

We were nowhere near being able to share an isolated nest in the bush. We were such a long way from each other when we spent any time together at all. The space between us could have been built in with bricks given how hard it was to communicate. But I couldn't seem to manage anything more, and The Golden Apple job was helping me work this relationship at the pace I needed. I didn't have the nerve to try to talk to her about it all. Wouldn't have known what to say anyway. Instead, I let enough time pass that any recriminations from the anniversary incident might be forgotten. When we did overlap in the flat, Wendy no longer even tried to talk to me. She spent all her time with her plants.

One day, though, after finding me at home when she returned from work, she did attempt to break into my world. It came as a shock. 'Why don't you get out there with your surfboard, Tim? The waves are amazing today.'

'Too tired.'

'Hmmm, I wonder why that would be. I never see you, Tim. When you do come home you fall asleep on the couch watching *Star Wars* videos. Don't you get bored of them?'

'No.'

'You know you're not fourteen anymore, mate! I know we want to save money, but this feels crazy. I never see you. We rarely talk. Are you ready to talk to me?'

It was inevitable that Wendy would eventually find the words. Didn't bother answering though. Couldn't. All I said was that I had to go because I was late for work.

———

I spent more and more of my time at Taronga and The Golden Apple. Wendy and I were trapped in some sort of holding pattern. A part of me knew I was still running off the energy of reactivity to everything I kept hidden in my spasming guts, but there seemed no way of interrupting this trajectory. There was no way of getting anywhere close to me. Not for anyone. And yet Wendy had the courage to survive on what few crumbs were left of our marriage. I'm sure she was guided by the profoundly intuitive compass she'd inherited from her father. Somehow, she knew that to keep in touch with what remained of our connection, she needed to keep her distance, as getting anything out of me was impossible.

When Wendy and I had any sort of conversation, it was always about our future farm—where to buy, how we'd run it, how many acres we'd have, how many animals. These conversations held our future shape as a couple, and we believed in them enough that they could withstand the obstacles in our relationship. Occasionally they gave us a glimpse of the companionship that had retreated from us so brutally. We could look forward to the farm as though that might solve the crisis of not being able to look at each other.

Then a property in the Southern Tablelands came up when we were trawling through *The Land* newspaper. We took a drive down there, passing through a nearby village on the way to the viewing. Bluestone houses, over 200 years old, lined the main street like stone sentinels, shadowed by brilliant yellow poplars towering behind them or in front of them. Sometimes beside them. Two pubs bookended the main street. I was to learn later that the locals sparred endlessly over whose pub was at the 'top end of town'. In this tiny community of under 300 people there were four stone churches: two Catholic churches on one side of the main street and two Protestant ones on the other side, all of them at least twice as big as any other building in the village. Except for the pubs.

A few locals hung around the main street. They were mostly either farmers leaning on the dusty doors of other farmers' utes, sharing flood or drought stories, or country folk meandering from the local shop to the post office and stopping for a chat with everyone in their path. There were a couple of young fellas on horses heading through town, their dogs circling them like blowflies. It seemed like a picture-postcard take on a perfectly friendly Australian bush town.

The small farm just north of the village was just as compelling, with great access to water, good soil and strong tree growth. With all of our boxes ticked, it only took six weeks for us to purchase the titles and the property was ours.

13

Revelations

The amount of work needed to get the farm operational distracted us from the gaps in our marriage. Water systems needed to be improved, weed-strewn garden beds needed to be dug up and restored, fences repaired. Wendy had already begun marking out the design of her vegetable gardens and quickly and completely got lost in her work. The rolling mountainous landscape that surrounded the farm was rugged and wild and breathtaking. For me, months of rumination opened into it like something subatomic on the move. The vast open spaces helped me release some of the intractability of the depression that had sluggishly settled inside me, bourbon in hand, and the physical work and fresh air even settled the grip the ghouls had of my guts. But when Wendy and I came back together after a day of work, while we would share the stories and problems of our day easily, our interactions still remained mostly brief and functional. We soon returned to our silences when we went back to the flat to work our Taronga shifts, and I was always eager to pick up extra shifts at The Golden Apple. Somehow, it was keeping me sane. It was easier to sit and listen to the abuse stories of the sex workers than follow up with a local fencer about our boundary problem at the bush block.

But at some point in the unfurling of pre-dawn light, when I was sitting at my desk at The Golden Apple, insight snuck up on me. It came for me when I had a cigarette hanging from my lips and a mug of sweet milky tea keeping my hands warm, appearing in my body as nothing more than a shifting of weight in my swivel chair. The thoughts it offered were clear and uncluttered and sat still while they showed themselves. A welcome relief from the loopy stew of reasoning Tom threw at me. It suggested that somewhere in trying to figure out why I was avoiding my own marriage, and why it was that I was taking refuge in the stories of broken young women, part of me was working out my own shame. The shame that existed in me as both the abuser and the abused. Shame about the many women I'd had sex with after Kea, women I never even attempted to make any sort of connection with. I never knew any of them by name. Not a single one. Shame that my own rape somehow had something to do with who I had become and the actions I had taken. It went on to suggest that by playing the role of protector, I could soothe my own shame. By giving something back, by helping others who had been abused, I was attempting to right my own wrongs. Insight then left through the same door it came in. Quietly and without a fuss, shutting the door on the way out.

On my way back to Taronga that morning, I started getting intense chest pains. This was the second time; I'd had a similar episode a couple of years before. The first time, I'd had to stay a night in the hospital and left in the morning with a diagnosis of pericarditis—inflammation of the heart. I thought I was going in there because of a fractured rib, but 'Pericarditis' was what was scribbled on the medical form I'd shoved into the glovebox when I drove home. So I knew exactly what was ahead of me when the pain returned even sharper and stronger.

Glenn later told me in the hospital that when he found me, I was unconscious on the floor of the chimp exhibit. 'Kicked ya first. Just to check if you were still living. Just a lump of meat though. Still, to be on the safe side, I thought it was probably a good idea to call the ambos.'

'Thanks. You're a good friend.'

Dr Victor Chang, Sydney's famous heart surgeon, was treating me. He was specifically called in because of the scars left on my heart by my first run-in with pericarditis. Dr Chang left me with a stark warning that my heart was unlikely to survive a third incident.

———

Wendy and I took some time off after my second hospital visit and headed to our bush block. Wood-stove fires, crockpots of long-stewed beef casseroles, three new guineafowl, quilted teapots, woollen blankets, and two new Chinese ganders all kept sanity within reach. But within two days of returning to the farm it was all one-word answers and checking the computer for emails.

As usual, Wendy found words for the loaded space between us. This time though, she'd had enough. 'For fuck's sake, Tim, are you ever gonna stop running away? You've been running since the day I married you. Two heart attacks, or whatever it was you had. What are you not telling me?'

This storm was breaking and I was desperately trying to hide in plain sight. I felt just as I had when I was a kid selling God's Word at the doors of strangers' homes.

'How many more heart scares do you need to realise how much stress you put yourself under just to try and get the fuck away. Your heart is quite literally breaking, Tim, and still you won't listen!'

She delivered razor-sharp insights that day the same way she might discipline a disobedient dog. It was how I needed to be told, though. For too long in our young marriage, Tom had taken the lion's share of my attention, keeping Wendy at arms-length, and it often felt too hard living in a marriage with three people.

'I can't help you. Your constant running. I see it every day. I feel it. Every day. It's like you have this force field around you and anytime I break just a little chink and get a little closer, you begin planning your escape.'

I stared into the fire. But I was sitting up straight in my chair. More than usual. A kid sensing detention coming.

'I reckon it's been like that since I met you, but now I can't even say anything without you biting. If I say anything, you get shitty. If you don't overwork yourself, you escape with bourbon, and if you don't do that, you get more night shifts at the fucking Golden Apple. If you're home, you just escape to wherever the fuck it is you go in your own head. You're always shitty, Tim. All day, and I'm fucking sick of it!'

I took it all in because I knew it needed to be said and it had been a long time coming. But all I said was, 'Yeah.'

'That's it? *Yeah?*'

'Yeah.' It came out as a mumble, but she'd already gone. She slammed the door on her way to her veggies like a mother taking refuge in her children after escaping her violent husband.

That night, thoughts slopped around in my head. Had too many bourbons while I stared at the fire. My drunk mate Tom told me his truths, that for sure this meant an end to our marriage. But Wendy had told me other truths that surely meant a beginning to our marriage.

I had been staring at the fire for hours when she came in later that evening, familiar and full of life, hair hanging over her face and a powder spray of black soil across her nose. She smelled of tomato plants and freshly picked thyme. I loved that she smelled of the earth. I looked at her and said sorry. No words. Just in my eyes. I walked to her and gathered her up in a hug. Then the words came: 'I really, really, REALLY love you . . . I'm so sorry.'

'I know, Tim. But you just gotta get some help, mate. Something needs to be unlocked.' She was a little more tender then, slowing the instruction to a suggestion, her body softening in my arms. 'Go and see someone. Talk about what happened to you. It's a fucking unbelievable story that you've gotta recover from, love.'

We held each other in silence for some time. There was a melting feeling inside. Ice to water, water to gas. I told Wendy all about the conversations I had with Tom in my head. About him telling me he was the only one who could really look after me, about all his ramblings. I told Wendy about the bullying he did in my head.

She wasn't surprised. 'Stop running, my friend. We're never going to find each other again unless you stop running.'

Revelations

The following week I went to see a psychologist whose main job was to provide therapy to the heavy-duty criminals in NSW maximum-security jails. Meeting him was confronting. He appeared from a doorway as a long stretch of a man with very pale skin and a warm smile. He slowly walked towards me with an outstretched hand, and he spoke so quietly that I hardly heard him during our verbal introductions. This guy seemed as innocuous as a bantam chook. Asking him to dig out my demons felt as useless as taking a pillow to a knife fight.

I was wrong about that, though. Very wrong. Dr S, as I came to call him, had a way of letting me speak without interruption. As much as possible. When he felt he needed to interject, he nudged me towards something that only his professional compass could intuit. I told him my difficult stories of being brought up inside a cult of religious dogma. That religious scriptures had flooded my life in the same way fairytales did for other children. Over a number of sessions, I talked him through the tales of my sadistic father and the outline of my broken mother. He pushed me towards my buried secrets. Tenderly. I was shut down tight. My heart started its hummingbird flap. Adrenalin was picking up pace and eventually ran king tides through my blood as I perched, pencil-straight and stiff, on the edge of my chair. But he could tell he was coming close. I could tell he was coming close. I always thought there was a stink that helped predators close in on their prey.

'Was there anyone you were particularly close to?'

'No one. Not after the rape.'

He took a steep breath. He was there. The jolt of a professional finding, uncovering a missing puzzle piece. He pushed himself slowly to the edge of his own chair.

What happened next was an unfolding. The mechanism he used was hypnotherapy and he took me directly back to the rape. 'As much as you can manage, Tim. No more. I'm here with you. You are safe.'

Sawdust shards, blood trails, sweat and rotting oranges, all of it running in split screens across my rolling memories. Breath picking up curls of freshly cut wood shards. I could see every grain. My head pushed down on the bench, fingers over my face. And then. Something strange. Something else. As the psychologist safely held me in this place, unfamiliar images filtered across the old storylines. The shift came in pieces. The synthetic scratch of a quilt took the place of sawdust. The sweat was still there but it was boy sweat, the sweat of Rugby tackle-and-rumble. The rotting oranges were gone, and in their place came the familiar dry smell of weatherboard and stale boy bedsheets. I was in my childhood bedroom. My head was jammed into the pillow fat of cheap synthetic quilting. I heard a groan from a newly broken voice as pain ran wild and bloody through my body. I knew that voice distinctly, too well. I turned as much as I could and saw my brother's head lurching back, his pale pimply skin blotching blood-red as he came inside me. I saw my brother. Steven.

I wasn't in my chair in the psychologist's office anymore. I was pasted against one of the walls, and there was a hole where I had put my fist through it. How could this be?! How could Steven have done this to me? Freak! I'd always hated him, and now I knew why. I couldn't believe I always thought it was my neighbour! How could Steven have done this, my own brother!

The next thing I was aware of was Dr S trying to reach out to me. 'It's okay, Tim. It's okay.'

'Back off, just back off!'

But Dr S was still reaching for me. He knew that my brain had long ago created a scenario that I could cope with, burying the truth. He also knew that this revelation would be absolutely terrifying to me. He took a step closer.

'Fuck off and leave me alone or I'll drop you!'

Getting as close to an edge as I was likely to get without killing someone, I ran outside. Tried to catch my breath in the car. I rang Wendy. Rambling, raging, words wobbling. '. . . fucking Steven . . . all this time . . . so fucked up! . . . own brother . . . New Zealand . . . kill him . . . John . . .'

I only heard pieces of her reply: '. . . I hear you . . . do you want . . . love you.'

———

That night I took a four-hour flight to New Zealand. I'd rung John before I'd left to let him know to expect me. I got into Auckland around ten o'clock then hired a car and drove the two hours from the airport to Whangārei, then on to John's place. On the way, ideas on what tool I would use to effect my revenge had time to brew, and I got so churned up that I took no notice of anything around me as I drove through the streets of my childhood. I decided on the most primitive of weapons. A baseball bat.

'Bro! Just settle down! Take a breath.' John handed me a bourbon and coke. 'Drink it. There's more.'

We were staring at each other, like we used to when checking to see if the other person had died after a jousting competition.

'Listen to me, bro, if you do this now, you'll never get out of the country. They'll have you for assault and you'll be no better off than your fucked-up brother. Besides that, check out the fuckin' car you'll be riding in, bro. A pink Honda. He's gonna think you're coming for a date!'

For the first time in days I laughed, a belly laugh, a rolling laugh. Rolling itself in bourbon shots and memories of my mate, like John and I jousting at the river. John had been there for me all my life and he was still here for me, making the best sense he could of the lunatic nature of all the shit that had happened to me. I would've thanked God for John if there was a God.

'I'll tell you what's so weird. I always thought it was one of the neighbours on our street!' I gave John the name of the guy I'd always thought had raped me. 'Did he even exist or did I just make him up?'

'No, bro, you didn't make him up. He did live in your street, though. Helped Dad with organising kids' Rugby. He was a gay guy. I remember he had a cracker of a sense of humour. Dad said he was a great bloke.'

Remembering how I'd vilified this man in my own mind frightened me. My brain seemed to have been making shit up as it went along. I guess my brain landed on him because he was gay and, according to the Bible, 'Men who practise homosexuality . . . will not inherit God's kingdom' (1 Corinthians 6:9,10), so I think I must have just put this guy among the 'banished wicked' and pinned the whole incident on him.

Later, when I returned to Australia, Dr S would tell me that it's a common mechanism for the brain, when it has experienced childhood abuse, and particularly when the perpetrator is within the family, to protect itself from the trauma of the actual truth by dissociating or creating a different story, one that it can cope with. But that night, after consuming a full bottle of bourbon with John, I couldn't make sense of anything. I fell into a stone wall of sleep.

John was up before me. His giant frame hovered over me like a storm cell. His own anger had had the night to brew, and diplomacy turned to strategy as we headed to Steven's place. When we arrived it was still dark, but the sun was thinking about getting up. When the curved rim of its golden rump finally broke from the horizon, Steven's house looked like a stage lit for this very occasion.

'Stay cool, bro,' John said, getting out of the car to better watch whatever was about to happen.

I walked up the driveway to the front door and banged on it like I wanted to break it down. A boy opened the door. He looked a lot like Steven did when he was young. So, his son. He must have been around the same age I was when his father raped me. It broke my brain a little. He just stood there and I just stared at him. After some long painful seconds, I offered, 'You don't know who I am.'

'Yes I do. You're the bad one.'

Fuck. The memory of my father's voice rising to the heavens, bellowing biblical banishment, crashed across my fragile brain. *'Banish the wicked man from among you.'* Having conspired with the heavens to arrive at his terrible sentence, my open-mouthed father-lizard was full-screen in my head. He was delivering his final judgement with splayed arms, as if he were Moses himself. But thanks to a different God, Wendy and John also felt close.

'No, I'm your uncle, Tim.'

I was ready to face my brother. The man who had condemned

my life to a living hell. Condemned it to cut-glass-edged emotions and hidden ghouls whose secrets made holes in my guts.

Steven appeared and pushed his son behind him. He had aged, and a common kind of middle-aged ugly hung off him. His chin was unchanged. That pimply pubescent chin and a newly broken voice would be forever in my head.

'I remembered everything you did to me and I'm here to have it out.'

His face dropped. With fear at first, eyes darting. I smelt the change as much as I saw it. Then he quickly shifted, just as he had done when selling Jesus. 'What! D'ya wanna fight?'

'No, I'm not here to fight you. I'm here to let you know that I remember and I'm dropping this bag of shit at your door now. And if I ever hear that you've touched your own kids, I'll come back and have you.' With that, I turned around and walked back to the car.

'Good on ya, bro! Good on ya!' yelled John. His fists were rolling and punching the air like he was at a bloody All Blacks game. He spat a sledge at Steven: 'I'll be watching you, freak!'

As we drove off, something gave way inside. It was like the space left behind when ice melts. I was light, so light, and I was holding my seat just to stay put. Then I noticed that John was only doing 60 km/h on the highway, slower even than Grandad when he used to drop me at Stagland. I couldn't stop the lunatic laughter that spilled out of me. 'We are a couple of old fucks now, aren't we mate!'

And then neither of us could stop laughing. Both laughing so hard we had to stop the car. How far we had come from the days of our galloping steeds' brutal jousting challenge, when life and death were always on the line, two alpha males facing off on a Monday afternoon. Our steady careful exit down the driveway played out in a thoroughly middle-aged way. Me and John, in my rented pink hatchback with its on–off flickering, as steady as a metronome.

'Good for you, bro. Tough thing to do back there!' John muttered this a couple of times as we drove back to his place. Then he said, 'Your Grandad's in hospital, bro, wanna go and see him?'

'Why's he in hospital?'

'Dunno, he is ninety-two. That enough of a reason?'

'Yup, wanna see Grandad.'

———

As we drove to the hospital, I watched the slideshow of my childhood through the window. The *Dominion* offices, the red-brick coffin-shaped Kingdom Hall, the greengrocer's store where I got veggies for my possum. But now I saw it all through a different lens. It was a kinder, more gentle view. It was like I had changed the channel during a newscast—same footage but different commentary.

'What are you doing in here?' I shouted from the door, Grandad watching me as I walked into his hospital room. All six-foot-three of me. His face broke free of its old age in a radiant Grandad smile. The same smile I used to hang around for, watching for any crumbs of self-esteem I could get when I was a kid. A brush with eternity, I felt that for sure.

I leant over and hugged him. Felt so very good. For a couple of hours Grandad and I chewed the fat. I told him what I'd just done with Steven, talked about what had happened when

I left Whangārei, the rodeos, the lemur presentation, Taronga, Wendy. With every new story, I saw the expression change on his face, as though he could feel everything I had gone through.

'I'm really happy for you, Timmy. Good for you, son.'

If it wasn't for Grandad, I may not have lived. That visit was the last time I would see him.

14

New life

On my return to Sydney, Wendy and I caught up on all we'd missed out on together, and the easy warm connection we had early in our marriage gradually returned. It was timid at first, like a child opening the door to the room his parents had angrily argued in only minutes before. But we eventually laughed more easily, shared observations, talk flowed, and after a few weeks, little interrupted us. I was home safe with Wendy and leaning into new feelings of trust. Not running anymore, or at least not running at that moment. But for me, anytime I felt that stillness, it was as if it could've gone on forever.

I continued to visit Dr S every week, and he was able to shed a bit of light on Tom's persistent presence in my head: 'When people go through the sort of trauma you went through, Tim, the brain does what it needs to do to cope. You had a lot of anger to deal with, so it could be that Tom was initially trying to help you manage all of that. But if we don't let go of anger after it's done its job, which is to alert us to an injustice or a threat, these voices can sometimes get stuck in our heads. Most people, actually, even without your level of trauma, have an overly critical voice, a "stuck voice", in their head giving them grief. They're just not aware of how invasive or destructive it can be.'

'Are you telling me Tom is someone I've made up?'

'Yes, Tim, but that doesn't make him any less real. And there's no reason to be afraid of or angry with Tom. His initial intention was only to help you.'

'I think I know that. He's always had my back, and I like knowing he's there, but he has too much of a say when I don't need his advice, especially about my relationships with people. He fucks everything up.'

'What I want you to do is to try and become aware of when he pipes up in the first place, because his ranting is closely linked to your bouts of depression. There will be certain situations that trigger him, particularly if he feels something or someone is threatening you. Can you just try and observe him without getting caught up in what he's saying? Just like you do with your chimps?'

'Ha! Tim and Tom, just chewing the fat on a sunny afternoon at Taronga! Kind of funny, hey!'

'And try not to immediately act on what he is telling you, Tim, because often what he is telling you is, for the most part, not true. And if, in rare cases, it is actually true, he isn't going to give you the best advice about how to deal with the situation. Unless of course you're being chased by a tiger, which, weirdly, could well be true in your case!'

'Getting him to pipe down can't be as easy as all of that.'

'It's as easy and as hard as all of that. Getting a handle on the workings of our own brains can be a very tricky thing indeed, Tim. Have you found anything that works to get him to quieten down?'

'Thinking about the good stuff I have in my life, my animals, my friends. I feel really grateful for people like Grandad. For Wendy and John.'

'Go there, then, when he's giving you grief. Go to what makes you feel good, feel safe. Call up those thoughts and feelings. Gratitude is a powerful tool as well, but it seems you naturally have that tendency anyway. All these approaches will protect you from getting so tied into his one-sided arguments'.

Dr S also talked to me about Tui, but I had already noticed I wasn't as angry when I thought of her these days. Since driving back through Whangārei and seeing my childhood from a distance, I'd realised just how crazy our lives inside the Jehovah cult had been. I got a sense that all of us kids were pretty fucked up and we were only ever doing what we needed to do to survive. Including Tui.

On my way home from my sessions with Dr S, I'd think about his take on Tom. How, according to Dr S, Tom had only ever turned up to help me. That somehow, my brain knew how to keep itself safe. How to keep me safe. I thought about Wendy too. How she just seemed to intuitively understand how to 'be' with all the broken parts of me. And how to stay with them, even though for a time, nothing about our relationship looked like it was worth that effort. These connections were as curious to me as those in Wendy's hidden plant worlds. Was it the sort of parallel universe of symbiosis that I often witnessed in the animal world? There was a wisdom there that I couldn't quite fathom.

In any case, since confronting Steven, I'd heard very little from Tom, and I was choosing to focus on what was in front of me at that moment.

———

Wendy and I took a few months off work on medical leave, to recover from heart attacks and job lethargy and broken hearts. We tacked on our unused holiday leave and spent months in the bush, and gradually the familiar nesting feeling started to settle in, for both of us. I began our animal collection. Goats, chickens and rabbits all happily thrived at home with my uninterrupted attention and care. And Wendy decided to start selling bags of different types of compost for garden beds at the local market, but it wasn't long before Wendy's black gold dust project and growing my collection of farmyard animals got turned completely upside down.

'We're going to have a baby!' Wendy broke the news over coffee when we were thumbing through *The Land* looking for goats. She put the little white plastic stick with its two innocuous-looking red lines in front of me and I sat there dumbstruck. The shock itself seemed to give me the biggest fright given that we had only talked about trying for a baby two months before.

'What?'

'Yup! A baby.'

We hugged one another. Actually, Wendy hugged me. She felt like a river flowing around the rock that stood in its way. She was all around me while I sat still in the middle of her, uncertain, bewildered, terrified, joyful.

I spent the next few months riding waves of terrifying

excitement and doubt. Not that different to the bronc rides during my rodeo days. The excitement was the simple and novel joy that I discovered came from creating a new life. I'd known I was a very good carer and nurturer of life when I looked after the broken animals in my bush refuge, and that continued with my work as a keeper. But the terror that gripped me rolled over questions about whether I could replicate those qualities for my own child. Role models were mostly unknown to me in my childhood. Tom even started a background babble suggesting I probably wasn't up for it, but I knew better than to listen to his catastrophising. Still, during these times, sleeplessness would get hold of me like a dog getting hold of a bone. How could I bring a child into this world? It wasn't just my own limitations as a parent that frightened. I wasn't confident our child would be safe on the human side of the fence.

Weeks, months moved along and Wendy moved conversations about her pregnancy at a pace she knew I could cope with, while I comforted myself with the idea that when I did retreat, it was akin to natural male ape behaviour. I had always been attracted to the extraordinary circles of support the females of any ape species gave one another when they were pregnant, so when I found myself spending more time at Taronga during Wendy's pregnancy, I told myself that was to be expected. That it was natural behaviour. But knowing the way my brain was likely working, Wendy would often challenge me to get more involved with the pregnancy: 'You can't hide in your animal behaviours corner, love. Silverbacks may retreat and let the females take over but that's not true of every primate species. What about the tamarins? The males take care of the babies the whole time, carrying them on their back through their infancy. They only hand them over to the females for feeding! Quite like the idea of mixing in a bit of tamarin parenting, don't you love?'

So I went with Wendy to the mothering classes, where we learnt about good birthing procedures. I also talked with some of the women at Taronga who'd had kids. This was a completely new world for me. But for Wendy it was as though all that had gone before was preparation for this very moment. She was utterly alive, present, focused. She surrounded herself with strong friends who tended to her rising bump like they were the parents themselves.

When a plump and tiny pinkish-blue little boy finally appeared after two days of painful labouring in the autumn of 1998, I felt not only immense relief that Wendy was finally out of pain, but also pride about the extraordinary strength she had shown to get through what at times looked like an impossible amount of pain.

When I first held our tiny son, it was a surprise as much as shock to realise that the wall I'd hidden my feelings behind was starting to break down from a mix of relief and shame. Relief because, to my way of thinking, this boy child wouldn't require too much of my broken care as a father. The shame part of the story was complicated, and it stung like a bull ant. It came from my belief that if the child had been a girl, I would have to protect her from the self-centredness of men. Men like her own father. But I never let myself live too long in my own damaged storylines, instead pushing myself towards being there for my son.

As it turned out, the connection and affection I'd so feared I would not be able to offer came more easily to me than I could have possibly hoped. And as always, it took a requisite dash of

Wendy wisdom to keep me on track: 'Strong men are made from parents who can speak authentically about how they feel, Timmy. Emotions don't belong just to women, my friend, and you, of all people, know how dangerous they are if you keep them locked up. That is not going to happen to our son.'

Wendy was completely in flow. Her heart opened, her nurturing, her care, all full throttle. I had only watched her dealing with pumpkin and zucchini seeds in the long steel plant holders on a verandah in Manly, and now I got to watch her reveal herself to our child. It was like watching a sunrise. The baby craved loving as much of her as possible with every day that life brought him.

One night Wendy woke from a dream all excited. She told me that in her dream, we had decided to call our son Jordan. 'It's a beautiful name don't you think, Tim?'

I did think it was a wonderful name. We both loved it.

More and more, I enjoyed coming home from work. Coming home to Wendy and Jordan. Our baby son was a surprise joy to me. One morning I watched while the little guy wobbled like a baby chimp from coffee table to couch. His tiny bow legs were so convinced of their ability to tackle novice flight that by the end of it, they'd broken into a runway take-off he had little control over. Wendy and I laughed a laugh so full of something other than funny that it took me a moment to put my finger on what it was. It was new and it was astonishing.

'It's hard to imagine we could love Jordan so much, hey Tim!' She had the words for life stuff again.

Wendy had always known how to feel, even before having Jordan, but there were so many emotions that were new for me with this child. I was struck with how quickly he was ready to smile at just about anything. In particular, his little chuckle got set off when I did anything with him. It was the beginning of a long connection with my son, where any one of a number of sometimes less than convincingly funny jokes found a welcome home with him. We would play on the grass, just watching ladybugs or listening for bird noises. He was profoundly absorbed by everything. I'd never known this in my own childhood. I had seen it among the lemurs. I had seen it in a number of other primate species. I remembered how curious the young of any species were when I observed them. How they would swallow whole every gesture and expression. I reflected that it could be because they felt safe, and to feel 'safe' involved both care and protection. And from that feeling of complete safety, the world seemed to offer infinite possibilities. Opportunities for exploration were everywhere for Jordan, and curiosity pushed him to find fascination with the simplest of things. It occurred to me that the stepping stones of life began with trust and maternal or paternal care, regardless of the species.

One day, Aunty Kez called from New Zealand. She was coming to Sydney to promote her latest book and wanted to meet us for lunch—Aunty Kez was becoming well known in New Zealand for her romantic fiction. We organised to meet at a pub in Woolloomooloo, not far from Circular Quay. Seeing Aunty Kez pour herself out of the bus, her lemon-yellow silk scarf wrapping itself around her face in the wind, filled me with sheer joy. She was dressed up pretty flash with her powder-blue blazer and matching skirt. Her hair was mustered into a mob at the top of her head, coloured feathered combs keeping it in place. Felt so good to give Aunty Kez a hug. She still had that synthetic apple blossom scent trailing her like a toddler. We had a cursory catch-up about what the family was up to but Aunty Kez knew vacant eyes when she saw them. Anything to do with family was dead-talk to me. And she was desperate to get hold of baby Jordan, so Wendy passed him over to her.

'What a little darling. Looks like you, Wendy! He even looks a bit like your own brother, Timmy!'

'Don't tell me that! I don't wanna hear that, Kez! Hate them both, you know that.'

'No, your REAL brother, Tim. Your twin brother.'

The silence that followed was heavy. Really heavy. 'My what?'

'You had a twin, Tim. Your mother never told you because she didn't feel it was something you needed to know.'

'I didn't need to know that I had a twin brother? What the hell?'

Aunty Kez put her hand over mine. Slow seconds passed.

'What happened to him? Did he die?'

'He died just after he was born. You know, Tim, after your mum's first husband died in the war and she was left to bring up their son Steven on her own, I think your dad thought he could tidy a few things up for her—especially when she fell pregnant again. But they waited a few months after you and your twin were born before they married.'

My thoughts were rolling over themselves, shock turning my body numb. 'Was my father trying to make an honest woman of her?'

I added that as a joke, but Aunty Kez's expression didn't change. 'Maybe, or maybe they were just waiting to see if you would survive. If you didn't, then your father wouldn't have to marry your mother.'

'That'd be right, whatever suits him.'

Then the penny dropped. I realised the whole thing had been a farce.

'Wait, what are you talking about? So, they weren't ACTUALLY married when Mum was pregnant with me?'

'No.'

'Is he even my father?'

'No, Timmy, he is not your father. I was sworn to secrecy, but the way your life has panned out I think it's good for you to know. Your real father was a travelling musician, I think his name was Leeroy. He was on his way through to Wellington.'

I noticed that Jordan's bottle had slid off his lips, and he had slipped off to sleep. 'So Dad was never my real dad.' That fact didn't seem to be able to land for me.

'That's right, my darling. But by God, that must come as some relief, hey!'

It felt like the ground was falling away from beneath me. Relief, was it? Shock and relief maybe. I think it could've been both but I couldn't think. But then it all made sense! Being singled out and bullied by my father. Time after time. Of course he didn't want me around. And my mum! What the hell did she go through? Was it shame that shut her up? Was it grief? Was she angry that I had survived and my twin had died? How I wish I'd known. I maybe could've helped my mum.

I went outside to get some air. Both Wendy and Kez followed me, Wendy holding Jordan. We all leant on the railing and looked out at the harbour. Aunty Kez lit a cigarette. 'It's hard stuff to hear, Timmy, I get it. But that's why your grandad and

I were so glad when you got away. Your mum never made it out. But you, you got yourself out from under his control. Got yourself away from that bloody cult.'

'I didn't get out. They chucked me out! There's a difference!'

'For doing something that any fourteen-year-old boy would be tempted to do. Especially when they had someone else showing them how to do it! You've really made an amazing life for yourself, for your family, for your animals. I'm really proud of you, Timmy.'

The apple blossom perfume was all over me as she leant into my shoulder. It was grounding. I think Wendy was as floored as I was by Kez's revelations. My father, not my father; my rapist brother only a half-brother; Daniel and Rachel only half-siblings; a completely new take on my mum. I had a REAL dad out there somewhere.

Aunty Kez finished her cigarette and then chucked the butt into the harbour. She stood straight up and looked at me. 'Do you wanna know something really kooky?'

'What you've told me not quite enough, Kez?'

'This one is really going to blow your socks off!'

Aunty Kez's humour was always pretty black. I looked at Wendy sideways, one eyebrow arched and my mouth drooping open like an idiot.

'Your mother named your twin before he died. She named him Jordan.'

15

Finding my feet

The bombshells Aunty Kez had delivered left me empty and quiet for some time. At first, childhood memories rolled around in my head like a ball still in play in a pinball machine. I couldn't stop the thoughts, nor could I make any sense of them. I did feel the rot of bad history falling away, though, and there were moments of clarity and relief that almost felt like stepping stones laid out for me. I liked to think it was by the mother I never fully knew, a mother who, it turns out, was as much a victim as I was.

Wendy was particularly aware of any changes in my mental health. She could feel my encroaching black sky just as clearly as she could sense one of her plants losing strength, and she knew what needed to be done to interrupt its progression. 'Maybe it's time to go out on our own, love. Freelance. Set up our own company.'

We began our own zoo consultancy in 2001, marketing ourselves as zoo specialists willing to do the jobs that no one else would touch. The zoos no one would go near, either because they were too neglected to repair, or they required too much hard manual work. I thought of them as the 'underdogs' of the zoo world. I knew what was required to pull someone, something, anything back to within the markers of what was considered 'normal'. Wendy and I also knew what it took to work hard and think outside the box, so by becoming something akin to the industrial cleaners of the zoo world, we were taking the logical next step. At that point, however, we had no idea how far into the dark corners of the world of exotic animal collection this idea was going to take us.

Our first consultancy job was with the National Zoo and Aquarium in Canberra. The new owners had found themselves in the difficult position of not being able to start their exotic animal collection due to their limited experience in zoo ownership. Serendipitously, the federal government had just outlawed exotic animal ownership in circuses, so when the Zoo and Aquarium people contacted me, I was able to offer them a solution by starting off their collection with some of the retired circus animals: brown bears, leopards, lions and tigers, among others. When the animals arrived, they appeared to be in relatively good physical shape, but they didn't have much spirit, and I knew exactly what to do. Within a few months the exhibits had been redesigned and various animal-enrichment ideas implemented. The brown bears foraged in extensive woodchip mounds for food, we started blood trails for the tigers and leopards, and we hid carcasses up trees. It was my first effort at curation, and within two years I knew I'd been successful—the National Zoo and Aquarium had acquired the reputational currency it needed to trade animals with other licensed zoos.

I worked in Canberra for only a couple of years, as it was too hard to be away from Wendy and Jordan every week, only coming home on weekends. But the experience provided an important psychological springboard for me. I had proven to myself that I was more than capable of directing and curating an international zoo, and it gave me the confidence to manage other, more complex projects.

———

My growing self-belief became a stepping stone, when, in 2004, Wendy and I received a letter from an organisation employed by the Queensland Government. From memory, it read something like this:

> *For the Attention of the Managers:*
>
> *There is a situation in Cairns where a wild animal park, which is 200 acres in size and has over 150 stock, has been abandoned by its owner. Over 35 staff have not been paid for three weeks. Animals have been neglected and the project itself is now deemed a risk to public health. The company has gone into receivership and many local Cairns citizens are owed hundreds of thousands of dollars.*
>
> *We are offering you a contract to bring the zoo up to international standards.*
>
> *Please let us know as soon as possible if this is a position you are interested in.*

This was a great opportunity to be involved in a project where the whole family could be together, so we jumped at the chance.

'I'll go up on my own first,' I said to Wendy. 'When I know what's involved, you bring Jordan up and we'll get ourselves set up there properly.' A few weeks later, I flew up to Cairns to start the job.

When I first arrived I noticed that any time I was in town, including at the airport, any mention of the bankrupt zoo among the locals, and specifically any mention of its one-time owner, sent an uncomfortable ripple through any conversation. The maintenance guy I found smoking a cigarette near a feeding station at the zoo explained it to me: 'Too many people invested their hard-earned money when the zoo first got set up. Lots of locals. There were small businesses and school teachers giving money! We were all so excited to have a zoo in our community. But where has all our money gone?' That was all he had to say to me.

Over the next few days I walked through the entire park, and what I found blindsided me. Neglect and suffering were both on exhibit. Hollowed-out and starved animals were struggling in 40-degree heat and were lethargically sprawled over dusty, balding patches of buffalo grass. Northern Hemisphere deer slumped listlessly within the thin margins of the shadows thrown by the eucalypts. Some macaques paced along fences, while others were so limp and sluggish they could barely lift their heads in the weight of the Northern Queensland humidity. There were only a few lions, none of which had the energy to come to the fence when I walked past. Some sort of curiosity would have been normal given I was the first new face they'd have seen in weeks. The cheetahs were the same: limp exotic lumps in the middle of regional Australia. The ungulates seemed in relatively good condition, but the sway-backs and misshapen heads were a red flag for inbreeding.

I finished my inspection feeling completely overwhelmed and went straight to a dingy, smoky pub to swiftly down a double bourbon and coke, after which I took a few long and deep breaths. The level of abandonment in this zoo triggered my own trauma as though it had happened only yesterday. As I sat reflecting on the neglect I'd seen, of not only the animals but also the local community, which had supported the zoo financially, I realised that the repair work was going to require a lot more from me than just tidying up accounts and fixing fences. Human self-interest had clearly been put ahead of the wellbeing of these animals. The self-serving nature of the human animal was still incomprehensible to me, hitting me the same way it had when I was a kid and the Elders had insisted there was no place in Heaven for animals.

I ordered a second double bourbon, and Tom piped up with talk of retribution, but I was careful not to take any of his rage-driven advice onboard, preferring to remember the more instructive and useful words of Len, Keeper of the Geese, words about our purpose as zookeepers: 'Our job is to try to give animals the best life possible on earth, and that should be enough for all of us.'

I pulled out a lined pad and a pen and got to work on a list of jobs. What was needed to repair this zoo could only be tackled in steps. When I called Wendy later that night, I told her everything was broken, adding, 'But we know broken, love, and we know we can fix it.'

Wendy and I came up with a plan for how to start the big clean-up. Our priority was the animals. They needed to be fed. Urgently. The next day, I approached supermarkets in Cairns. They let me have any food that was out of date. A local chicken company gave me all their carcasses. A local dairy farmer said I could have any of their euthanised bobby calves (male calves born to the dairy cows). Lions, bears, tigers, cheetahs, they all chowed down on out-of-date chicken parmigiana from Coles and frozen pies from IGA. It was a long way from the diet of the wild, but we were filling the empty stomachs of some very hungry animals and that was all I cared about.

I organised an interview with the local radio station and used it to speak to the community about how we were trying to get the zoo back on its feet, and that any help from local businesses and the community itself would be greatly appreciated. Over the next couple of weeks, donations poured through the gates of the zoo, including used lawnmowers, chainsaws, tools for construction, fencing material—even coffee machines. To see how people were pulling together for their own community, as well as for the animals, was a buzz for me. I'd rarely been exposed to it, and it felt like a safe landing of sorts. Whenever the Jehovahs had come together at difficult times to pool their resources, the Elders would use the community's grief as an excuse to finish unrelated jobs, like fixing their own sheds, or their driveways, maybe replastering leaking walls at Kingdom Hall. These particular zoo donors were remarkable because they were people who had been seriously skinned. It was my first look at a community gathering for the sake of animals.

Salvaging the sinking ship that was the northern Queensland wild animal park kept me bone-tired busy for the first four months. From repairing over fifteen kilometres of fencing that swayed dangerously when I leant on it to monitoring the feeds we were delivering to the malnourished animals, I was at work from dawn until dusk. Wendy and Jordan's arrival gave me a much-needed boost. For Jordan, the park was magical. He was entirely bewitched by having his very own farm full of some of the world's biggest and most exotic animals. Wendy set herself up in the office to get all the accounts into shape and manage the volunteer rosters, as we were getting lots of calls from people willing to help in any way they could. She also worked on the grounds as a keeper. Often in the mornings, I would see Wendy and Jordan completing the morning's feed. Wendy would be pushing a barrow full of chaff and hay around the exhibits, with little Jordan often perched on top of the load like a baby lemur. Nothing completed me quite as much as seeing them together like that.

———

We spent the next couple of years making sure all aspects of the zoo were brought up to international standards, which involved a number of changes. The signs of inbreeding were everywhere, so working out what was ground zero in terms of animal genetics was one of our first steps. Another was to ensure all the animals were then genetically registered. Many of the animals at the park had falsely registered microchips. The previous owner had done this by extracting a microchip from a legally registered animal after it had died and implanting it in the zoo's illegal animal collection so as to get them past legal zoo registration. The process of cleaning up a collection's genetic lines was quite layered and in this place, quite shocking.

Diet always came near the top of our list of priorities. The carnivores' previous diet of chicken feet and dry dog biscuits was replaced by a diverse range of fresh meats. We expanded many exhibits and introduced behaviour-enrichment programs in order to emulate the animals' particular behaviours in the wild: we hid calf legs up in the trees for the tigers, hid nuts in tree trunks and fallen branches for the monkeys, and we scatter-fed the pygmy hippos. Scatter-feeding means spreading food all over the exhibit to extend the animal's mealtimes and provide mental stimulation throughout the day. We also made a point of chucking the hippo and rhino dung into the carnivore exhibits every day. This stimulated the carnivores' sense of smell. I started leaving blood trails around the lion exhibits, and when the weather peaked in summer we gave all the apex predators what we called 'bloodsicles'—big ice blocks of frozen blood—to lick throughout the day. Given that carnivores are the ultimate protein processors, this served to keep their protein levels up as well as keep them cool. It was successfully balancing the animals' physical and mental health that got them passed by vet checks in 2006, our third year there.

The park's rhino and hippo collection was based at a Northern Territory cattle station so another of my jobs was to retrieve them and bring them back to Cairns. After a couple of weeks of wrangling and mustering, we were able to get the two rhinos into the stockyards as well as successfully crate the numerous hippos. Convincing the hippos to move comfortably into the crates—where we could trap them—took the full two weeks as daily we coaxed them in there with delicious northern Queensland fruits and fresh grass. We finally loaded two white rhinos, four common hippos and four pygmy hippos, then took the long trip back to Cairns. Returning to the animal park felt relatively peaceful after leaving the Jumanji adventures up north.

Jordan, meanwhile, was growing up fast. He was six when he started at the local primary school, which had an enrolment of around twenty kids, mostly Aboriginal kids from the Djabugay mob. After his first day, he tucked his shiny new black school shoes under the assembly hall bench—he'd seen the other kids run out of school with bare feet, kicking up sand in their race down to the river to do some fishing. He never went back for his little black Grosbys, which stayed under that school bench for the five years we were in Cairns.

Kids seemed to love Jordan's company. He made friends as easily as he took breaths. He found a big mob of local Aboriginal kids to hang out with, and they all loved every chance they got to come and check out the zoo. Show-and-tell got a boost at Cairns Primary as, every week, all the kids in Jordan's class hung out to see what little Jordan would bring in next. One week it was a deer antler, the next a tiger's whisker or a lion's tooth, and he especially loved to throw in stories about Nelson the rhino, who he was quite sure was his best mate.

Both Wendy and I tried to teach Jordan as much as possible about animals when we were working with them in the zoo, as Jordan showed an early and unusually sensitive interest in animal care. His ability as a young fella to retain detailed information, and repeat lessons back to us word for word, stood out to me as exceptional. And his dinnertime offerings gave us our daily entertainment, often arriving as a trail of obscure facts he had collected from *The Pictorial Encyclopedia of the Animal Kingdom* I had given him. The very same one that had kept me company in my childhood. 'Did you know that polar bears actually have black skin?' . . . 'Did you know that giraffes stand up all their lives?' . . . 'Do you know that frogs can freeze without dying, and how about that pandas pee upside down?'

I couldn't help but compare our stories. How differently we

had started out in life. Father and son. Where I'd hidden myself under blankets on my bed reading animal books while living out my childhood inside a religious cult, Jordan was in the world, making friends, exploring his environment. My son was fully present for his own childhood. I was awed by how Jordan—or actually the young of any species—when given the chance, could open so naturally to life. This was how life was meant to start, safely and with care. All I could feel at those moments was gratitude that it wasn't Jordan who'd had to suffer the trauma that had swallowed me whole as a young boy.

Over the last couple of years we spent at the zoo, Wendy and I enjoyed the rewards stemming from all our hard work. Most of the animals were in peak health. We eliminated all the inbreeding, and the strong flow of donations kept coming from the local community, only getting stronger once we got national zoo accreditation. We could now give high-quality food to all the animals, particularly the apex predators.

The zoo itself was sold at the beginning of our fifth year in Cairns. When the new owner first met all the staff, he seemed to say the right things in terms of zoo-speak, especially that animal welfare was at the top of his list. I could physically feel the relief among all the keepers at that first staff meeting.

For a few months we helped the new management team get the park fully operational and then decided to hand in our resignation. But before our departure, the park gave us one more adventure.

'There are eight lions out here, Tim!' The radio message came through from Wendy, who had been out near the zoo's restaurant, showing the landscapers where to plant trees, when she'd noticed a lioness casually strolling along a pedestrian pathway. When she radioed the feeding station and asked for someone to check the lion exhibit, that person radioed back that eight were missing. We had just experienced a powerful category-three cyclone, a weather event that wasn't unusual for Northern Queensland, but the flooding had been so extensive that the river had risen over the tops of the fences around some of the exhibits, which meant some species were simply able to float out.

As I raced out the door of my office to get my tranquilliser gun, which was kept near the zoo's entrance, I came face to face with a one-tonne male hippo. The hippo was more startled than I was and took off into the bush. I decided on the spot that eight lions loose in the zoo grounds had to take priority over a rogue hippo. Luckily it was a Monday and there weren't many tourists around. As I tore down the pathway to the zoo entrance, I radioed Wendy and told her to call the vet.

Fortunately, most of the lions were fairly apathetic about their escape and were loping slowly through the grounds, which made darting them very easy. We got them all except for two big males. I had a feeling they were around the back of the big shed where the feeding station was located. I said to the vet, who was new to the area, 'Look, if the two lions are around the corner, don't turn away, don't make any fast moves. We'll dart them and then step back and wait for the drug to work.'

She agreed, nodding her head, anxiously. Sure enough, we went around the corner and the lions were there. I looked back to see the vet running for the shed. 'Sooooorrryyyyyyyy!'

The sound of fleeing prey stirred hot blood through the young lions in the same way that a whisky shot might stir a teenager. They stood up, their heads high, their necks stretched, ears forward, and started trotting towards me. I slowly walked backwards with my eyes locked into theirs and my rifle cocked. No fear allowed in the locking of eyes. No fear. I made sure all my movements slowed down to slower than slow. Then I'd slow them down some more. The slower I walked, the more slowly the lions followed. Finally I got into the feed shed. The lions were still following, but slowly, eyes still locked onto mine. The vet was standing in the middle of the shed, her tranquilliser gun dangling from her hands. Without losing eye contact with the lions, I whispered, 'Get on top of the cool rooms.' Then I yelled 'NOW!' We scrambled onto the roof of a cool room just as the two males began an explosive charge, falling just short of taking a piece out of the vet's leg. I darted both and within fifteen minutes they were asleep on the cement.

Another radio call came in. It was Frank, a very experienced keeper I'd brought up from Taronga. Frank told me that he and Wendy had recaptured the last three animals that had 'floated' from their enclosures—two hippos and a particularly buoyant rhino. That evening, Wendy told me of the terror she and Frank had experienced when several 200-kilogram tranquillised lionesses in the back of their park buggy started waking up. I was both horrified and in awe of their courage as Wendy talked me through how she, Frank and a volunteer had endured hauling these animals back into their exhibit while they were regaining consciousness.

It was a miracle that none of us suffered a full-blown lion attack that day. The postmortem of the breakout revealed that the skirt of the mesh fencing that was required around every lion exhibit hadn't been connected to the upright fence when the zoo was first constructed. I was surprised that it had taken a cyclone for us to discover it.

Jordan was nearly eleven when we were finishing up at Cairns, and his animal knowledge was enormous. He was still offering gems at the dinner table like, 'Did you know an eagle has a grip ten times stronger than that of humans?' So when four journalists turned up with our local MP to do a story on the park, I decided to catapult Jordan into the position of 'Guide'. It all went smoothly, I thought—until the following morning, when Wendy and I realised how creative our son had been while showing the group around the park. The second page of the *Cairns Post* read like a movie review:

Behind the scenes with Jungle Boy

It's not often you get to see behind the scenes of what goes into the running of a zoo, but Jordan Husband was brilliant in revealing what was involved . . .

The article went on to reveal that the young jungle boy had taken the group to the cool rooms to view the deer, pig and horse carcasses hanging from hooks and dripping fresh blood onto the white tiled floor. He'd also managed to take them via a bridge over a moat and into the actual hippo exhibit, suggesting that they might get a better view that way.

'What did you think you were doing Jordan? I've told you that moat is out of bounds, and didn't it cross your mind that live animals might have made for better viewing than the dead ones?' Knowing the visitors had been exposed to a potentially fatal hippo attack, I was steaming.

'But we couldn't see the hippos, Dad, and I knew that we would get up closer to them on the island!'

'Not that bloody close!'

Jordan was hurt. But not that hurt. 'What's wrong with showing them what the other animals eat? You've always said that matters. Dead animals are so cool, Dad!'

It was at this point that Wendy jumped in to help out Jordan. 'Yes Jordan, what's wrong with showing them a food chain! All part of nature's cycles we've talked to you about many, many times. And if I was an ELEVEN-year-old boy trying to impress my father, I'm sure I would have thought that getting up close to the hippos was a perfect way to get a better view. Don't you think, TIM?!'

—

As we came to the end of our contract, I noticed the many ways in which this zoo fed back into the community, as well as the other way around. It was incredibly satisfying. I was amazed at how Wendy and I had been able to make such a difference to the lives of this neglected collection of animals and their carers. Before I left the office for the last time, I pushed some photos and newspaper clippings about Jordan the Jungle Boy and the lion escape, and our successful role in restoring the northern Queensland wild animal park, into a large envelope and addressed it to:

Mr and Mrs Brake,

Stagland,

Whangārei, New Zealand.

16

The lion park

I received a phone call from the New Zealand Government soon after Jordan's eleventh birthday, asking me to come and sort out a lion problem.

'Mr Husband, I work for the Ministry of Agriculture and Forestry.'

'I'd recognise that accent anywhere.'

'Yes, but this isn't just a call from a fellow countryman. I'm hoping you might be able to help with a concerning situation we have here at a lion park in New Zealand.'

A week earlier, I'd read in *The Sydney Morning Herald* about how a South African keeper had been killed by a tiger in that particular lion park. As it turned out, the park happened to be in Whangārei. 'Yes, I do know what you're referring to.'

'It's a complex situation we have here, Mr Husband, as we . . .'

'Call me Tim, please.'

'Thank you Tim. The difficulty is that this park has an

extensive media following, as the fellow who runs the place has developed a TV series. This show is a HUGE hit in the UK as well as in NZ. He is quite a tricky fellow to deal with because of the relationship he has with these big cats, but also he is embroiled in a court case, with a relative contesting the park's ownership. It's a mess for sure, but something's not quite right in the park with the killing of a very experienced South African keeper. The New Zealand Government has set up an inquiry and we have completely closed down the lion park. We would like to fly you here as soon as possible to head the inquiry.'

'I'll be there Monday next week.'

⸺

I arrived in New Zealand on my own. Wendy happily stayed home, at the farm—Jordan had started at the local high school and she wasn't keen to uproot him in his first year of secondary school. I was met at Auckland airport by the government official I'd spoken to. He handed me a thick folder full of documents, which I tucked away in my briefcase, and then we headed to the lion park.

It was the first time I'd been back in my hometown since I'd come face to face with my brother, my abuser, my rapist. I had been unsure of how I was going to feel about that, but I was a little bit proud to be travelling in a government car through the streets of Whangārei. I was a zoo specialist representing the New Zealand Government as the head of an inquiry into what was potentially zoo corruption. Dad was right when he suggested I was a contagion in my community. I *was* contagious, but in a good way. 'How well the banished wicked seem to be coping beyond life with the chosen few,' I muttered under my breath.

On the way to the lion park my memories drifted in and out, but this time I could see and feel them without being hurt by them. This time, I could only feel compassion for the child I'd been. The suffering child whose early life was so broken. The memories seemed to surface from everything that flashed past my window. They were attached to roads, buildings and bus stops. It was as though I was watching someone else's story on film. With a shiver of both gratitude and sadness, I felt a sense of wholeness for the first time. Even though Grandad was gone, I sent him a little prayer. I think it was to say thank you. I thought of Dick Brake and John, Mick and Len, and also sent them my thanks. This new feeling in my body seemed to throw up gratitude just as easily as it had thrown up anger, revenge and spin-cycle thinking when I was at my lowest. These people had been my stepping stones across a monster of a river that held the powerful currents of my childhood. Without them, I never would have made it to the other side. And this felt like I was on the other side.

We arrived at what appeared to be a zoo setting completely built for TV. There was something about the place that was chilling, that was all surfaces and illusion. The sense of this was heightened by the lack of people milling around, as the place had been completely shut down. The park's owner eventually emerged from an open office door. He was dressed in a faded navy-blue safari shirt and canvas pants, his long dark hair caught in a loose ponytail that was a clear nod to animal whispering of some sort. He gave me a summary of the park as though he was advertising it for TV. I was immediately wary of the way he talked about the lions. He had marketed his identity as being 'one with his pride', but the manner in which he talked about the lions themselves was unnerving.

I did meet one of his big cats as he led me to the exhibit where the African keeper had been taken. A white Bengal tiger apathetically slipped off a couch in the owner's office and proceeded to plod heavily behind us like a disgruntled toddler. There was no fight in it. A life force lost. I noticed that its back legs splayed out in its gait, and its head sagged in a submissive droop. I assumed that either the lions and tigers were drugged or maybe the owner had hand-raised them and managed some sort of connection that way. However, the tiger's splayed gait alerted me to the fact that something much more sinister was at play.

The following day, I spent time with all twelve of the park's lions and tigers. They accepted me with the indifference a domestic cat might show in a household. The fire, the wildness were entirely drained from this group and there was behavioural apathy. They moved around me with organised resignation. The only time they got excited and spontaneous was just before a meal, and even then the prospect of food raised barely a pulse. As I picked up their paws, I was horrified to realise that every one of them had been declawed. Declawing had been outlawed in all developed countries for the past ten years. It was still thriving in the dark corners of dodgy international circus practices, but as far as I was aware, not in any mainstream accredited zoo organisations. To declaw a big cat means amputating everything from the last of its knuckles on, including the claw. It's like cutting a person's finger off from the end knuckle to remove the nail. This affects the animal in a catastrophic way later on in their life. They have trouble walking because their legs become splayed. They no longer have value in any breeding program because they can't defend themselves against other lions or tigers. Trying to place them in any other accredited pride would be like taking a dove to a cock fight.

So this was how the owner controlled these cats for the anthropomorphic appetites of his television audiences. And there were millions of viewers. Once he'd declawed the carnivores and subsequently suppressed them, these apex predators spent their day napping on a sofa in his office. In his TV shows, he delighted in passing morning tea biscuits to these beasts in his office and throwing out lines such as, 'Morning gorgeous Pearl, how's my favourite pussycat this morning?'

With the carnivore's limbs amputated, the only other threat came from their mouths. I realised that it was more than likely that the South African keeper who had been killed would not have realised that the carnivores were declawed and, given this particular keeper's substantial training, he would not have been seeing their mouth as the first threat. He would have known that a carnivore will hold their prey down, their claws operating like hooks in their victim, before using their jaws, so all his attention would have been on the claws. He died because he was killed literally by a single bite to the head and then dragged into a corner of the exhibit.

I spent a couple of weeks overseeing safety upgrades to the animals' exhibits, which mostly consisted of dividing the enclosures so there were areas where keepers could safely introduce feed or clean up after a feed without being endangered by the big cats. I also spent a lot of time consoling the keepers who'd had the bad fortune to witness the attack. The advice

I gave to the New Zealand Government was to categorically condemn the lion park. I exposed the cruel declawing, specifically highlighting the broken nature of the animals given their very limited future, both physically and genetically. The park was subsequently permanently shut down by the government, and the New Zealand papers were awash with stories about the fall of 'the man who lives with lions'. When my few weeks of work on the lion park inquiry ended, it was a huge relief to finally head back to the farm.

On the plane home, I reflected on the owner of the lion park and more broadly on what I had witnessed of carnivore ownership. I thought about the men who aspire to it. How, more often than not, they seemed to be driven by the need to dominate and control these animals. It felt to me that big cats attracted men who were making up for some sort of testosterone deficit by not only owning lions but robing themselves in lion and tiger vestments and paraphernalia. Much like the Elders did with their elaborate robe preparation before a church service. This carnivore deification embraced the full spectrum of worship, devotion and servitude, everything from lion tattoos all over the cult leader's body to the ownership of full-blown carnivore collections.

The toxic smell associated with this particular zoo owner followed me home in the virtual world. I was unprepared for the extent of the backlash. The online vitriol continued for months. The TV shows about the lion park had had an online following of millions of people all over the world, and some of them were dangerously loyal. Almost as dangerously loyal as the Jehovah followers were to their Elders. They sent me messages like, 'If I see you on the road I will run you over!', 'Lion Man wannabe, I know who you are!' and 'Fuck you, mate, hope you die!'

After reading through pages of troll threats, and after the initial bracing when I imagined my life could possibly be in danger, it occurred to me that I'd dealt with this sort of shit my whole life, starting with my Jehovah's upbringing. Bullies and fundamentalists. The lion park trolls were completely unable to see a failing in their 'god', and the only way they could preach their judgement to those they believed threatened his image was by delivering threats in the virtual world. They were just another version of my father and the Elders. When other people failed to see the world through their lens or failed to adapt to their moral code, they were very quick to point the finger. The very opposite of what a compassionate god of any faith would surely advocate.

Eventually I developed a rhino hide against the incessant backlash from maintaining a focus on animal welfare rather than pandering to the powerful people who owned the animals, or their followers. Besides which, the farm was always a nest, a sanctuary, a hideaway. Returning there felt like the same safe landing it had always been. Tucked deep in scrubby forests of callistemon and eucalypt in the Great Dividing Range, Wendy, Jordan and I could easily shut out the world just by turning off all technology and spending time together. Quiet, uninterrupted time together. Doing puzzles, reading, tending chickens, weeding, drinking tea, watching sunsets, walking, swimming. Sometimes doing nothing. But doing it together.

———

Aunty Kez rang one night to tell me that Steven had taken his own life. Gassed himself in his car in the family garage, apparently. 'I'm sorry Tim, love.'

The news had difficulty landing for a while, but when the shock finally receded, all I felt was numb. 'Don't be. I'm not.'

Aunty Kez could've been telling me that she and Lou were moving to the South Island. Other than relief for his kids, no feeling, nothing, not one way or another. I did wonder why he'd done it though. Maybe Steven had been triggered because I was all over the press in New Zealand when I was investigating the lion park. Perhaps seeing the 'Evil One' close up and in a position of power frightened him. Shocked him. Reminded him. Shamed him. I would never know. What I did know is there would be no Kingdom of Heaven for Steven.

17

Training keepers

A few months after Jordan started at his new high school, Wendy told me he was having trouble adjusting. She told me he was struggling to make friends. 'He's not the cool kid anymore, not called Zooboy anymore, love. These young fellas are sons of shearers and mechanics and I don't reckon a crocodile tooth hanging around Jordan's neck interests them too much.'

My ability to understand my son's journey was often limited, although I did my best. As a young teenager I stared at vinyl water-stained walls and thumbed through encyclopedias in my rat-infested caravan. I hardly even saw anyone else to interact with, let alone respond to the challenges of those communications. The cone of silence I hid within, I never challenged. Silence was my retreat, my safe place, my home. So I had a lot of trouble understanding what Jordan might be going through. I often thought it was better not to offer much at all in terms of parental advice. Just to listen and hope that Wendy would find a way to resolve the problem. But as usual, Wendy never let me hide in my history. She insisted I always be there for Jordan when he needed me.

That afternoon I found him alone with his Nintendo on the couch. I sat down next to him and gave him a cuddle. 'School's hard, yeah?'

'I miss my mates up north, Dad. This mob is tough.'

'Don't let them get under your skin, mate. Sounds like some of them are bullies. Ignore them if you can. If that doesn't work, try and make a joke of it. Or use one of my jokes. Nothing like a dad joke to frighten off a bully.' We chuckled and he pushed deeper into my side for a cuddle. 'You know bullies never amount to much in the long run, love.'

We sat there for a while without speaking. It felt good to be creating a new normal for my son. By pushing my brutal history behind me and rewriting the story in the moment, I was changing an actual default setting. There were hard-wiring changes happening. I was creating a reality where my boy could talk to me about his troubles and feel heard. And most importantly, feel connected. Never alone.

While I was at home, we got a call from a zoo in Bali, Indonesia. Denpasar Animal World needed a new curator who could offer them 'special expertise and assistance with its animal collection'. They also wanted to offer Wendy a job as manager of their Education and Conservation Centre.

At first I resisted, as I knew that Indonesian zoos could be among the most challenging in the world in terms of compromised management, often with little attention given to animal welfare. But there was something inside me pushing me to go—maybe Daktari, or young Tim saving injured roadkill.

The drive to rescue animals from dismissive owners seemed to have gathered steam for me, despite the industrial level of neglect we had already uncovered. Wendy was more than keen to accept the offer, particularly given that Jordan was still struggling to settle into his new school. So we made the decision to start the new project and see where it took us.

———

Jordan was twelve years old when we arrived in Indonesia in 2010, nearly the age I was when I got thrown out of home. As we walked through Denpasar airport, I felt a deep sense of gratitude, once again, that my son's early experience of the world was so profoundly different from mine.

What we found when we arrived at Denpasar Animal World we were entirely unprepared for. The park was much more developed than either Wendy or I had imagined. We were both stunned to see the level of detail and care in the organisation and design of the park. This looked like it was going to be a completely different venture for us, less cleaning the scum from the bottom of the barrel and more creating a world-class zoo from the ground up. We were very excited. The bare bones were all there to make something world-standard.

On a balmy pink Indonesian evening, Wendy and I clinked bottles of Bintang together in celebration. We were sitting on the verandah of the zoo's treetop bungalow that initially was to be our home. There was little else but the maniacal laughter of hyenas and the breathy guttural roars of faraway lions to break the silence. Happiness buzzed all around and inside us like a drug. Beneath our mango wood verandah was a waterhole where

208

small herds of antelope, giraffe and wildebeest milled. Within the herds, I spotted three Grévy's zebras drinking, and there were also some impalas. I'd already been impressed by the level of species integration in the exhibits I'd seen from a distance on the way in, but this felt like the real thing. I remembered reading one of my encyclopedias when I was a kid and it felt like we had landed somewhere inside the chapter on Africa.

It was a sweet sleep we all slept that night, soaking in the sounds of the Serengeti plains. The morning was sticky and humid. Through the thick smog that hung like a roof across the city, new smells reached us. The hot sweet scent of frangipani and banyan tree, the woody dry odour of sandalwood, and the crisp edge of peanuts frying in sesame oil, all found a way onto our verandah as we sipped our thick sweet coffee. Wendy and I felt a sense of relief at having finally arrived at a place that looked to be managed thoughtfully, and with a depth of care that we hadn't known in the past eight years.

We dropped Jordan off at the International School that first morning. As we said goodbye to him at the doors, kids who looked to have been drawn from every curve of the globe gathered him up to go inside. He was as excited as I'd ever seen him.

For me, that first day at the park was full of introductions and animal inspections. I had meetings organised with the heads of all the animal collections and the correlating vets, as well as a board meeting. As curator, I was to be comprehensively in charge of the extensive animal exhibits. It was a new frontier for me, not only as a curator, but as the manager of a vast staff. Denpasar Animal World was a zoo with over 200 staff and 2000 animals, so I was, at last, to be tested on every level. Gaining respect and trust from staff was going to be the steepest of my learning curves, and the challenge of the test made my circuitry buzz. I couldn't wait.

The head vet narrated the animals' history and genetics as we drove around the park during the initial inspection, but the monologue turned into background noise as we got a close-up look at the animals and I quickly realised what was in front of me. The telltale signs of inbreeding were everywhere. The cleft palates of the lions, the splayed legs of the tigers, the warthogs with deformed heads. Many species were noticeably stunted due to generations of inbreeding.

'Who is in charge of the animal selection!'

'Management look after this, Mr Tim,' said the head vet. 'But they have been aware of the many problems we have here. This is why you are here.'

I felt the burden of the project landing on my shoulders, as if someone had literally thrown their full body weight around my neck. I hated to see the extent of the health problems that resulted from inbreeding. At this point I knew it was crucial to keep Tom out of the picture so I could stay focused on what was in front of me. I had to let the adrenalin of anger in my body come and go, as I knew it would. I needed to put my mind to how to solve the myriad challenges in terms of the animal collection.

The board meeting started late. A table of ten men formally welcomed both Wendy and me. They were dressed in dark-green tunics, which were buttoned at the wrist and the neck and had fresh Animal World logos intricately threaded in gold on their right top pockets. They sat silent and gargoyle-stiff in their chairs, and their uniforms sat over them like boxes. All impossibly pressed and untarnished. We sat down and were offered coffee.

The operations manager spoke first. 'Mr and Mrs Tim Husband. Welcome to Denpasar Animal World and welcome to Indonesia. Just before we start, is there anything you would like to ask or comment on having been around the park?'

Wendy ripped in right then with a vigorous summing up of her day, a habit that always made me melt with love for her. 'Thank you, everyone. Already loving Animal World! I had a very good session with the girls today in the education team. The women are receptive to my suggestions and I think we have some very good education ideas and approaches to conservation to begin work on.'

What followed was an unsettled shuffling in chairs among the group as Wendy continued to summarise her initial observations. We were later to learn from my PA and translator, Ketut, that it was considered inappropriate for Wendy to answer the board members' questions before I had had a chance to. It was going to be one of those customs that, for anyone who knew Wendy and me, would need to be abandoned very early on.

'And you, Mr Husband, your thoughts?' asked the operations manager.

'Thank you and good to meet you all. There are some things I am very impressed with here at Animal World. Your exhibit sizes are very generous, you have some terrific multi-species exhibits, and your infrastructure is the best I've come across. However, the animal collection is in very bad shape.'

The atmosphere became heavy again, but after a long pause I waded through it, driven on by how angry I was. 'The amount of inbreeding is out of control and it's going to take a lot of work to pull these animals back into some sort of acceptable and accreditable breeding program.' The silence that followed became increasingly uncomfortable, with everyone in the room appearing to readjust both their breath and body. 'I think it's important we all understand what we are aiming for here with the park. What I have in mind is that we aim to make Denpasar Animal World the best zoo in Indonesia. And to be the best means we need to not only attract locals but also international tourists. To attract tourists, we need to pay attention to standards, and that means paying particular attention to animal husbandry standards.'

One of the men, who had heavier gold embroidery on his pocket, finally spoke. I was later to learn he was the managing director. 'We are aware of the problems you point out, MrHusband. This is one of the main reasons we would like your expertise. Meeting these standards for accreditation. What does this involve, in terms of expense, I mean?

'There are many high standards that we need to meet. These are in areas such as animal enrichment, animal nutrition and animal husbandry. I have noticed for example that the animals are only being fed chicken carcasses at the moment. This is not enough for apex predators, for the animals that are used to being at the top of a food chain. Haemoglobin, iron, red-blood cells, these are all crucial in the diet of carnivores and other apex predators. As well, many of the exhibits have not been designed with behavioural enrichment in mind. An animal's good mental health is crucial for good physical health.'

'Could you explain, exactly, what sort of costs we are talking about here, Mr Husband?'

'Whatever the cost of good animal health is!'

As we left the meeting, there was a slightly more anxious tenor to the handshakes and back pats.

Later that evening, when we shared the same Bintang combo with a different noodle dish on our Serengeti verandah, Wendy said, 'Management is hearing your frustrations, love. It's a good sign. You need people to listen if you're going to lead this project. It's huge!'

A couple of thoughts struck me later that evening while I reflected on the day. First, to be fair to the managers of this Indonesian project, they had specifically brought me in to deal with the difficulties they were having, and that was a testament to the care they were showing towards their animal collection. Second, I'd managed to shut down Tom very early during the wave of rage I'd experienced when I first saw the extent of the inbreeding. Just as Dr S had suggested, I let the anger come, let it do its job, and sat with it, all the time trying not to react to it, and it eventually passed. I was then able to respond to what the anger was trying to alert me to, an injustice or a threat, with much more strength. With a firm and compassionate hand. The tail, the sting, the endless rumination after the event, were no longer there. I seemed to be expressing my anger in a very different and more effective way, and that made me feel incredibly strong.

It WAS going to be a mammoth task to pull this animal collection into shape, and I knew that the way in which I led the many staff was going to really matter to the success or failure of the project. Here, managing staff was going to be a particular challenge because it involved many differences in culture. I knew from experience what it was like being surrounded by people who thought they were the only ones who had a handle on 'truth', and that it was important that I try as hard as I could to be tolerant and learn from the different cultural sensitivities within the staff.

I pulled out a scrappy and stained piece of lined A4 paper tucked away in a side pocket in my briefcase that had my writing scrawled all over it. I found a pen and added point number fifteen on the second page: 'Respect cultural differences, and if you can't, learn to live with them.'

When I turned the paper over to recap the first seven points on how to be with people and how to lead them, I had a gentle chuckle. They were all the ideas I'd picked up from watching Mick and Dick Brake all those years ago. As I read out loud the words sprawled across and down the page in the same drunken-spider handwriting I'd developed at fourteen, I felt a really weird sense of tenderness towards little Tim.

People behaviour and respect

1. Always pitch in to help, whatever your management level is.
2. Always treat people with dignity.
3. Respond, don't react.
4. The person at the bottom doing the hard manual work matters just as much as the person with the ideas at the top.
5. Take time to listen.
6. Get people's respect enough so you can teach them why animals matter (Kingdom of Heaven on earth).
7. Be encouraging to people when they are really trying hard.

They were pretty basic, but I regarded these first seven ideas as my seven best commandments on the best way to lead people. The rest were ideas I'd taken away from Canberra, Taronga and Cairns but which I seemed to refer to less. And so, during my first few months in Denpasar, I would make a point of introducing myself to and talking with each of the keepers individually. It was important for me to understand what each of the keeper's motivations for animal care and further learning were, so I knew how to encourage them. I was driven to help them find an authentic and enduring connection with the animals they kept.

———

Getting the animals healthy was now my top priority. I called Glenn Sullivan, who was able to get in touch with a fellow in Sydney who supplied kangaroo meat internationally. The roo meat was needed to replace the chicken carcasses that had been the mainstay of the apex predators' diet. However, after a few weeks of feeding the various species kangaroo, I was confused to see a lack of weight gain among them, and stumped as to why the apex predators' health had not improved.

'Keepers like it too, Mr Tim. They take it first.' Ketut was letting me know where all the replacement meat had gone.

I gathered all the keepers and calmly but sternly let them know what my expectations were of all of them. 'The health of these animals has to be our top priority.'

Ketut, who when translating my words had very quickly become a wizard at mimicking my facial expressions, body stance, rolling eyes and exasperated breathing, delivered my expectations to the group with a performance worthy of an

Oscar. There was more performance in Ketut's telling than actual translation, which I quietly enjoyed, purely for the theatre.

I was fairly confident that the choreographed castigation would do the trick, but week after week, the same thing happened. Carnivore bellies were still hollowed-out hides hanging off skeletons, and the animals continued to be listless and breathless. The bears were the same. They were not being fed nearly enough food. In fact, when we did their monthly blood analysis, there was no sign of kangaroo meat in their diet.

'Kangaroo is very delicious, Mr Tim. Vets like it too.' Ketut managed to point me, yet again, in the right direction.

My next step was to put a call through to Australia and ask for the kangaroo meat to be treated with vegetable dye before it was shipped. The next shipment contained three tonnes of blue minced meat swirling in turquoise blood. Job done. No more theft. Full bellies and robust play returned for many of the apex animals in their exhibits.

One morning when I was doing my early morning rounds in my buggy, checking on both the animals and the keepers, I came across a keeper charging towards a group of elephants while shouting and holding a burning branch of bamboo high above his head. The old matriarchs turned in terror and ran towards the elephant shelter for cover.

'Put that thing down!' Ketut shouted in a remarkably and unsettlingly similar pitch to my own. The elephant keeper was a kid—right then, a terrified kid.

Later, I addressed 25 elephant keepers who I'd assembled in the education room for a lesson on animal husbandry: 'Elephants are animals, just like us. They feel fear, they can feel it when a keeper is angry. They understand and feel it when you are calm.

Animals will connect with you if you show them respect. If you treat them like shit, they will distrust you, and if they distrust you, they become unpredictable.'

Ketut slowly translated this to the group. Most of the keepers stared at me with a mix of terror and curiosity while Ketut choreographed my talk. I already knew that Woko, the head elephant keeper, was hungry to learn as much as he could about elephant behaviour. He took everything in, on every level. I saw myself in Woko. He was clearly head keeper because he'd found a way to care about the animals as much as he cared for himself. He also knew their behaviours inside out. He knew when they were likely to be more aggressive—when the males were in musth or when the females were protecting calves—and he knew when it was safe to be with them. I had already noticed that the elephants were more responsive to him, much calmer in their behaviour when with him than with any other keeper. I would video the interactions Woko had with the elephants and play them back to the other keepers so they could see what it was we were aiming for.

'So no more hoses, guys, okay? No more spraying them with jets of water to get them to move. No more flaming branches. Work gently with them. Treat them with dignity and respect. Imagine they are part of your own family. Work with them when you're feeding them. Trust comes when you treat them well. Especially when you don't need them to do something for you. It matters. I know you can do this, all of you, because I know you have come to work here because somewhere inside, you care for animals.'

I shared this approach with all the keepers of the various species. One of the more astonishing success stories was that of one of our reptile keepers. He had established a very unusual bond with his Komodo dragons, a species widely recognised as being particularly aggressive. Because he respected them, while not fearing them, they allowed him to comfortably move around them in their exhibits. This allowed him to keep a close eye on any changes of behaviour and easily address their changing needs.

Over the course of the next two years, I spent many hours working with the keepers. Most of them had had very little schooling. One of the keepers told me that the boys chosen for this work had usually finished school at around fourteen, while the girls, of whom there were few, were lucky to make it to twelve before leaving school, and even luckier to be chosen as keepers. So I knew my teaching approaches needed to be considerate and clear. Our husbandry lessons were extended to every animal species at the park. Wendy and I implemented the first structured zookeeper course in Indonesia at Denpasar Animal World, which gave many young Indonesians a step-by-step approach to further their education and skill level.

Importantly, they learnt to see the animals they kept through an observational and conservational lens. Specifically, they learnt that, when it came to sharing an understanding of animal behaviours with tourists within a zoo setting, instead of 'entertaining' the tourists by teaching the animals to engage in unnatural acts—like teaching the orangutans to ride bicycles—they could focus more on natural behaviours, like watching how an orangutan broke open a coconut, or how it brachiated—swung from branch to branch. Every group of keepers was given substantial instruction on how to connect and work with the particular animals they were caring for and, most importantly, to work with them in a way that was respectful and gentler to the animals themselves.

The results were immediate. Animals became less stressed, more interactive with keepers, and were more easily persuaded to move from their exhibits if needed. The connection that I always got a real kick out of witnessing was the one the keepers had with themselves. Connection wasn't just one-way. Once the keepers no longer treated the animals with fear or condescension, they were happier and more engaged with not only their animals but with themselves. I was often reminded of how animals had grounded me when I was young—both when I looked after them in my bush refuge and when I cared for the lemurs and other Stagland animals after my rodeo weekends. It was a circle, a perfect feedback loop.

We eventually moved out of our safari bungalow—as they were originally designed for tourists—into a flat five minutes' drive from the park. But each morning, those five minutes could easily stretch to 45. Long lines of traffic snaked slowly through the back streets of this smog-filled city that was crawling with scooters, their passengers often only a blowfly's breath away from the windows of our own car.

The car trip to work was also often interrupted by every manner of festival. Daily Hindu festivals popped up like grass after rain in Bali, and they celebrated all aspects of life. Trails of the devoted led by gold-and-red-silk-robed celebrants threaded ribbons of colour through the traffic. Some were men shaking tambourines who wore headdresses wrapped in coloured layers, and some were women balancing wobbling trays of fat mangoes, jackfruit and jellied sweets on their heads on pedestals. All carried symbols of worship and gratitude to their gods. The people watching were often showered in flowers. I'd watch the faces of the onlookers lapping up the shared joy just as a child might when stepping through their first breaking wave. The colour, the food, the textures, the rituals, all fascinated me. Joy and religion were two concepts that I didn't think sat easily with one another, yet here they were on show and as naturally symbiotic as a buffalo and an oxpecker.

I transplanted the young boy I was here amid the festivals and music, and wondered how things might have turned out if I had grown up inside a different religion, especially one that appeared to be life-affirming and generous. I was in awe of the power of the spectacle and rituals, the connections within the community, the shared celebration, the wonder. I felt just as I used to when I'd watch Dick Brake with his big family on Sundays, all together, laughing and sharing stories over a roast lunch. It was immediate solace when the ripples of warmth, connection and care they had for one another found me and spread through me like hot sweet tea on a cold day. I had that very same feeling here. Even if it was still from a distance.

———

The Australian vet whose employment I'd specifically requested, and who I'll call Anna, finally arrived. I'd become less than entirely confident in the level of professionalism among the local vets after twice observing one of them struggling with how to use a catheter, so I was keen to have someone new oversee that process. Anna had worked as a vet in the Northern Territory and was full of frontier life force. She'd had more than her share of boundary life in Northern Queensland too, wrestling bulls for castration, inseminating mares and dealing with colic in stallions. Nothing much frightened her. She was taller and had a stronger build than most of the male vets at the park, but most importantly she was a straight shooter and had impeccable attention to detail. It didn't take her long to sort out where weaknesses existed in the team.

'Where the fuck do these guys get their vet accreditation from, Tim? Yesterday I was trying to anaesthetise an antelope and the vet I was with had absolutely no idea which drug to use or even how to insert the bloody thing! I can't imagine what these animals have been through!'

I had suspected that at least some of the local vets had received questionable training, so I was very glad to have Anna overseeing the department.

A few weeks later we employed another new vet, a local woman called Hera. We were very careful to research her academic and practical history before taking her on. Hera proved invaluable, so much so that I began to use the expression 'BH' as a guide to when things were really bad at the zoo. 'BH' meant 'Before Hera'. BH, the aquarium was losing up to a hundred fish a week, including some incredibly rare ancient species that any Western zoo would be desperate to get their hands on. We still had a deteriorating school of three lungfish and an extremely rare pair of bowfin fish, two species mostly considered extinct in other parts of the world. Hera applied a microscopic eye to her work. She covered every detail impeccably, like a bower bird on blue. Feed quantities were meticulously monitored and prepared. Water temperatures were taken three times a day. AH ('After Hera'), the turnaround in fish numbers happened quickly. The increase in the number of lungfish and bowfin was particularly exciting. Not only did we stop losing fish, her meticulous management made it possible to hold more and more species together successfully.

When I reflected on the female keepers and vets I had worked with over the years—Hera, Debbie Cox, Lisa Naylor and Anna among the many good examples—it occurred to me that women seemed to make better keepers and vets than their male counterparts. What struck me in particular was that with the female keepers, there seemed less of a need to dominate animals while interacting with them, a tendency I'd observed to be widespread among the male keepers. There wasn't that same need to use force or strength to control or manipulate the animal. Women were more patient and able to work with the animal's temperament and idiosyncrasies. This allowed for a different relationship, one that involved deep levels of trust and respect.

Anna, unfortunately, seemed to appear in my office a little too often for her, or my, liking. 'I'm not sure if I can take this for too much longer, Tim.'

'Oh no, what's happened now?'

'Rather than euthanase an animal in a terminal situation and in pain, all the Hindu vets sit in a prayer circle around the animal waiting for it to die! What sort of compassion is that?'

'So not that unlike what we do back home. Only back home, we euthanase animals who are dying while suffering terrible pain, and we sit around waiting for humans who face the same intolerable terminal situation, slowly and desperately suffering, to die. Look, I get it Anna, I do, but these customs and religious rituals are centuries old. We have to respect their ways.'

I did get it. I never liked to see an animal suffering, and

I struggled with many of these religiously informed practices at the zoo as well. But from my experiences on the human side of the fence, I knew that morality was a slippery concept that involved a complicated mix of ideas informed by religion, culture, power and gender, as well as the very human need for belonging. The way this often played out in the world was through well-established practices and rituals. For the most part, I tried to steer clear of telling people what the right thing to do was in their own country. Anna's ethics, on the other hand, were hardwired and rusted on, and she wasn't going to compromise them for anyone.

Anna only stayed for six months, eventually returning to a Northern Territory cattle station where she could work comfortably within the boundaries of her own standards.

Wendy's work at the Education and Conservation Centre, meanwhile, was attracting a lot of attention. She had managed to triple the number of locals who came through the centre in the two years she'd been managing it. Wendy had designed a museum for indigenous conservation, which taught locals about what needed to be done to secure protection for domestic endangered species. Her exhibits provided a closer look at bird species, specifically the Bali myna, along with pangolins and other domestic animals that got sold through the illegal markets in Indonesia. Many exhibits had storytelling at their core, with a focus on both Indigenous culture and contemporary science, and most were interactive. The local community were encouraged to take more of a role in managing their indigenous species and their habitats.

The design of the exhibits played to Wendy's strengths. She told me that when she'd been preparing them, she'd been influenced by a Taoist proverb she'd once heard. 'It's the teaching how to fish thing, Tim.'

'And what's that?'

'Give a man a fish, you feed him for a day. Teach a man to fish, you feed him for a lifetime.'

Despite occasional run-ins with the vet department, every aspect of the zoo began to improve, from nutrition, genetics and conservation to husbandry. Animal enrichment was developed in every part of the collection. We introduced hidden caves for the lions. We addressed and improved the climbing structures and privacy barriers in all the primate exhibits. We scatter-fed the elephants, encouraging them to move around their territory searching for the pellets, fruits and vegetables that we'd hidden. And we continued with carcass blood trailing for the carnivores. We even managed to mimic hawk shadows over the meerkat exhibits, prompting them to stand in a line and make their distinctive alarm call. All behaviours that are endemic in the wild.

Meanwhile, the number of tourists coming to Animal World continued to grow. Explosively. Five thousand visitors daily, a number that doubled, then tripled. The most satisfying of our achievements was that I was able to prove to management, by way of numerous profit increases across all aspects of the business, that when animal welfare is prioritised, a feedback loop is created: tourist numbers improve, job satisfaction for employees improves, there are fewer problems with animal health, and so the cycle continues.

In our fourth year, we were accredited by the South East Asian Zoos Association, gaining the status we had long aimed for. The first of its kind in Indonesia. Journalists across the country were now covering Denpasar Animal World's success.

'Foreign Managers Turn Zoo into Gold'

'Best Animal Park in Indonesia'

'Global Success for World-Class Animal Park'

Whenever I read these accolades in the press, I continued my habit of taking newspaper clippings and putting them in a file marked 'Dick Brake'. Once a year, I would send it all back to Stagland.

—

One of the more extraordinary adventures I had while I was in Indonesia was overseeing the transportation of a cargo-plane full of exotic animals from Australia to Denpasar. It began when one of the owners of Cairns wild animal park rang me one afternoon.

'Tim Husband?'

'Yes.'

'Hello, we bought the Queensland zoo not long after you left. We have been trying to make it into a commercial success but have been struggling.'

'You're probably doing everything right then. Animals cost a lot of money if you're looking after them properly.'

'Yes, we've discovered that the hard way. Anyway, we're selling up, and I wonder if you are interested in buying our collection.'

'The whole collection?'

'Yes.'

'What would the cost be?'

'A hundred thousand dollars, US.'

I knew that collection had been in very good shape when I'd left that park. I knew exactly what we would be taking on, and I knew that US$100,000 was an incredibly small price to pay for an entire collection of exotic animals. In any other zoo in the West, a single rhino alone would have cost US$70,000.

'In short, yes. I'm very interested. There are logistics involved, though. Can you give me 24 hours?'

This opportunity was indeed exciting. I was confident that the protocols I had introduced in Denpasar meant that the collection would be coming to a safe environment enriched with genetically sound animals. The idea of buying the Cairns park animals was well received by the zoo board at the emergency 9 am meeting I'd called late the night before, and we got the go-ahead. Two weeks later, me, my trusted elephant handler Woko, and forty of the park's better keepers were in Cairns.

The project was massive any way you looked at it. Adding to the logistics of moving a collection of 132 exotic animals was the fact that it had never been done from Australia before. Flying this number of exotic animals in a cargo plane out of Australia attracted a significant amount of media attention, both in Australia and Indonesia. A documentary team from the ABC covered 'the crossing', along with a plethora of independent journalists who seemed to be lurking anonymously everywhere around Cairns. Hundreds of crates arrived at the park, having been built all over Australia. They had been designed specifically for the crossing, lined in steel and heavily fortified with iron cores.

There were two methods for transporting animals that were accepted practice. One was to tranquillise them all before loading them, and the other was to get them used to being in crates. I insisted on all the animals being 'crate-trained' as this was the best animal husbandry practice. This was because some species suffer from a condition called myopathy, which causes their heart to stop if stress is brought on too quickly. If we tranquillised the Cairns animals and they woke up in crates mid-flight, not knowing where they were or what the hell was happening to them, it was very likely many of them would die.

The crate training required a staged process. First, we put the animals' feed in the back of the crates at mealtime, so the only way they could access their food was to go in there. To start with, they would snatch the leg or carcass or whatever feed we were giving them and take it out into the open to finish it. But after a week or so, they would stay in the crate to finish their feed and then come out for water. Sometimes, they even fell asleep in the crates. In this way, we crate-trained rhinos, hippos, monkeys, bears and lions over a two-week period.

Very late into the night before the flight, we crated and then freighted all the animals to Cairns airport by road. Lines of semi-trailers carrying cargos of exotic animals snaked ribbons of red light down the coastal highway in the black night. I was already in Cairns, holed up in the Marlin Hotel, where I was to spend a mostly sleepless night. The morning of the transfer, I was up at 4 am. The cargo plane was to arrive at 5. It was only going to be available to us for three hours before it was scheduled to take off. Every one of the forty staff I had brought over from Indonesia knew exactly what they were required to do minute by minute, having rehearsed this a number of times over the previous fortnight. We couldn't afford for anything to go wrong, due to the animals' very limited threshold for dealing with this type of stress, so we had set a precise time for getting every animal into a crate and onto the plane. Fortunately, it all went exactly to plan.

When the loading process was almost complete bar the rhino and hippo crates, I went and sat in my ute. I was in the middle of taking my first real breath of the morning when I heard a knock on the driver's window. Two men from the Cairns council were standing on the tarmac clutching clipboards. One was an inspector from the Queensland Pasture Protection Board and the other was from their marketing department, or so said their name tags. It turned out they were checking whether a bullet-point checklist put together by the National Exports team had been correctly adhered to.

'You'll need troughs in all your crates,' said the Pasture Protection guy. His companion then leant in and gave a bit of muscle to the question: 'Got troughs in all the crates?'

'Yes, where possible,' I replied. I was still only partly paying attention as I had finished enjoying the sense of relief that we had actually managed to get all the animals on board without any serious problems.

'I noticed you didn't have a trough in the rhino crate,' said the Pasture Protection guy.

'What?' I looked straight into the hot glare of the morning sun and caught the inspector's silhouette. He was persistent, of that there was no doubt.

He continued: 'I want you to put a water trough in the rhino crate.'

'Look mate, there is no way that will last more than five seconds before he tramples the shit out of it!'

'I don't care. I would still like a trough in there, as per the regulations.'

He had my complete attention now, and I got out of my ute to get a better look at him. Hot lines of breath were pouring from my nostrils in the early morning cold. Refusing to look me in the eye, instead preferring to focus on the pen poised over his clipboard, he insisted that I adhere to his requirements. As per the regulations.

'Okay, mate, you come with me, and bring your buddy with you. You can get a good look at what you're ticking off on that list of yours.'

They followed me like automatons across the tarmac. We collected a hard-plastic trough from the crate truck, which was made from industrial plastic similar to that used in road-construction barriers. There was quite the racket at the rhino crate, with multiple tonnes of one hundred million years of Rhinocerotoidea evolution snorting, groaning, trapped. Not happy. Woko and I awkwardly lifted the trough of water and sat it on the lip of the crate. Woko then slid the door open just enough for me to push the crate in. I was just pulling my arm out when there came a sound like a building implosion and I found myself flying metres into the air, upwards and backwards, as if I'd been electrocuted. The inspector also took to the air, careering backwards and losing his clipboard and multi-focal glasses mid-trajectory. As litres of water poured out of the crate, we eventually regathered, gingerly, and stood at the back of the crate where the hullabaloo seemed to have finally quietened down. I took a quick look inside the tiny viewing window, then suggested the inspector take a look. At first, he would've just seen grey leather, a sparsely haired rhino hide flush up against his multifocals. Then, when the rhino lurched forward, he would've caught a glimpse of a decimated mess of plastic shards that had once been a water trough.

'I think you better listen to him, mate,' his marketing mate offered.

Once all the animals were finally on the cargo plane, I went back to my ute, pushed my head up against the steering wheel and closed my eyes. Quiet there, space away from micromanagers and bolshy rhinos. But my sweet solitude was interrupted by a very broken version of 'Happy Birthday' being sung somewhere on the tarmac. I opened my eyes in confusion. Woko was knocking on my window. He pointed to one of my staff who was carrying a cake. The rest of my staff were shouting, 'Happy birthday, Mr Tim!!'

'Is it my birthday?'

I checked the date at the top of the flight sheet: 20 May. Bloody hell. It really was my birthday. Wendy had apparently organised for the cake to be delivered to Cairns, complete with 38 candles. I had completely forgotten it was my birthday, but then again, it was only during my life with Wendy that I'd had a birthday to pay any attention to at all. Wendy never forgot my birthday. Wherever I was in the world, she made a point of celebrating the day, filling it with festivity and friends. Every year. Even the knowledge that she would remember it was like a slow life drip for my own sense of belonging. I continued to find it remarkable, the power connection had, when someone you loved remembered your birthday every year without fail. Everything I never knew as a kid.

Nine hours later, we finally arrived at Denpasar airport with our precious cargo. The animals were settled when they were released into the holding pens. We gave them a good feed and then began the gradual process of integrating them with the established animals at Animal World—a process in which the keepers had been given extensive training. The next morning I saw a couple of Australian newspapers with front-page coverage about our effort. One read:

Green Tape Fails to Ground Airborne Ark

Australian zoologist ships largest load of exotic animals to ever leave Australia.

Another read:

New Age Noah

Tim Husband is counting them off: 23 lions, two Bengal tigers, a pair of pygmy hippos, one rhinoceros, white. Spider monkeys, brown bears, ostriches, hippopotami and ring-tailed lemurs are being loaded on the chartered Boeing 474 to take them from Cairns to a new home in Indonesia.

Once the animals had settled in, we noticed they were pulling even greater numbers of tourists into the park. We had managed to create an extensive and diverse collection of genetically sound and healthy animals, and I felt deeply satisfied that I had been a part of that.

———

By our fifth year, we had achieved what we had set out to do at Denpasar Animal World, and we were looking for an excuse to get home to reassess where we were going from here. Around this time, one of our young keepers was killed by an elephant, which caused widespread and intense distress, particularly for Woko: 'I tell him, Mr Tim, not to go in when elephant in musth! I tell him! He very young, Mr Tim. Maybe not see musth.'

I knew Woko would replay this event throughout his life. 'Tell me exactly what happened.'

'He go in. Elephant charge, he drops food and run, but elephant fast. Catch up, knock him with his trunk. Wheelbarrow go into moat. Elephant just tread on him, Mr Tim! Over and over! He make him flatten over and over again into ground with foot. We all running in and wave to push away elephant and elephant run back in trees and we drag out boy. Boy very floppy, Mr Tim.' Woko was in tears.

'I'm sorry Woko. It sounds like he made a very bad choice, but he was young and just learning. It's not your fault. It was an accident. A very sad accident.'

I had come to have an unusually strong trust in Woko and his word. He was a very honest man and he had a deep connection with the elephants he looked after. Woko went with the injured boy in the ambulance to the local hospital. The pain of watching a young keeper suffer was clearly very hard for him, and watching a great keeper like Woko go through the agony of self-recrimination was very hard for me, particularly as there was no Debbie Cox, no Lisa or Glenn here to support him. For Woko, there would be very little comfort from his team, for these young keepers were only on the cusp of learning the true value of the animals they kept.

It was time to go home. For good. Wendy finished up her recycling project with the team at the conservation centre, where she was teaching locals how to make luxury fibrous paper out of rhino and elephant manure, and we booked a flight to Sydney.

Home, like always, felt like a different dimension. To get back to the peace and quiet, the predictability of our small farm in the Southern Tablelands, was like stepping into a parallel universe of some kind. I loved that there was nothing to check on my phone, no emails, no texts. Wendy's crèche of plants was waiting for her as if she had never left. Rows of berries still stood strong with only a season or two of fruit missed. Lines of compost bins with softly bubbling swill were still fermenting and sending their rotting stink around the garden as a whispered promise of the next season's crop. Fruit trees, speckled with untreated fungus, still stood sturdy. Everything was a little more neglected than when she'd left, but with roots deep and strong, the plants didn't suffer too much, having waited for Wendy's return like loyal little pups at the back door.

Our time was soon swallowed up by cooking and by composting gardens, chopping wood and tending to our small animal collections. Wendy was busy with jar sterilisation for pickling, and she had taken to dying fabric with vegetable dye and tannin, which she had learned a bit about in Indonesia. I built a narrow-framed glass box in which I was able to finally hang up all of Grandad's medals. The display hung proudly above my armchair on the verandah. He would always be with me because 'in the going down of the sun and in the morning' I would always remember him. Plus I loved knowing he was close by when I had my morning cuppa.

After a few months, however, restlessness began to peck at the edges of my day. I increasingly found things to be annoyed about. I was definitely more irritable with Wendy and Jordan.

I was even giving my chickens a hard time for not being easy to round up at night when I wanted to put them into their shed. I knew from Dr S to check in with my thoughts to see what was going on when any sort of strife like that came up. When I did, I realised Tom was back. He had helped himself to another bourbon and had his feet up, once again watching a live feed of my life in the theatre of my brain and constantly yelling at the screen. He had a dig about me being too young to stay put. He had a dig at my family life verging on normal and that I was never going to get away with that. He told me another bourbon would help. He told me it was time to get on the road. Although I could still be persuaded by some of his arguments, I was much more cautious now when I knew he was around. I found myself using the approach that had been so helpful when I'd successfully managed him in Indonesia. I let him rant and tried not to engage. I sat with him like I might've done with Jordan as an overactive toddler, and then, when he began to trail off like he always did, I said goodnight, calmly asked him to turn the lights out when he went to bed, and closed the door.

'As easy and as hard as all that,' as Dr S would often say.

This time, though, it was particularly tricky to manage Tom because I was always at my most vulnerable between jobs, and the debilitating sense of drift I'd often experience was a known trigger for my depression. Wendy pleaded with me when she saw my irritability return: 'You're not getting caught up in your head with your old mate again, are you, lovey? Tell him to piss off if you are. You can do that with brothers you know. Just enjoy home, Timmy. Let's just enjoy being home. Enjoy having Jordan home. Our sheep, your birds. Let's enjoy the rest while we can.'

'No, he's not running the show anymore. I'll be alright. And what do you mean by "brothers" anyway? He's not my brother.'

'It's a possibility though, hey Tim? It always made sense to me that the voice in your head could have been your twin. I mean you'd shared a room with each other for many months before you were born. Did that ever occur to you?'

'I don't know. I don't think so. I do know that Tom has always told me he was there to protect me, but he just got stuck in my head. Stuck pushing everyone else away.'

'It makes sense that he is trying to protect you. Any brother would. Maybe that's where it all started from. Just a thought, but it's quite a powerful one, isn't it?'

The idea that the voice in my head was some sort of living connection I still had with my dead twin made the hairs stand up on the back of my neck. And the possibility that my twin was trying to protect me from the very early abuse of another brother (only a half-brother) rattled me for some days. Maybe it was comforting. Either way, Tom had become larger than life and I knew he wasn't always giving me the best advice. Even now he was still trying to have a crack, telling me I wasn't worth much. I did my best to let his monologues play—white noise. Besides, I now knew I was worth something. Maybe to species that couldn't tell me I mattered, but I knew I was still changing lives for the better. There was a big part of me that belonged with animals in trouble and I still wanted to protect them when they were vulnerable to indifferent zoo owners. Added to this, the zoo industry felt like another family to me. I felt that the better pieces of me belonged with the animals and my industry colleagues while working inside a zoo. Or maybe, that I couldn't be at my best unless I was there.

18

Billion-dollar safari

One morning I took my coffee outside to sit in the old armchair on the verandah, which I typically did, especially in autumn, and I began working my way through my emails. Among all the spam, the ads selling tractors and chainsaws, sheep drench and superphosphate drums, was an email with the subject line, 'Dubai Municipality'. It came from the office of 'His Royal Highness, Dubai Municipality, UAE', and requested my 'unique skills' to assist the municipality to move a number of exotic animals to a new 'state-of-the-art' zoo in Dubai. 'We will also be hoping to engage you in overseeing the initial set-up stages of the International Dubai Zoo. Your services will be required for the length of time you deem necessary to undertake this project.'

'That's a long way from footrot!' I said out loud.

My armchair spent most of its time swallowing the last of my depleted energy, but now I almost leapt from its grip. Dubai was a place I had never really considered for my next project, but I knew there was a part of me that was very ready to get my teeth into another job, and I made up my mind before I even had the chance to finish my coffee. Wendy was as excited as I was, as much about the location as anything else.

I was in Dubai within a week. Standing on top of a 100-metre-high sand dune in 52 degrees Celsius heat, I asked the zoo's operations manager, a Dubai sheikh, 'So where is it?'

'It's right here. I mean it WILL be right here. Where we are standing!' The project manager then pointed to the white sand beneath me.

I looked to the horizon across what appeared to be miles and miles of a corrugated sand sea, then looked down at how it lapped the base of the massive sand dune we were standing on. The heat was oppressive, heavy, like I was being held down by something.

'So, none of it even built yet?'

'Not built yet, no, Mr Husband, but it will be built in the next two years.'

'And this is the whole site?'

'Yes, Mr Husband, sir, this is the site. This used to be Dubai rubbish tip. That's why it's so much higher than all the city. There's all of Dubai's building waste under here. Under our feet!'

I looked down again, this time at Dick Brake's boots, then to the finely contoured lines of sand sloping down to the flats. It was hard to imagine that the elegant sweep of the sand lines that bordered this dune hid the waste from decades of this modern civilisation's rabid concrete consumption.

'I don't know anything about where these animals are going. I would like to look at your plans,' I said.

'Yes, of course.'

237

Over the next week, I looked at the available plans for what was to be the Dubai Safari Park. I made practical changes to aspects of the design and in terms of workable livable spaces for the animals. Within two days of my suggestions being submitted, I was called to the head office of the director of the municipality.

'We would like to expand your job description and responsibilities, Mr Husband. We would like you to become director of Dubai Safari Park.' Not once did the director look up to see if I was interested. He merely continued with his list of accompanying responsibilities: '. . . animal collection, staffing list and structure, guides, keepers, etc. The full budget could extend to over a billion, so we will be monitoring your use of funds but will give you full rein . . .'

As I watched this impeccably dressed Arab man continue to outline my job description, oblivious to my response, my focus sharpened. His crisp white cotton tunic drove straight lines across him like it had been chipped from marble. The long white headscarf he wore was secured by a crown of black rope and shadowed his earnest face.

I felt so very far from Whangārei. I took some time to sit at the bus stop with the broken kid from Smith Street after everything and everyone he'd known in his life shut him out like a light switch in a bedroom. As the numbers and responsibilities connected to my new role flew around me like a swarm of blowies, I recalled the memory of that same boy at Stagland, that fourteen-year-old who had a straw-chewing stag to keep him company as he swept shit out of exhibits. I remembered how he would get lost in dreams of zoos, of owning animals, of buying animals, of looking after animals and running zoos. And then I drifted back to the moment.

'. . . oversee a staff of 500 . . . international recruits . . .' And the meeting came to an end. 'Your car is waiting for you outside, Mr Husband. Keys to your apartment will be given by your PA.'

And that was that. Message delivered. There was no room for a reply. It was just taken for granted that I would accept the position. I could have just as easily been told they would require extra water troughs in the gorilla exhibits. I returned to my onsite cabin with a set of keys and the address of an opulent apartment in the city.

That evening, I sat in my air-conditioned cabin looking out its expansive window at what appeared to be an infinite tide of sand corrugations disappearing off the edge of the world. The temperature had dropped to a balmy 39 degrees, and the burning yellows and humid greys of the day had faded to purple. A bruise finally given room to spread. As I stared out at the desert, I thought about how, within weeks of arriving in Dubai, I had been made director of a billion-dollar zoo that didn't yet exist, and I was to oversee its design as well as its construction, through to completion. I silently reeled. A circuitry overload. At that moment, however, my stronger sense was that everything I'd done in my life was only ever in preparation for this moment. I was feeling capable and in control, and although I faced a staggeringly steep learning curve, I knew I had everything required to pull this thing off. But it was going to take all of me. All the knowledge I had learnt about people and management from Dick Brake, all the fearlessness and hard-headedness it had taken to ride a bull's rump week after week, all the straight shooting and no nonsense it had taken to stand up to religious fundamentalists, and all the rigour and courage that came from being a survivor of sexual assault.

The most exciting part was that I was building this project from the ground up, which meant all of my most cosseted ideas of utopian zoo design; good nutrition, sound husbandry, strong and respectful staff management, all the ideas that had animal behavioural enrichment and welfare at their core were finally going to get their time in the sun. There was even a possibility that I could develop some of the ideas I had for designing exhibits that specialised in mutualistic relationships—larger exhibits that potentially mimicked wild habitats that would naturally have symbiotic interactions at their heart. I was determined to approach the project holistically, from an operational as well as a sustainability point of view. Every area I developed would feed back into the zoo operation at every level. 'Thinking in circles' were the words Wendy used.

⁓

Over the next few weeks, I put my head down and tackled the detailed work of planning the project. I made lists, mountains of them. All around me, in the office and at the apartment, torn pieces of A4 paper covered with lists piled on top of each other in pitched heaps. Lists of the collection plan for the animals, lists of the species breakdowns, dietary requirements, exhibit dimensions and veterinary supplies. I made lists of staffing numbers, for guides, keepers, vets, vet nurses, security and operational staff. The building requirements were bullet points outlining what was needed for the vet hospitals, car parks, canteens and amenities. Throughout the entire process, every detail seemed to appear exactly when needed. It was almost as if, when I was a kid in my caravan, I'd created the templates needed for this very moment. The days on end I'd lose being completely absorbed in making up countless lists of dietary and exhibit requirements for non-existent animals in imaginary zoos, it all must have been filed away somewhere in my mind only to reappear for this moment in the real world. I felt a strange sense of ease during the days I spent preparing the plans. It was the same sense of flow I'd felt years before when I made the national rodeo team. I was exactly where I was meant to be, doing the thing I was meant to be doing.

On the ground, I started with the practical knowledge I already had and worked up from there. One morning, I walked the entire 25-square-kilometre site, placing pieces of the zoo. I only managed it very early in the morning when the temperature was only 40 degrees because not much physical work could be done by the time the heat clocked close to 50, which usually happened by midday. Physically walking through all the zones gave me a strong sense of how the animal exhibits would work best organically. Later, I mapped out the drive-through safari, then the African area and where it was possible to design a walk-through, and the same with the Asian area. I looked at the best position for a petting zoo, and of course the local Arabian area, which would exhibit camel, oryx, gazelle and Arabian leopards among other animals. Daily, I added to the busy map of the park layout that splattered across the whiteboard in my office like something spilt. It was jammed with arrows, sticky paper bullet-point reminders, and columns of highlighted animal divisions.

Early morning was my favourite time of day. I woke at five o'clock, the gentlest part of the day, keen to see the jewels offered by the rising of a desert sun. It turned out to be more incredible than anything I'd seen from my animal books in my caravan.

I watched while a burning orange crown broached the horizon, all the while sending its blazing golden spires spilling down the fine lines of the dunes.

I'd often say to Wendy during one of our early-morning phone catch-ups, 'Wish you and Jordan could see what I'm seeing, love. It's like opening a box stuffed full of gold. And I get to open it every morning!'

Those first few months, while I was still soaking up the detail of all that was required in terms of construction materials, my right-hand manager, Abdullah, worked with his teams supporting all the initial stages of the project on the ground. Bulldozers were creating roads, cranes were dropping in palm trees, expansive fencing projects had begun. Every day I was between the planning and the project. But the conditions were confronting. The 50-degree heat brought a swath of concerns, ranging from those that seemed insignificant, like raising my windscreen wiper blades to stop them from melting, to those that were about life and death, like checking that all the animals had operational water walls in the holding pens when they first arrived. Given the heat and the topography, I was constantly pushed to think laterally about how to solve problems. I designed cool pads under artificial cement rock so that all the animals, in particular the carnivores, had some cool places to lie down in during the day. Every one of the animal exhibits had spray mist over at least a third of its area. Added to this was air conditioning in all the overnight dens. The ungulates from Europe, whose resting core temperature was five degrees, were going to need an extreme amount of innovation in their exhibit design to keep them from dehydrating. All these aspects we would have taken for granted in any of the other zoos I had curated.

Our first shipment of animals eventually arrived from South Africa, and many of the ground staff dropped whatever they were doing that day to enjoy the spectacle of sleek impala springing off the back of the transport truck like a hundred slinkies, headed for the waterholes. There was a real buzz among everyone that day, replete with back pats, fist pumps and hollering. Eventually, more of our antelope arrived safely from Golden Game, an animal park in South Africa, along with a cargo of zebras. All were well and healthy, and we actually had their exhibits finished and ready, which was always pleasing. The ungulates had nearly four hectares to live in, replete with carefully positioned motion-triggered water sprays. An air-conditioned night enclosure was built underground to keep them cool. When everything operated smoothly like this, in terms of transport, exhibit design and settled animals, I always felt satisfaction at a job well done, and the quiet contentment that comes with completion.

With the park's momentum building, every day felt dizzyingly exciting. There were the inevitable hurdles, those that had come with most of the zoo operations Wendy and I had been involved with, but my first really significant obstacle came in the form of interactions with one of the park's administrators. We differed on what we felt the priorities of the park should be. Our first big falling-out came after they'd insisted on recruiting locals for the most pivotal of the parks' positions, as this was Emirati protocol. But I didn't believe these uncredentialled locals made the animals or zoo-keeping staff enough of a priority. None of these recruits had a background in zoo ethics or zoo management, nor, indeed, an iota of animal experience. I wasn't happy that we were unable to get the expertise and the management skills needed in order to make the most of the competency of our staff. And I wasn't happy that the animals would bear the brunt of the inevitable poor decision-making. They, on the other hand, put their interpretation of Emirate protocol above all else.

Our philosophical differences seemed to rile this administrator as much as they did me, and they'd enjoy cautioning me: 'Watch your step, sir. It's not the way we do things here!'

———

Work was now underway on every aspect of the zoo's construction. Dubai was known internationally for its awesome architecture, and none of it was lost on the design of Dubai Safari Park. I watched as the giant iron frames of the zoo's contemporary aviary structure pierced the greys and blues of the UAE sky. Below the aviary, the structure of the Exhibition Centre was coming together. It was designed to mimic the skeleton of an ancient mammoth, with vast arcs of steel rising out of the desert like the rib cage of an ancient colossus. It was the work of a young female Emirati engineer, and daily stopped me in my tracks. The elegance, the innovation, the reality. It was breathtaking.

I'd also designed a place of prayer and worship for the 500 international workers. The large, fairly utilitarian building provided a space for the broad diversity of religions practised. Despite my own difficult experience with religion, I knew that for many people it was an essential part of keeping their mental health strong, so I considered a place of worship essential. Every Sunday there was a Hindu, Christian, Jewish, Buddhist or Ahmadiyya ceremony of some sort. Added to that, the services on Sunday provided a meeting place for many of the international workers, one of the very few opportunities they had to meet other people and send messages home.

I wondered what my father—actually my stepfather—would think if he could see me, the most evil of his sons, who never was his son, 'corrupting' others. I wasn't even patching up broken zoos anymore. I was building one of the world's biggest zoos from the ground up because I could. What's more, the international and local workers who staffed it were building a community within the safari park that was strong and very supportive of one another. I was good at my job and I was trusted and I was honest and I was proud of all of those things.

I was assigned a personal assistant called Akilah, or Aki as I came to call her. She was extremely capable and paid exceptional attention to detail, and she became indispensable. She was there to explain cultural issues to me that I didn't understand. She helped me grasp some of the power jostling among the Emiratis. She took me to the airport, assisted me with animal transactions. She helped me cope with the corrupt animal dealers who crawled out of their holes when they learnt a billion-dollar project was underway in Dubai. Aki was always ready to roll up her sleeves and get her hands dirty—and I loved how she always wore jeans and runners under her abaya so that she was ready for anything that might be thrown at her. She even helped me wrestle crocodiles. Whenever and whatever I needed, she was there. But the thing that proved most crucial for me was that she helped me figure out how to better understand and manage UAE culture.

After my first few years in Dubai, with Aki by my side, my work settled into a rhythm and many aspects of the project really came along. Now, when Wendy and I talked on the phone each morning, I skipped through events in their recounting rather than offering the wading-through-weeds retelling that was more typical of my first few months in Dubai. After our early-morning catch-up, I'd lose myself in my own quiet deity: watching the sun rise. Witnessing it shimmer and shiver and pull itself over the skyline every morning was how my energy was restored.

With much of our local animal collection already acquired and waiting in holding pens across the continent, we discovered the construction teams were more often than not behind their timelines for finishing projects. Unfortunately for the animals, the problem was only properly acknowledged when a newly arrived cargo load of African buffalo started losing consciousness in the 50-degree heat. 'Inshallah,' the crew would say to me, meaning 'God's will', and with a shoulder shrug they'd return to work that was at least three weeks behind schedule. It took around-the-clock vet care over several days to attend to the dehydration the buffalos had suffered.

I was never pleased when contractors used God's name as an excuse for their own laziness, rather than taking responsibility themselves. Indeed, religious norms continued to show up in my life every day, most of them confronting. They often posed challenges at the park, particularly regarding my efforts to tilt everything towards sustainability. When I'd had to replace 500 metres of the meditative green herringbone carpet I'd chosen for the prayer rooms in the building dedicated to worship, because the herringbone wasn't facing Mecca, I was livid. I let Aki cop the fallout: 'Why didn't someone point that out to me? Anyone! I'm not Muslim, I don't know these customs. I've had to pay for religious practices quite enough in my life, and it blows me away that this far from Whangārei it's still happening!'

'Breathe deeply. Breathe deeply, Mr Tim.' Aki, never too ruffled by my reactions, steadily steered me back to focus on the job at hand.

The deputy director of the municipality was given the task of overseeing the Dubai Safari Park project for Dubai's royal highness and became a good friend to me. His name was Essa and, for me, he was a rare balm for the complicated power hierarchy within the municipality. What I noticed in particular was that he recognised his own knowledge of animals was limited, and so he was constantly driven to learn more about them. Essa, like me, was also very keen to create spaces for animals as close to their natural environments as possible, which would allow them to flourish. Essa's questions about animal care lined up for me daily like kids in a tuckshop queue.

Every evening after work, before going back to the opulence of my apartment, I would sit in my office cabin in the softening heat as the pink evening cooled further into the night, staring out at the desert horizons. Often, Essa would join me and we would share a pot of mint and sugared tea. It was during these times that I felt I could ask Essa about his religion. I was never quite sure why. Something about him seemed free of the hard edges of orthodoxy. Some strange quality, particular to Essa, left him open to other possibilities about the world and its peoples' various beliefs and interpretations of God— or their more secular ideas on 'truth'—while still firmly yet gently holding his own beliefs. I had rarely come across such an anomaly. Essa and I would sit together watching tiny sand corrugations chase each other over the disappearing lines of the horizon. It was usually the first time in the day I could really take a deep breath.

We often sat for an hour or so, saying very little at all. Eventually, one of us would say something.

'At times, I struggle with how things are done here, Essa.'

'You'll get used to it. You're here because you are strong and we need someone who believes in what they are doing. In all aspects of what they are doing.'

'It's sometimes a real fight.'

'I understand.'

'You are open to the best welfare of the animals, Essa. I don't come across that much.'

'Well, I have wells of compassion in me, not limited to any of God's forms in particular.'

'Sounds more like Buddhist philosophy to me.'

'I am not a Buddhist. I have a deep belief in the Qur'an.'

'Is it true that the Old Testament in the Bible is identical to the first half of the Qur'an?'

'That's right, Tim! How do you know that?'

'The first thirteen years of my life were completely devoted to the Bible.'

As Essa gave me a look filled with both intrigue and wonder, I told him all about my childhood. He listened with a compassionate intensity. At the end of my story, he took a deep breath and just turned to stare out the window at the sand sea.

I eventually asked him, 'I would like to know more about the religion that is the foundation of your society. Would you lend me a Qur'an to read?'

'I'm surprised at you, Tim. Surprised you want to go anywhere near another religion!'

'Well, if I'm to honour my name, I must keep my mind open.' Essa tilted his head, his eyes sparkling and curious.

I continued, 'Timothy! It means "One who honours God" in Hebrew!' I laughed. A humour that felt both complicated and ironic.

Essa chuckled too. 'I actually think that, in a way, you do honour God, Tim. You have learnt tolerance the hard way. According to Chapter 17, Verse 70 of the Qur'an, "Everyone's God-given human dignity must be respected, regardless of his faith, race, ethnic origin, gender, or social status." God embodies tolerance, Tim. Even after you've been so hurt by your own religion, you keep an open mind. I am very impressed by this.'

We both watched the wind play with the sand, curling and unfurling in tiny tornados. Essa continued, 'Essa means "A God's promise" in Arabic!'

'Woah! We have quite the religious genealogy between us, Essa!'

Our laughter was rich and explosive. Baritone blasts from deep in our bellies. We poured another mint tea and once again turned our gaze towards the desert's horizon, sharing the silence.

Later that week, Essa brought me his English translation of The Noble Qur'an, which I would spend some months reading from start to finish. We would talk about ways in which our two books were similar and how they were different. We talked about how the books shaped our different worlds. I don't think our stories could have been further apart, both of us irrevocably shaped by these two books, and yet through the sharing of our histories we found that, regardless of our religions, we could see and respect the path of the other.

———

One morning while I was on the phone to Wendy, I recounted another run-in with the administrator and told her how exhausted I felt a lot of the time. I sensed her concern sitting heavily in the silences that filled our conversation. I had managed to keep myself relatively steady with this project as far as Tom was concerned, but occasionally both he and my black sky threatened, and Wendy was well aware of the havoc Tom could wreak should I fall into his grip.

Creating a world-class zoo that had animal welfare at its core was the reason I'd come here in the first place. Wendy reminded me that everything else was 'white noise', and her advice was always to contain my focus to the animals, to not get distracted by political roadblocks. 'Ah love, you need to be more careful! Stick to the zoo and the animals, lovey, and keep away from politics. Please! It's too dangerous.'

The long silences continued throughout our conversation. That was unusual. I thought she might be making her mind up about something but I wasn't sure what it was. She eventually told me that, in two weeks, she was going to bring Jordan over to share my purple-and-gold embossed apartment. That she was ready to come and so was he. 'It's the right thing to do now, Tim.'

I put the phone down, put my head in my hands, and a wave of relief consumed me. I realised just how much I had missed them both. They felt like they lived in my body somewhere. Like blood or bones.

⟵

When Wendy and Jordan arrived late in 2016 I wasn't able to join them for their first few days in Dubai because we had multiple shiploads of animals arriving at that time. But they wasted no time uncovering the jewels of the city. They discovered not only where the best street markets were in Al Fahidi in Old Dubai, but there, they managed to find stalls of explosively colourful offerings of exotic spices and scents. In Al Fahidi they also came across the world's first traditional wind towers. Jordan later told me that Old Dubai was full of them, that they stood tall and defiant, like giant belltowers, with their long open windows on all four sides. While reading from a brochure, he went on to inform me that they were built from sandalwood, teak and gypsum, and that they worked by allowing hot air to escape while capturing the cooler air that was directed through the channel to the inside of the house. 'A timeless architectural feat,' he announced imperiously, clearly thoroughly impressed.

Wendy and Jordan also travelled across to Kalba, where they explored the desert mangrove swamps that had been attracting a fair bit of international press because of their potential contribution to combating climate change. Wendy rang me to say: 'Did you know mangroves are carbon-capturing plants, Timmy? They call it blue carbon!'

They even managed a climb up Jebel Jais in the hope of getting a view of Oman. Wendy and Jordan did more in three days than I'd managed in a whole year.

The day I was finally able to make time to get away from the park, Jordan had gone to the city centre to look for tripods for his new camera, and I followed Wendy through the street markets like a storm chaser, watching and witnessing. Having swept up paper bags somewhere along the way, she'd fill them with dates, figs, nuts and myrrh gathered from the sprawling stallholders' tables, hand the bags to me, and then, using both

251

hands, she'd shove overly generous amounts of dirham into a surprised vendor's outstretched palm. When she asked one of the vendors about the origins of the powerful-smelling myrrh, the woman told us it was a resin from an indigenous tree and it was prized for its cultural significance in the UAE. The woman added that Sheikh Zayed, the first leader of the Emirates and the 'Father of the Nation', had celebrated myrrh as a symbol of the power of women, which he believed should never be underestimated. She leant in close as she completed her cultural offering, at the same time sending a wry look in my direction.

We discovered the ancient market of the Spice Souk, with its powerful fragrances of cinnamon and nutmeg and its baskets brimming with brilliant red and orange aromatic saffron and mace. Vibrantly coloured combinations of potpourri, cardamom, shisha tobacco and nuts were also on display. Wendy bought a bottle of frankincense oil. We later found a stall filled with Dubai sweets and ordered one of the larger boxes. A vendor opened a gold-plated acacia box and we saw it was filled with lines of layered and honeyed baklava thickly sprinkled with grated lime-green pistachio. There were other treasures in there too, like almonds and dates dipped in chocolate and dusted with what smelled like shredded cinnamon quills.

'Oh my god, Tim! Have you ever seen anything so luscious?'

It had taken Wendy's arrival, her perspective, to take me inside this culture in such a different way. I was enjoying getting to know Dubai outside the demanding operations of the Safari Park. The three of us spent the rest of that week driving around Dubai taking in the sights that Wendy had scoped out and which I'd not yet seen. And there were many of them. We met people that week who Wendy had already connected with in Australia.

Most of them were conservationists who were on the front line of permaculture projects in the UAE. Wendy was squeezing them for all their knowledge on sand and soil composting, and in particular on growing plants in a desert environment.

Jordan was completely engrossed by 'the new' because, like his mother, he delighted in the possibilities that different cultures threw up. Daily, he walked around sucking in the unfamiliar sights and sounds. His newly found love of photography meant we would lose him to a compositional idea for a photograph in the same way Wendy was swallowed up by new ideas for the best growing conditions for plants.

After Wendy and Jordan joined me in Dubai, I grew stronger and began to feel my feet touch the ground. I knew I had the strength and capacity to see this incredibly extravagant project through to its end.

—

There were still holes in my animal collection which I needed to deal with, so Johann from Golden Game in South Africa was supplying me with a stream of species, including elephants, giraffes and rhinos. I could be completely sure of the background of the animals we were buying when I bought through Johann, confident of not only the strong bloodlines in the animals he supplied but also their sound genetics. Three months after I'd signed off on the rhino deal, however, the animals still hadn't arrived, which worried me. When I rang Johann, he said they were keeping them a little longer, as there were two pregnant cows among them and they had been stressed from their trip down from Kruger National Park. As it turned out, that seemed to suit our team, as the UAE construction group was still behind schedule on completing the rhino shelter. Then, about two weeks before the rhinos were due to be shipped to us, Johann sent me some photos. Two dead pregnant rhinos lying in pools of their own blood in their quarantine enclosures. Both had bullet holes straight between the eyes. Their lengthy horns had been butchered from their heads, leaving gaping holes where their skulls had been slashed open.

I took time out. Left the office and went home. I showed Wendy the gut-wrenching photos. We had some tea. Didn't say too much. Didn't have the words. I eventually contacted Johann and he told me that apparently someone in the export office in South Africa had informed poachers where the rhinos were being quarantined. The poachers had come in the night, shot the rhinos and taken the horns. 'Fucking arseholes,' exclaimed Johann. 'I'll get you some more, man. And I'll get the fuckers who are behind this, don't you worry.'

Johann did both those things. He bought two more pregnant cows and told the South African Government where he was quarantining them, in the usual holding enclosures. But then he took them to a secret place known only to himself and his offsider. That night, the poachers came again, but instead of two rhinos in the quarantine enclosure they found a mob of police waiting for them. Johann's strategy managed to flush out not only the poachers but also the government mole who'd been informing them.

Reconciling such brutal attacks on these animals was very difficult for me and threw up existential quagmires that my rolling thoughts could barely make sense of. One night, soon after the rhino attack, two international workers were caught throwing blocks of cement at the giraffes. Abdullah had watched the incident unfolding and immediately rang me. I was so incensed by the meaninglessness of it that I drove straight to the park and caught one of the perpetrators as he was trying to run away from the holding pen and the gathering security vehicles. I dragged him to the elephant pools, which were nearby.

'Did you do this?'

'No, Mr Tim.'

'Are you telling me the truth?' I was holding him a mosquito's wing away from the water, threatening to drown him.

'It wasn't my idea, Mr Tim! I just came along because of my friend!'

I told him that if I ever heard of anything like that happening again I'd report it to State security then put him on a plane home with no pay.

I replayed that incident in my head. It played out in my sleep. In my waking hours. The disconnect—no, worse, the disrespect and disdain some of the workers had for animals—was beyond my comprehension. It was one of those dark puzzles that just got stuck in the rat runs in my brain, and the empty corridors of my guts, simply because it was so incomprehensible.

What made someone want to pick up a rock and throw it at an innocent animal, a species they'd never seen before, unless they were clearly its prey or their life was on the line? How could someone think it was fun to hurt a giraffe? Was it cultural? Religious? Did they enjoy cruelty? I doubted that the Indian staff would have ever put themselves in that situation. They respected animals, most of the gods they worshipped were animals. I always remembered Gandhi's quote: 'The greatness of a nation and its moral progress can be judged by the way its animals are treated.' Regardless, treating other animals with dignity often seemed a highly underrated concept among the human species.

———

Whenever there was too much stress at work, like the month the giraffes were attacked and the rhinos mutilated and murdered, I would go somewhere with Wendy and Jordan. Both Wendy and I knew when my black skies were shadowing me, and we did everything we could to disrupt their usual cycle. We went to the markets. Or to see a film. Sometimes we went for a weekend in the Central Asian country of Georgia, which was only an hour's flight from Dubai. Sometimes we just spent a quiet few days at our apartment.

One night, Wendy returned to the apartment later than she usually did. I'd been concerned, and I said, 'Where have you been?'

'Zumba. Love it! It's great!'

'What's Zumba?'

'It's a dance class but it's for fitness. Very cool. Remember I used to do it at home? So different here. These women are wild. It's a line-dancing thing we've all got going.'

'Line dancing in their abayas?'

'Nooo, Tim, they throw them off as soon as they get down into the basement of the gym. All their abayas are lined up on hooks, and they're all wearing their activewear underneath! It's a hoot, Timmy. I love it. I love these women. You've gotta meet them. There's a kind of sisterhood and energy about them that I don't think I've come across since my days at Taronga. Beautiful big spirit in these women, and can they ever dance!'

I was enjoying how Wendy and I were looking at the heart of Dubai through contrasting lenses, and in doing so we got to see different aspects of this culture just by sharing our stories.

19

Ready, willing and able

With most of the animal collection and the majority of the infrastructure completed, I could focus on the next major step of the project, which was filling the 500 staffing positions. The task was enormous. I would be travelling the world, sourcing employees. I flew to the Philippines, Indonesia, Kenya, South Africa, Nepal, India, Pakistan and Singapore, specifically looking for a broad background of interests to fill the diverse multitude of vacancies we had: vets, vet nurses, keepers, guides, security staff, maintenance people and more.

Accompanied by two Emirati officials, I arrived at our first stop—the Ibis Hotel, Nairobi, Kenya. There, we were told that hopeful applicants had been waiting all night to see us. However, according to the project organiser, they were not properly prepared. 'But it is not good! They are too scared! Please, go to them and share stories, Mr Husband.'

Sure enough, when I walked into the Ibis conference room

the next morning, hundreds of job applicants—men and women, young and old—were shuffling nervously from foot to foot as if an arctic wind had found them. There were no prerequisites for most of the zoo positions we were offering, so the jobs were open to anyone to apply, and that meant that for these applicants, too much was at stake. I saw the desperation in their faces—it was very raw. The stink of fear was all over the room, in the sweat clogging up second-hand suits and synthetic church dresses. Their hope quivered inside them like blown-up balloons. Too much hoped for and too much empty inside. These people were underdogs, and my heart opened to them all.

Warmly and sincerely, I said to the group, 'You've got to really sell yourself. If it were up to me I'd hire all of you, but I've got two other people here who are Emiratis, so you really have to sell yourself hard. We have a quota we have to meet from Kenya. I wish you could all get a job but only the best will get them!'

The next morning, they came in for their interviews filled with personal stories, smiles beaming and laughter booming. I loved that they were able to let loose. Many of the Kenyan women who turned up were single mums with one or two kids, often from some of the poorest neighbourhoods in Nairobi. They were there to make life better for their kids. One of the women I hired used the expression 'Stop the circle', meaning once her kids had access to better education, the circle of poverty and hardship would stop. Being in a position to help her make that happen gave me a profound sense of purpose.

On the last day of the interviews, a woman came in wearing army greens. She was tall and thickly built. No nonsense. She sat down and slammed her file on the table in front of her. It was a thick file full of photographs and documents. Then she leant back in the chair, hands behind her head, legs sprawling, and just waited for us to talk.

I opened the file and looked through the first few pages. 'You were a ranger on rhino patrols in Kenya! Wow! That's pretty hard-core. Did you have any specific conflict experiences?'

She looked at me as if I was a kid in primary school. 'Yes. I was a patroller. I often had times where poachers were shooting at us.'

'What did you do?'

She pulled her file from my hands, flipped through some pages, then spun the file back around and dumped it in front of me. There was a close-up of a dead guy with a bullet hole between his eyes. 'I shot them in the head.'

'Mmmm, so you did.'

I leant over to my colleagues and whispered, 'I really like this woman, I'm going to hire her, but I'm not sure if it's because she clearly has the balls to be able to do any job I offer her or because I'm too scared not to hire her!'

We then flew to Manila where we had two days of interviews before moving on to Kuala Lumpur. We were picking at least a hundred staff from those countries. Given the success of the interviews in Kenya, I went out and gave 'my talk' to all the other groups. I think it helped the groups of hopeful applicants.

After a month spent interviewing in various countries, we returned to Dubai for a week to collect a shipload of rusa deer. A Nigerian woman walked into my office one morning. She was tall and broad—she would have been taller than most of the men I had interviewed. She had an expression like someone who had just started a twelve-hour shift at the most boring job they'd ever had. I summed her up as humourless but tough. Life had obviously knocked her around, but I reckoned she gave as good as she got. I'll call her Nelly.

I asked Nelly, 'What's your background?'

'I've got a degree in marketing. At the moment I'm just a labourer, but the fucking employer doesn't pay us.'

Blunt and clear, a straight shooter. I liked that.

She felt comfortable enough to continue: 'I hate my fucking job. I just want a new start. I've got my daughter back home and I wanna give her a decent education.'

I knew exactly where I wanted to put her. 'Actually, I'm looking for someone who can oversee the office management in the vet hospital.' After Denpasar, I had become suspicious of supposed exotic animal vets, and I knew I needed to keep a close eye on them. Nelly would be perfect for overseeing the vet department.

She looked through the job description. 'I can fucking do this!'

'I'm sure you fucking can!'

She was brilliant—so much so that I would later put her on as the manager of the vet hospital. She didn't take any shit. She was able to knuckle down and get everyone organised. The Emiratis didn't like her, though. If people were doing the wrong thing, she told them exactly how she saw things, way too many times.

A couple of months after Nelly had started work at the park, one of the vets came to my office. 'Sir, I would like to speak.'

'Yes?' I knew this particular guy. He was always finding excuses to not do something.

'You must relieve our manager of office. Put her in a different position.'

'Why?'

'I find her chest and bottom very distracting in the office. They are both too big.'

'Well, here's an idea: stop talking to her chest and start talking to her face. That's where all the really big things come from. Like her good ideas. And none of us can afford to be distracted by those. Now go back to work.'

———

After a couple of months of travelling, we had filled our quota and employed 500 people from across the world. They all came with different levels of experience, some with very little, and I had a unique view of how adaptable, or not, various cultures were in this very unusual employment setting. Luckily, I was able to bring in some people with substantial training. I was particularly happy to secure the employment of a lion keeper who'd worked in Rotorua. She had gained a strong international reputation as a great professional. Her name was Susie Jansen. When I watched Susie work, I was able to observe all the markers of a great keeper. She had an acute attention to detail—she knew she had to clean the walls as well as the floors of the lion dens to cut down aggression. She had an unwavering respect for the lions and by treating them with dignity there was connection between her and the pride. She also made a striking manager as she was able to insist on these standards for the lion keepers who worked under her.

By my third year, most of the staff had settled into their different positions. This gave me time to work through some of the recycling approaches that Wendy and I had become known for in other animal parks. Keeping the Dubai Safari Park's carbon footprint as light as possible was very important to us. We had created sustainability and recycling loops in Indonesia and Cairns, and we were determined to create them here.

'Whatever you have left over, reimagine it and put it back into the pot. Think in circles, Timmy.' Wendy's motto for composting always showed up for me when I thought through how to run the budget of a zoo or a park.

Wendy and I developed a complex recycling system where we could collect waste from the animals and then reuse it as compost, thereby creating what we called 'sweet soil'. We imported an industrial-capacity compost machine from Germany, which could cook all the animal waste, both food waste and hay. After 40 hours of cooking, it would produce a potting mix, which could be used in the park's landscaping. It was an innovative way of balancing out the heavy composition of animal waste and sand at the park, thereby creating soil fertile enough to provide for the many horticultural needs for the animal exhibits and tourist areas. We also installed hundreds of solar panels on the roofs of the undercover parking lots, which had a collective capacity of 10,000 cars, and they ran energy back into the park for all the pumps and filtration systems.

The backlash against these ideas could be intense among a few of the office staff. The main problem, as I saw it, was the perception that we were awash with money, so why worry about sustainability? This created endless roadblocks among the staff, and it stalled any creative thinking, particularly when it came to making decisions that were good for the environment.

A case in point was when a shipment of three hippos arrived. The animals proceeded to boil in the ever-increasing temperatures of the transportation pool. But rather than ordering ice from our own newly acquired industrial ice-making machine, one of the staff decided to order it from a Dubai petrol station. Five truck loads of five-kilogram ice bags arrived, having been transported from ten kilometres away. The environmental waste due to the plastic alone was staggering.

When I found this out, I was seriously pissed off at the staff member. 'Why did you buy ice? Did you forget the recipe?'

Aki interjected: 'Breathe deeply, Mr Tim, breathe deeply.'

I continued: 'We need to make what we can, when we can. We don't just spend money because you think we have money.'

It occurred to me that money had great power to stem innovative thinking. And then I remembered Len, the Keeper of the Geese, once telling me that 'Necessity is the mother of invention'. At the time I had no idea what he was talking about. Now I reckoned that 'necessity' was exactly what we were lacking at the park.

20

Storm brewing

My battle with the administrator was evolving. It was like a metastasising storm cell that had begun life as relatively benign. At first, not too many of our confrontations rattled me. Not enough to interfere with my day-to-day work, anyway. However, a few white and slightly bruised puffy clouds on this particular work horizon quickly grew into an extreme weather event. I was becoming increasingly concerned by what I perceived were unempathetic decisions they were making regarding the staff.

A few occasions stood out in particular. One was when a group of male workers came to complain about not only being housed next to Dubai's sewage-treatment station, which resulted in their clothes always smelling bad, but also that there was nowhere to keep their clothes in their rooms. The men said they were too embarrassed to go to their religious ceremonies on Sundays. These concerns were dismissed by the administrator as trivial and the men were reported as troublemakers. Another was when a female guide reported that she had been molested, but the administrator didn't believe her as they deemed that the perpetrator was a 'good Muslim' and therefore incapable of committing such an offence.

But perhaps one of the most brazen provocations from this particular Emirate employee occurred one afternoon when they secured one of the park's trams in order to take a few visiting diplomats, who they were keen to impress, for a tour around the park. Instead of letting the visitors take the normal Dubai Safari Tour with one of the park's guides, they decided to direct the tour, insisting the driver follow all their instructions. When the tram was crossing an open stretch of grassland within the cheetah exhibit, the driver was ordered to stop. The administrator then insisted the doors of the tram be opened so the group of diplomats could step out and take a walk. Five VIPs, heavily clad in thick white cotton tunics and stork-walking through dense seagrass, were spotted by our head carnivore keeper, who was working nearby. Unknown to the VIPs, stalking them in long grass less than 50 metres away were three cheetahs. It took quick thinking by the head keeper to avert disaster. He drove his jeep at over 100 kilometres an hour, picking up some airtime to cross a sand gully, in order to cut the cheetahs off.

I immediately confronted the administrator: 'You could have killed those people with your careless actions! You know nothing about the behaviours of these wild animals. If you want to take people around the park, you come through me and you observe the protocol of the park. This is my jurisdiction: the animals, the park grounds. MY patch. You need to run it by me first.'

We sparred like silverbacks that afternoon.

Storm brewing

Despite these confrontations, I continued to enjoy being at the helm of this vast UAE project. With Essa and Aki beside me, I oversaw the extraordinary development of one of the world's largest animal parks. One of the most profound feelings I experienced was the satisfaction of knowing that many of the international workers, who we had recruited from the poorest curves of the globe, had managed to not only get a foothold for themselves through their jobs at the zoo, but also were able to send money home in order to support their families. The knock-on effects of these jobs were like a million ripples reverberating and expanding from a single pebble dropped in water. But the connections I continued to enjoy more than any other were those the keepers had with their animals. Regardless of nationality, once the keepers learned the skills of animal care and opened themselves up to treating animals with greater dignity and compassion, I saw the way these deeply powerful connections took hold of them. Many of them developed an interest in wildlife conservation, and I loved seeing them try to find ways to be more involved with conservation projects. The joy of witnessing these connections filled me up the way watching the lemurs come to life at Stagland had.

Wendy and Jordan stayed with me in Dubai for a couple of years, spending part of that time travelling around Eastern Europe working as WWOOFers on various farms. The WWOOF program, an acronym meaning Willing Workers On Organic Farms, is an international volunteer program that offers work in exchange for food and board. Wendy saw it as a terrific way of learning about different methods of organic farming, as she was intent on plying herself with as much knowledge as possible to take back to the farm in New South Wales. Jordan and Wendy would return to Dubai 'between volunteering jobs' and then shoot off when another adventure presented itself, maybe in the highlands of Georgia crushing grapes by foot in wineries, or working on garlic farms in Hungary.

But by our fourth year in Dubai, Jordan had decided he wanted to get his teeth into some study to become a paramedic, so he and Wendy both returned to our farm. There, Jordan researched and applied for various courses, while Wendy began adopting all the new knowledge she'd gathered.

———

Nearly five years after my arrival in the UAE, Dubai Safari Park was finally ready to open. But before admitting all visitors, we held an opening day just for the locals. When the municipality assigned the date, I knew we were not going to be finished in time and insisted that we delay the event until we were completely ready, but the municipality decided to push ahead. The aftermath was confronting for me. In one day, 23,000 people came through the park. Fragile landscaped areas were compromised. There weren't enough staff for tourist services, nor nearly enough facilities to cater to the thousands of people who came through. And the interactive exhibits, where animals were involved, had not had enough time to adapt to such enormous numbers of people, so the animals were stressed. It was difficult to go through, particularly because I felt that if we'd had a bit more time, we could have avoided some of the more destructive elements of the day. But in another way, I was grateful. The day itself revealed some of the problems in the operational flow of the park, and this gave me the chance to correct them.

The municipality was sympathetic to the challenges that had been presented, and gave me the time and budget I needed to make repairs and prepare for the official international opening.

When the official opening finally happened, in December 2017, it was very well received by the international press and deemed a great success by the municipality. The reviews were good, but mostly all I felt was exhaustion and I retreated in a way that was new for me. I stayed in my office the day of the opening with my door locked and drank mint tea. Thoughts and reflections clamoured over themselves in an effort to get my attention. I had spent the last five years living out the dreams of fourteen-year-old Tim. I had built and created one of the world's largest animal parks, one that had animal enrichment and conservation at its core. And that was such a big achievement that I struggled to really digest the nature of it. It did, for sure, give me a sense of pride. Great pride. But it had come at a cost. It had required a lot of fight and resilience. Not a Tom type of fight but a different type of fight. A fight that required me to step up for the things I valued—for the animals and their keepers. It was as close to an understanding of fighting for 'truth' or 'justice' as I was ever going to get.

It occurred to me that night that anything of any worth on the human side of the fence necessarily involves a struggle. And the animals that gave me my first sense of family were indeed worth fighting for. I'd learnt from one of our keepers that Buddhists talked about approaching life with a strong back and a soft front. I interpreted that as having the courage to stand up for what matters to you, while never losing your compassion. I reckoned I was trying to fit somewhere into that mix.

In my fifth year in Dubai, an unopened letter sat sparkling

in my in-tray. I knew it was official because of the embossed gold writing and the seal on the back, and I'd also been around the UAE long enough to know a gold seal on a letter was either a very good sign or an ominous one. I nervously opened it. The letter came from the office of the prince of Saudi Arabia and invited me to be at the helm of a similar project in the Kingdom of Saudi Arabia—a project ten times the size of that in Dubai, with a considerable increase in remuneration. It finished with a touching paragraph that read something like, 'We will give you time to consider, but please know this: we would consider it a great honour should you choose to accept our offer.'

I folded the letter very carefully and put it back in the envelope. *Breathe, breathe deeply, Tim.*

That evening after work, I went home and poured myself an (illegal) bourbon and reflected on the last five years. The nightly cacophony of animal noise had begun, the same as the sounds of bedtime at Stagland in my caravan. The towering steel structures of the new aviaries now obscured the sinking of the sun beyond the sand dunes, the sight that had so mesmerised me in the early years. Everything was changing, and so was I. I had a last swig of bourbon and rang Wendy. We went through all our options.

The next morning I went to the office of the director general of the municipality and gave him my resignation. He was very surprised. 'We thought you would be with us for life, Tim. Why?'

'It's time for me to move on. You know, Essa once told me something your great prophet once said and I think it really resonated with me. "Be in this world as though you are a stranger or a traveller along a path." I am ready to move along that path. Besides, we've built a great park together!'

270

The director general, the head of security and another official all stared at each other, then at me, and for a moment a memory interrupted my thought train. In it, three Jehovah's Elders screamed at me about truth telling, busting their arteries to condemn me to some sort of living purgatory. And here I was now, talking to these three elders of Dubai and telling my own truth to them. My integrity was completely intact, and this time I knew it. It was a perfect recasting of a horrible scene from my childhood.

One of them finally said, 'Could we ask one thing of you before you leave us?'

'Of course.'

'Could you write a review of each of the park's employees, across all levels, from cleaners to managers, and give us an honest assessment of their positions.'

'Of course.'

Over the next few days I completed a review of each employee. I was careful not to use anyone's name, only ever referring to their positions—for the purposes of political sensitivity. My reviews were informed by how an employee's professionalism, or lack of it, might affect not only the smooth running of the zoo but also the animals' welfare. I also noted the potential effects on the welfare of the myriad other people who cared for the animals. All part of the cornerstone of my ideas of best operational practice.

While I was finishing up my packing, I was called to the local police station. I thought it was a matter of tying up financial accounts and wasn't particularly troubled. However, when I arrived at the station and found the administrator and their lawyer in the waiting room, I realised something more sinister was afoot. The Emirate employee had reported a crime, with me as the criminal. Apparently, they hoped I would be jailed for 'Unlawfully questioning Emirati professionalism'. Neither of us made eye contact as we were ushered into a meeting room. Dubai's chief of police eventually joined us and, without sitting down, he announced that the case had been dismissed. He had read the accompanying papers, which had confirmed that the municipality had asked for the staff assessments to be completed as part of my resignation requirements.

I offered my adversary a loaded goodbye. We were both fighters, I knew that, but I think I had learnt how to pick my battles.

21

Damned, again

I'd returned to Australia, but in my head I was already in Saudi Arabia. My grid books laid out the sketches for my and Wendy's next adventurous project in the desert, filled with drawn-up plans of all the primary and secondary buildings. Holding facilities would be needed, as would staff accommodation, vet hospitals, exhibit design, aquariums and aviaries. The list was endless. Excitingly, because of its size, the Riyadh safari park would have a considerably higher budget than the one in Dubai, so I would have many more opportunities to explore animal collections and environment-enrichment ideas. Just as in Dubai, I was interested in creating larger exhibits that mimicked how animals lived in the wild. Educating people on how animals connected and worked mutualistically within their wild habitats remained as important to me as showcasing their existence as individual species. I couldn't wait to get started. We both couldn't wait to get started. While we were in Australia the Saudi group had also invited Wendy to work on a desert rejuvenation project they had underway.

Our neighbours and good friends, Rob and Deb Kane, would oversee our farm until we could sort out new tenants for the five years we would be away. There were a few minor repairs to do in the house, and some of the fencing on the farm needed attention. But I had trouble concentrating on that, as the Saudi project continued seeding ideas in my brain like a fish laying eggs. Hundreds of them. Endless ideas on what was possible. And what was impossible. I wrote those down too because I had learnt from experience that most things were entirely doable once you actually had a go and worked out the way to do it. As Walt Disney famously said, 'It's kind of fun to do the impossible.'

On 3 March 2020, Wendy and I boarded a plane to Saudi Arabia from Sydney, with our only stop to be in Abu Dhabi, UAE. While we were waiting there to board our flight to Riyadh, I was pulled aside by the UAE Criminal Investigations Department— the CID. One of its officers said to me, 'Mr Husband, there's a case filed against you in the UAE so you cannot board this plane.'

Two heavily built men stood behind me while another cuffed my wrists. I had a sneaking suspicion my friend the tenacious administrator was behind this, but given what had happened at the Dubai police station, I wasn't too alarmed. I was, however, seriously pissed off. I suggested to Wendy that she keep going, telling her not to worry, that I'd been through this before. I knew this person's handiwork and I knew from my last run-in with the law that it didn't hold much water. The next flight to Riyadh was in four hours time and I was certain I'd be on it.

Wendy was anxious, however. She'd sometimes reminded me during our time in Dubai of the Greek myth of Icarus, which often woke her at night. Icarus was a boy who, forgetting he had wings made of wax, overreached his own limits by flying too close to the sun. She was often anxious about how close I flew to the sun when interacting with the UAE political process, fearing that one day I would be burnt. She would say to me, 'These people have their own ways of doing things, Tim. You are playing with fire.'

More often than not, I'd reply: 'That doesn't necessarily make it right if the animals and their keepers have to cop it, and they ARE always the ones that have to cop it.'

It was two in the morning, and I was taken to a holding facility in the airport. A grey air-conditioned room with a few chairs and very little else. I sat waiting patiently for several hours, reworking some of the drawings for the Saudi Arabia park on my phone. But as more hours ticked by and I knew that I'd missed at least two flights, I became worried. I rang the Australian consulate to tell them what was happening, and they took down all the details of my story. I now had only ten per cent battery life in my phone. Eight hours after being arrested, my phone was dead, and I was really feeling the heat of this unknown and unlawful detention. I had been left in this grey box with no food and nothing to drink and no clue as to why I'd been detained.

My isolation continued throughout the following day and into that night. Whenever an official of any sort, even a cleaner, went by, I would rush up to the window and shout, 'What am I here for? How long am I going to be here for?' But no one said anything to me. My head began telling stories that took strange turns. Tom rose like a phoenix in my mind, and I was actually relieved for his company. I knew the signs of panic and agitation as my leg started to tic nervously and my thoughts wouldn't stop. Wendy would be in Saudi Arabia by now. There was no Wendy here, no Aki here, there was no 'Breathe deeply, breathe deeply'. I channelled all my thoughts to Wendy anyway and this managed to soothe my agitated mind for a few hours, but as the second night came down and still I'd had nothing to drink or eat, nowhere to go to the toilet, and had not been contacted in any way, I began to feel like a new hell on earth was about to swallow me whole.

Finally, late that second evening, a couple of security guards unlocked the door. Words fell out of my mouth already shredded: 'Who . . . why . . . water . . . what the fuck!' Still not a word back. No answers. I was bundled into a van and taken to an industrial block of a building fenced in wire mesh and guarded by soldiers with guns. Lots of them. I knew it was a prison. I was taken inside in handcuffs.

'Why am I here? Please just tell me why?'

They stripped me of my watch, my belt, my glasses, phone and wallet, and I was led to a cell. I smelt it before I saw it. The acidic smell of animal piss and sweat was something I knew only too well from cleaning out night dens for animals for the best part of my life, but the acrid stink of human body odour mixed in with their shit and piss was a special new hell for me. The cell was less than fifteen metres long and about five metres wide. It was dark inside when they pushed me in. Immediately, I became aware of eyes that bore into me from the shadows. Later, I learnt that there were sixteen other guys in there, but that night all I was aware of was a haunting shuffling of feet. All I was given when I entered the cell was a five-centimetre-thick foam mattress. It stank and it was stained with every imaginable body fluid, as were the two blankets that were thrown at me before the cell door was locked.

I grabbed at the bars and yelled, 'Just tell me why I'm here!'

Nothing, no answers. I did, however, get an orange and a cup of lukewarm tea that, after two days of no food or drink, soothed my parched, cortisol-dried mouth. Then I found a spot against a wall and drifted off to sleep.

It was a few hours later when I woke, sensing someone closing in on me. I opened my eyes to see one of the other prisoners leaning over me like a scavenger over a carcass. He was a hyena's breath away from my face and he stank. His eyes were glucy, and I caught glints of yellow in them. He was holding my Blundstone boots in his hand. Adrenalin tore through me and Tom took over. Tom, my fighter, my friend, all the broken pieces of me in full flare. I swung out at the thief, who moved back, so my punch hit him in the neck. He went down screaming like a wounded goat.

'What the fuck do you think you're doing? Where do you think you're fucken gonna go with those? We're all in this fucken jail together!'

He dropped the boots. Everyone was awake now. I turned to look at the shadowy ghostly figures in the cell, still shuffling from foot to foot. I yelled at all of them, 'Now fucken leave me alone!'

My shoulder had come out of its socket and hurt like hell. I lay down with my arm stretched out, knowing I'd dislocated it; the other arm had my boots tucked tightly under it. After some manoeuvring and an incredible amount of pain, I was able to pull the shoulder back into its socket. It had happened before, in my rodeo days, so I knew I was in for a couple of days of intense pain as my shoulder began to repair itself.

Next morning, when the lights went on in the cell, I discovered there were no windows in this Abu Dhabi dungeon, so I had no way of being able to tell what time of day it was. Walking around, I also saw there were no toilets or toilet paper, just two holes in the ground, and beside each a small jug with a tap beside it. I guess that was for washing your arse. There was a shower. But no sink, no towels, no soap, nothing else. The smell of shit and BO only got more intense.

Every day, the guards would do a roll call, but instead of my name, they just called out, 'Ostralie? Ostralie?'

I'd go up to the bars and shout, 'Do you know why I'm here? Why am I here?!' Same thing every day. Still no reply. A few days into my incarceration, the only communication I'd had was with a teenage Pakistani boy in the cell.

'Why are you here?' I asked him.

'Not sure, something like I'm a robber. Not me. You?'

'Same. Not the stealing bit. Just that I shouldn't be here. My wife is in Saudi Arabia. She won't know where I am.'

'I leave tomorrow. I call her for you?'

'You'd do that?'

His courage and selflessness completely overwhelmed me and I felt hot fat tears well up in my eyes. Wasn't gonna let those break in here, though. 'Thank you, thank you, my friend.'

An old scrunched-up receipt appeared from his back pocket. I scrawled Wendy's number on it with my finger, using the fish fat from the gluey soup scum at the bottom of my cup. 'Let her know I'm okay and to contact the Australian embassy. Thank you my friend, thank you.'

Next day, my Pakistani mate left the prison.

Damned, again

That first week was long. Longer than anything I'd experienced in the caravan. The Saudi Arabia safari park had retreated from my thoughts. I just lay on my stained mattress for most of the time—some of my own stains were on there now. Tom was talking endless shit to me about the difficult administrator. Ranting. About how it had to be them. Tom had saved me once already from the boot thief, and just then I was more than happy for his company. But the black sky, in the stink and the rank rot of this prison cell, opened cavernously inside me, and I fell into its void without a fight.

In the second week, a vast loneliness bloomed and ached inside me. It felt irreconcilable and brutal. It felt like I was hurting for the vulnerability of the human spirit itself. At some point in this soup of day–night time that drew up ghouls from all of the saddest parts of me, I knew one thing for sure: the human side of the fence was the more dangerous side. It seemed our potential to hurt one another had no boundaries. Our voracious desire to protect power at all costs made us, as a species, our own worst enemies.

I missed Wendy. It physically hurt me. My guts were ripped through and it hurt when I pressed them. But Wendy was there with me enough to help me to sleep for an hour or two at a time.

One day someone from the Australian embassy came to the cell. She must've been in her early twenties. 'Do you know why you're here?'

I shuffled forward. 'No. Do *you*?'

'What do you want us to do?'

'Your job.'

I returned to the back of the box, back in the shadows with the rest of the vacant-eyed mob. This was all protocol. I knew ticking boxes when I saw it.

By the tenth day, actually the twelfth day if you count the two days spent in the airport waiting room, I was shrinking from my own stink. I was in the same clothes, no washing, no shaving, no brushing teeth. The only food I got was offered a couple of times a day: a bit of rice and a sliver of chicken or some fish soup, one orange, and a polystyrene cup of warm tea.

Then, one day, a guard called out, 'Ostralie! Ostralie! Time to go.'

I was put inside a van, where the light hurt my eyes so intensely that I kept them closed for most of the drive. I was comprehensively numb as I was delivered into a courtroom. The judge who was overseeing the proceedings read out the charge: 'Someone from the Dubai municipality has apparently insisted that Mr Timothy Husband needs to be incriminated for insulting a member of the government circles.'

So it was, indeed, the administrator's work.

As the statement was read out to the room, just as in the police station, it sounded like it had been taken from some disagreement in a school playground. And the outcome followed exactly the same trajectory as before. Astonished that revenge could have effected such astounding levels of destruction, the judge looked directly at me. Using a tone heavy with apology, he said, 'I'm humbly sorry, Mr Husband. I have read all the documents pertaining to your case. This is not a case at all. On behalf of Dubai and on behalf of the people of UAE, I offer you our apologies. We will make a complaint about this person. Go back to Abu Dhabi. Get your things and go.'

With the larrikin in me flattened like road kill, I couldn't even dredge up an acknowledgement of the official apology, even though I did feel the relief. Staring at the empathetic judge, it appeared to me that we seemed to understand each other in that moment, and our tacit agreement was that, yes indeed, life was shit.

I took a taxi back to Abu Dhabi and retrieved my passport and my phone, which had been damaged. I then collected my suitcases, and booked myself into the hotel at the airport so I could have a shower and a proper rest. Then spent some hours having a good cry before ringing Wendy.

'Tim? Oh my God, Tim! Is that you?'

'Yup.' I hardly recognised my own voice, it was so small and shredded.

'Ahhh Timmy, very hard for you, love . . .'

We didn't say much else, just sat in the immense relief of having the other person still alive at the end of the line.

———

The next day, I tried to book a ticket to Riyadh. This was the moment I realised the true extent of the COVID-19 pandemic. Saudi Arabia had just closed its borders, and so had Australia. I booked a flight for a week later—surely something would shift within a week. In the meantime, a fully decked-out room in an airport hotel chain was complete luxury for me, and I spent a lot of time asleep. There was only one place to get food in Abu Dhabi because of the pandemic, and it happened to be the airport McDonald's. I had fish burgers and fries for a whole week. It was heaven.

I talked to Wendy every day on the phone. She said she'd read in the press that it might be as long as two weeks before the pandemic alarm would be over, and then we could get on with our lives. The Saudi Arabian team, she thought, should then be able to get the restrictions lifted for me so I could enter their country and get the project started.

Two weeks dragged into a month. One month into five. I'd added chicken nuggets to the fish burgers and fries menu that I'd consumed every day for nearly half a year. Strange how the luxurious hotel room turned into another cell for the living dead in the space of just a couple of weeks. My takeaway food similarly became a rote meal that I forced myself to eat just to keep myself alive. On top of this, because I was in Abu Dhabi without a visa, I had to go through a police check twice a day, so they could verify I hadn't tried to escape. Every single day, without fail, they knocked on my door dressed in full hazmat gear.

The staff of Dubai Safari Park had heard what had happened to me, and many of them reached out to me through emails. Some of the Kenyan contingent said they would put some money together to help me get home, but I told them to save that money. I told them they were supposed to be sending that money home to their families.

My link to life at home in Australia was my good friend Rob Kane, with whom I'd talk once a week. But as the months passed, I spoke less and less. My black sky had filled me in completely. More and more, it sounded to me like Rob was speaking to me from behind glass or in water. Later, he told me he felt it was like trying to save someone from drowning. Rob also guessed my shoulder wasn't repairing itself the way it should. And so, in every phone call, he kept pushing for me to come back to Australia, suggesting I come and live with him and Deb until I recovered. He thought I needed to live with close friends for a while, people who could take care of me. But

I wasn't ready to let the idea of Saudi Arabia go. I later learnt that the Saudi officials were doing all they could to try to get me out, but because of all the pandemic chaos, with borders closing and airlines shutting down, there was little they could do. Along with many others, I was caught in the crosshairs of all the confusion.

Finally, in July 2020, I was ready to take a flight out of the UAE back to Australia. My departure felt like a scene from *Midnight Express*, only it was my mental health that I wrapped inside me instead of cocaine. Once in my seat on the plane, I swaddled my arms around my body, as though I wore a straitjacket. I rocked my body backwards and forwards, and waited an interminably long hour for the plane to finally start moving on the tarmac. With my eyes closed and my guts still terrorised by the idea that I would be swooped on by another situation I never saw coming, I held my breath—until I felt the glorious thud of the jet's wheels tucking in under its belly as it swept up into the sky. I finally let out the breath that had been trapped and undecided in my throat since I'd boarded the plane. I opened my eyes and looked out to the blue sky outside my window. Salty tears found their way to my lips and I realised I'd been crying. My cheeks were completely sodden as I watched the United Arab Emirates slowly recede as we climbed into the clouds.

All those years ago, when I'd looked out from the lemur exhibit at the passing tourists at Stagland, I'd intuitively understood that human behaviours were far more complex, chaotic and dangerous than those of most of the animals I took care of. Now, as my plane climbed higher and higher, I felt that a big part of me was still on the wrong side of the fence.

22

Home

When I arrived in Australia, it seemed the officials knew something of my story. They showed me a lot of concern and compassion. 'We are so sorry that you have to quarantine for two weeks, Mr Husband. AGAIN!' said one of them.

I was just well enough to find my sense of humour: 'Just two weeks? Easy!'

I was soon diagnosed with PTSD by Dr S, who I'd started seeing again. Together, we worked hard to put everything that had happened in Abu Dhabi behind me. It was particularly difficult for me not to ruminate on the havoc the Emirate employee had subjected me to. Not only was I traumatised by my stint in jail, but given the unpredictability of the pandemic and all the closed borders, it looked like I'd lost the opportunity to get the Saudi Arabian project underway.

We also worked hard to settle Tom. I knew Tom had done his job because I needed no more reminding about how unjust the last year had been. But I also knew that whoever Tom was, whether my twin, a maniacal echo of my stepfather's voice, or my 'supposed' treasured protector, he didn't have the destructive power he'd once had. I was also finally learning, the hard way, just how little control over outside events I actually had. With time, I was getting better at understanding that when Tom and I sat together in my head, shared mint tea, had the odd laugh, looked after each other when we fell, we managed life a lot better.

My first few months at home, after emerging from quarantine, were spent recovering with Rob and Deb. Wendy had a few months to go with her contract in Saudi Arabia, although she was trying to get home earlier. She was making lots of progress with permaculture groups on a program called Greening the Desert. Every night on the phone, she would talk excitedly to me about what an untapped resource desert plants were. 'We need to learn, Tim. Because of climate change, we all need to know more about being sustainable in desert environments. Deserts are not stark, they're so rich with potential and possibility. We just have to learn how to be in them.'

Jordan was living in a town to the north of the farm, with an old friend from school, and working as a volunteer for a refugee centre and at an arts collective. He came to see me at the Kanes' place once a week. We took walks, he talked about his little apartment, his work. Making a living seemed to be little more than a minor intrusion on how he wanted to spend his time. He did tell me that he was going back to study later in the year, but that his thinking had changed.

'What happened to the paramedic idea?'

'Not for me Dad, it's too intense. I'm thinking about

becoming a fireman. Good hours I think, and I can keep my volunteer jobs going.'

'Okay. Why a firey, then?'

'I don't know. There's an adrenalin rush. And you get to help people, you get to save lives. I like that.'

'And I like that you like that. You're more like your old man than you could ever have imagined, hey!'

We had a chuckle and a hug.

The Kanes were very careful to give me the space I needed to recover. Rob took me everywhere on the farm with him in his ute, along with Beanie, his border collie. I helped him with sheep work and with the bush domes he and Deb were building for a bushwalking retreat. I needed both the physical work and the silence. And the slow toxicity of the half-lives of McDonald's burgers was slowly soaked up by Rob's delicious bush cooking. For four months, it was all venison curries, slow-cooked casseroles, homemade sourdough bread and drinking home-brew beers after a long hot day of work.

Deb, as an artist, spent her time painting and writing, only connecting with me when she intuited that I wanted or needed to talk. It was everything and all I needed. I was grateful for the distance she gave me and sensed that perhaps she had some understanding of the nature of trauma. So much so that I was able to share parts of my story with her when she'd take breaks from her work and join me for a cuppa. That was when I recognised that I could trust Deb with my story, and then I asked if she would be interested in writing my whole life story for me. That was how this book came to be.

One Saturday morning, I went into the local store to pick up a weekend newspaper. The owner had *The Australian* spread out on the counter behind her. It was open to the story of an Australian zoo director in Dubai who had been, according to the headline, 'Treated Like an Animal'. The irony that my life's work was about getting better treatment for captive animals all over the world wasn't lost on me.

There was a picture of me on the opposite page with a galah sitting on my arm. 'Is that you?' said the store owner.

'Afraid so . . .'

'Wow, that's a crazy story. Amazing you got through it! Incredible.'

As I handed her a five-dollar bill to pay for the newspaper, she said, 'We never get celebrities coming through this store!'

———

Tup was a seven-week-old black-and-white border collie pup I'd bought once I'd decided I was strong enough to go home to our property. He slept on the passenger seat of my old ute as I drove to the farm, curled around himself like a little black-and-white bagel. He was very young, but he had an intelligence in his eyes older than many animals I had cared for. Our connection was, at once, warm, loving and nurturing. For him as much as for me. Over the four months before Wendy came home from Saudi Arabia, Tup and I spent every day exploring the hills and rivers around the farm. Tup was never far from me. When I slept, he was there curled up on my bed, and when I walked, he jogged along beside me. He was a little bouncing ball of puppy, and every time I looked at him I smiled.

I'd also found a juvenile galah that had been left behind in some tussock after a lightning strike had taken the rest of its siblings along with the tree. I took it home and fed it parrot milk, which is a milk substitute I'd bought in a local pet store that imitates what a mother bird would regurgitate when feeding her young. I called the bird Lady Gagulah. A couple of months after that, I found two magpie chicks at the side of the road. What was left of their parents was two bloodied feathered blobs that had been squashed into the middle of the road. I took them home too and fed them some crushed-up worms and a little bit of mince.

I now felt as close to a sense of home as I'd ever come, like when I lay on the riverbank with my possum as a child. Every morning we would all walk to the river . . . well, I walked, Tup bounced, the magpie chicks would hover above us, and curious Lady Gagulah would explore the sky in ever-expanding circles of flight. In the evenings, in my old armchair on the front verandah, we would watch the sunset together, Lady Gagulah teetering safely on my shoulder, the two magpie chicks perched on my boot, and Tup lying at my feet, all of us witness to the changing of the light, all of us just waiting for Wendy to come home.

Afterword

Let there be light

Whichever side of the fence I have been on, either with wild animals or with human animals, I've worked hard to learn what it takes to belong. And I have learnt much, particularly from the many people in my life who have accepted me without judgement, despite all my brain bullies, my gut ghouls and my crazy mood swings. But what I have found most meaningful in the world is what I have learnt from the animals whose company I have taken refuge in since I was a child. In particular, the lemurs, whose companionship I sought when I was at my most vulnerable. Animals were the first to accept me as one of their own, and from that space of belonging, over many years, I have witnessed the many sophisticated ways in which various species live in and organise their environments.

The compass animals use to navigate their worlds is intricately connected to the earth's biorhythms, to its ecological health and its ability to regenerate, and, unlike humans, other animals do not seem able to exploit the myriad systems that sustain them. A female kangaroo will hold an embryo in stasis if she senses the coming season will not provide enough resources for her young. Elephants move on from a grazed area when they know the plant life needs time to regenerate. Baby turtles produce and respond to sounds of other unhatched turtles to coordinate the timing of their birth from inside their eggs on a beach, and by doing so they give the entire clutch the best possible chance to reach the water once hatched.

Extraordinarily, animals appear to only ever behave selfishly if their natural environment is out of balance, which generally tends to be because of human activity. My favourite example, probably because of my love of the underdog, is the dung beetle. Dung beetles become disoriented when navigating landscapes if light pollution from human habitation prevents them from seeing the stars. It hardly seems fair to me that the tiny creatures doing all the shit jobs to keep everyone's ecosystem healthy, all the jobs that go unnoticed, are not allowed their celestial compass—their view of the stars.

Humans as a species, by contrast, seem to live their lives apart from the ecological environments that sustain them. We are a devastatingly invasive species that has destroyed countless of the earth's vast ecologies, and has the unique ability to destroy its own kind. As if that isn't frightening enough, we are a species singularly consumed with our own trajectory, tirelessly congratulating ourselves on our own success.

To me, it's the same as preaching phoney stories at flyscreen doors. It's still dogma. It's following the phone lines again. The human species is like the alpha kid in the playground, the loudmouth with lots of sycophantic mates. Like Nathan Barrett, we are so busy with our own self-promotion that we don't bother to listen to all the quieter conversations, the often more interesting and sophisticated stories that bubble away at the edges. Like Wendy's stories, her hidden worlds. Her exploration of nature's complex cooperative fungal networks and microbial symbiosis is a quiet side story whose only mark on the world is a strong line of fruit trees or a lush crop of brassicas. Quiet, unassuming, connected.

I believe the natural world is a lot more interconnected than we could possibly imagine, and that should we, as a species, find the humility to look for meaning sideways, then we might find a new sense of belonging that isn't solely measured by status, religion, wealth or nation—or any of their various combinations—but is, first and foremost, a connection with the earth and all its inhabitants.

My advocacy for both animal welfare and conservation has often come under attack. Len, the Keeper of the Geese, told me that perhaps the best we can ever do is give animals the best life possible while here on earth, to make life on earth their Kingdom of Heaven. But although all the keepers I have worked with have learnt to treat animals with dignity and respect, as though they were part of their own family, we were all still pawns in a bigger power play. The 'Kingdom of Heaven here on earth' is an idea always just out of reach when humans prioritise their own power and status. I first recognised this in the Jehovah's Witness teachings, when animals were denied the right to a place in Heaven, and I saw it in some zoo settings, where animals lacked not only the most elemental rights, like the right to good water, food and security, but also the right to be treated with respect and dignity. Surely, these rights should apply to all animals, on both sides of the fence, not just the human animal.

When zoos are done well, with animal enrichment at their core, they act as a living ark for the many animals that are rapidly disappearing in the world due to climate change and the explosion of human populations. Without zoos, we would lose the genetic diversity necessary if, one day, we were able to put animals back into their wild habitats. And the role zoos play in educating people about various animal species is critical. We never know which young kid's heart and mind will be ignited when they visit a zoo. The same kid might one day make crucial decisions that will protect whole species from extinction.

Along the way I have discovered the importance of determination. Even when I felt completely alone and all the odds were convincingly stacked against me, I somehow knew how important it was to have the courage to go on. I've had to reconcile some hard truths. Life isn't fair, I know that for a fact. Not for most animals and not for a lot of people in the world either. But wherever you start, you have to find a way through, because there's just no bloody choice. I intuitively knew there was great power in not giving up. And I also knew that if there was something worth fighting for, then you had to have that fight. That it mattered.

I've also learnt that fundamentalist thinkers of any kind, both religious and secular, are dangerous thinkers. Less because of *what* they 'believe' or 'know' and more because of *how* they believe it or *how* they hold their knowledge. Making absolutes out of knowledge or belief systems of any kind seems to cause havoc among the human species. Essa was a true exception to this rule. He was able to hold his beliefs deeply but lightly. Nothing ever threatened how Essa understood himself in the world. He was always open to different ways of thinking even if those ideas challenged his own. He carried his capacity for tolerance with immense grace and unfailing good humour.

It took me a long time to find a reason to want to belong with humans, particularly when faced with so much dysfunction and disconnect, but when I finally did, it was profound. When I reflect on the people, with no connection to me whatsoever, who gave when there was no expectation to give and who never once waited to be thanked—the Pakistani teenager in prison who risked so much to take Wendy's phone number; the people in Cairns who contributed to the zoo there, having already been skinned; the keepers from Kenya who were willing to sacrifice their family money to send me home from jail; the judge in the UAE who reached out to me so sincerely—my hope for the species remains strong. Experiencing these acts of compassion and generosity gives me courage to live among this strange and most violent of the ape species.

Maybe it all comes down to having a bigger heart. As the first functional organ that develops for all living beings, its vitality is what the rest of the body depends on, and it is the only organ that the body can't do without. The steady drumbeat of all animals' hearts sends a life force to every cell in their bodies. It seems to me the human species could do well by aspiring to having a bigger heart. A bigger heart would send out more of the good stuff—the messages of connection, communication and compassion. I often remind myself of how simply Jane Goodall put it when she said, 'Only when our clever brain and our human heart work together in harmony can we achieve our full potential.'

I like to think I have been, unknowingly, following the heart's messaging all my life. It's the secret language I share with my animals, and which Wendy shares with her plants. And I have an inkling that, unless you're bent on greed or power, it's written into the DNA of most living things.

Acknowledgements

Tim

To my long-suffering wife, Wendy, 'It's been a journey.' Thank you for sticking with me. To the people who have been there to advise me when I was stuck, your gems of wisdom often helped more than you will know. To my mate Rob, who can always find the humorous side of most situations and can always find the time for a chat, thanks for being there, mate. Thanks to all the animals who were the first to give me a sense of belonging. Lastly, to Deb (whose name should have been in larger print on the cover), thank you for the long hours spent being my ghostwriter. Without your perseverance in telling my story, this book would never have seen the light of day. Your wordsmithing is fantastic.

Deb

Thank you to my late mother for her love of literature. Often, my five siblings and I would lose our mum to an afternoon 'kip', which really meant retreating to bed with armfuls of library books and a swiftly emptying box of Quality Street chocolates.

Thank you to Tim for entrusting me with your courageous and, at times, very difficult story. I share your wish that this book leaves other sufferers with the hope and belief that early traumas can not only be survived, but that decent and meaningful lives can emerge from that chaos.

As always, my thanks go to my generous husband Rob and my darling daughter Tess, for your constant encouragement and support.